Corporate Governance in Africa

This book discusses the issue of limited stakeholder recognition and protection of stakeholder interests within the Anglo-Saxon corporate governance model practised in many sub-Saharan African countries.

The volume argues that the relative success of the Anglo-Saxon model in developed economies is attributed to the presence of functional institutions, such as effective legal systems, active external markets for corporate control, and organised civil societies, among others. Many African countries, such as Nigeria and South Africa, have adopted the UK corporate governance framework despite facing challenges occasioned by an inefficient legal system plagued by systemic corruption. Given the challenging institutional contexts in African countries, this book proposes an alternative corporate governance framework – the functional stakeholder model (FSM) – for the banking industry in countries facing similar institutional challenges; the FSM aims to promote stakeholder recognition and the protection of stakeholders' interests. The book draws on stakeholder and institutional theories in designing an alternative corporate governance model, the 'FSM' for banks operating in challenging institutional contexts.

The book will interest regulators, bankers, auditors, academia, policymakers, and researchers in comparative corporate governance and financial regulation, especially banking regulation and stakeholders in developing and emerging markets.

Victor Ediagbonya is Lecturer in Law at the University of Brighton, United Kingdom.

Routledge Studies on Law in Africa

Social and Economic Rights in Africa
International and Public Law Perspectives
Nsongurua Udombana

Financial Inclusion Regulatory Practices in SADC
Addressing prospects and challenges in the 21st Century
Edited by Howard Chitimira and Tapiwa Victor Warikandwa

The African Continental Free Trade Area Agreement
The Development of a Rules-Based Trading Order
Kofi Kufuor

Corporate Governance in Africa
Victor Ediagbonya

For more information about this series, please visit
Routledge Studies on Law in Africa – Book Series – Routledge & CRC Press

Corporate Governance in Africa

Victor Ediagbonya

Routledge
Taylor & Francis Group
LONDON AND NEW YORK

First published 2025
by Routledge
4 Park Square, Milton Park, Abingdon, Oxon OX14 4RN

and by Routledge
605 Third Avenue, New York, NY 10158

Routledge is an imprint of the Taylor & Francis Group, an informa business

British Library Cataloguing-in-Publication Data
A catalogue record for this book is available from the British Library

ISBN: 978-1-032-73370-8 (hbk)
ISBN: 978-1-032-75534-2 (pbk)
ISBN: 978-1-003-47441-8 (ebk)

DOI: 10.4324/9781003474418

Typeset in Times New Roman
by Apex CoVantage, LLC

To, Blessing Obasuyi-Ediagbonya my loving wife and our lovely children, Abiemwense, Eronmwon, and Omoregbee.

Contents

Foreword

Corporate governance is no doubt a popular subject in scholarship, policy, and practice. While corporate governance as an interdisciplinary subject has generated a plethora of commentaries, with diverse perspectives, the Anglo-Saxon shareholder model is a dominant narrative. Nonetheless, as the G20/OECD Principles of Corporate Governance 2015 acknowledge, '[t]here is no single model of good corporate governance.' Context is, therefore, crucial for 'good corporate governance.'

One of the effects of a contextualist approach to corporate governance is a growing acknowledgement of the role of formal and informal institutional factors. As a result, the Anglo-Saxon corporate governance, which is underpinned by neoliberalism, may be unsuited for certain jurisdictions, including some developing countries. The relative success of the Anglo-Saxon corporate governance model in the United Kingdom, for example, is due to the availability and effectiveness of its institutions. Transplanting the corporate governance model from such a developed economy may not yield the desired results if the peculiarities of, and challenges in, the institutional environment of a developing or emerging economy are not taken into account. Another lesson from contextualism is the need to consider the type and nature of sectors in the formulation, adaptation, and implementation of principles, rules, and standards of corporate governance. What works well in one economic sector, such as manufacturing or mining, may not be effective in the banking industry, even within the same jurisdiction.

Victor Ediagbonya's *Corporate Governance in Africa* is, therefore, a welcome contextualist contribution to corporate governance generally and to the limited scholarship on the corporate governance of African banks. The book is a fascinating and thought-provoking work that considers the role of corporate governance in the country, regional, and sector contexts. Providing fresh insights on the shareholder-stakeholder debate, especially in the context of developing and emerging markets, the book offers an intriguing yet contemporary account of corporate governance. Nigeria and South Africa are used as case studies of developing and emerging African countries to assess the recognition and protection of stakeholder interests in the corporate governance framework of banks. It examines the legal, regulatory, supervisory, and institutional environment for banks in the two countries to aid better understanding of the challenges in developing and implementing effective corporate governance in African countries and other developing and emerging markets.

A key argument in the book is that the shareholder-focused Anglo-Saxon model, which underpins corporate governance in the African banking industry, provides little room for advancing some stakeholder interests that the institutional environment in the region and sector may need. The proposed functional stakeholder model as an alternative corporate governance framework for African banks is an innovative, and potentially defining, contribution to corporate governance scholarship. Drawing on institutional and stakeholder theories, the functional stakeholder model recognises the context-dependent nature of corporate governance to offer suggestions aimed at longer term and effective balancing of the interests of critical stakeholders of banks operating in challenging institutional contexts.

I recommend the book as a distinctive and timely contribution to corporate governance, corporate social responsibility, corporate law, banking regulation, development studies, and political economy scholars and postgraduate students as well as policymakers and practitioners within and beyond Africa.

Professor Onyeka Osuji, PhD, BL, FHEA, FAcSS
Dean and Professor of Law
Essex Law School
University of Essex
Wivenhoe Park
Colchester
Essex CO4 3SQ
United Kingdom
14 August 2024

Acknowledgements

I would start by expressing my profound appreciation to Almighty God for granting me the fortitude to complete this work. I am sincerely indebted to Prof. Onyeka Osuji and Dr. Anastasia Karatzia, my esteemed PhD supervisors, for their invaluable guidance and unwavering commitment in overseeing the thesis that formed the foundation for this book. I extend my heartfelt gratitude to Prof. Ebenezer Adodo for his rigorous examination of my PhD thesis. His invaluable feedback has significantly enhanced the quality of this book.

I am deeply thankful to my mother, Mrs. C. Ediagbonya, and all my siblings, especially Kingsley, Oghogho, Frank, Osaretin, Osariemen, Josephine, Osagie, Bernard and Ekundayo for their love and encouragement. I am also very grateful to Dr. Eghosa Ekhator, who consistently motivated me, was always available for discussions, and provided valuable insights and materials. His guidance kept me motivated throughout my PhD journey and beyond.

I would also like to express my gratitude to Dr. Folashade Adeyemo, Cailin Morrison, Dr Stefan Speckesser and Dr. Adaeze Okoye for their outstanding support and encouragement. Finally, I extend my sincere appreciation to my friends and colleagues, particularly Princess Philomena Iheyen, Dr. Jobson Ewelefoh, Augustine Iremiran, Jude Imagwe MON, Hon. Kenneth Adodo, Rufus Aigbogun, Yusufu Aruna, Tracy Nkano Ekpe, Dr Ejike Ezeja, Freddy Igbinosa, Osagie Obasuyi, Ehigie Ogbebor, Taibat Olajire, Ehigie Igbinosa, Dr. Comfort Tioluwani, Dr. Fikayo Taiwo, and Dr. Godswill Agbaitoro for their unwavering support, which has been truly remarkable.

Abbreviations

AMCON	Asset Management Corporation Nigeria
BCBS	Basel Committee on Banking Supervision
BOFIA	Banks and Other Financial Institutions Act
CAC	Corporate Affairs Commission
CAMA	Companies and Allied Matters Act
CBN	Central Bank of Nigeria
CCGTI	Code of Corporate Governance for the Telecommunications Industry
CEO	Chief Executive Officer
COB	Chairman of the Board
CFRN	Constitution of Federal Republic of Nigeria
CIBN	Chartered Institute of Bankers of Nigeria
CSR	corporate social responsibility
DMB	Deposit Money Bank
EFCC	Economic and Financial Crimes Commission
ESV	Enlightened Shareholder Value
FSCA	Financial Sector Conduct Authority
FHC	Federal High Court
FRCN	Financial Reporting Council of Nigeria
FSM	functional stakeholder model
ICPC	Independent Corrupt Practices Commission
JSE	Johannesburg Stock Exchange
LFN	Laws of the Federation of Nigeria
MSME	Micro, Small and Medium Enterprise
NAICOM	National Insurance Commission
NCC	Nigerian Communications Commission
NCCG	National Code of Corporate Governance
NDIC	Nigeria Deposit Insurance Corporation
NPLs	Non-Performing Loans
NWLR	Nigerian Weekly Law Reports
OECD	Organisation for Economic Co-operation and Development
PENCOM	National Pension Commission
SARB	South African Reserve Bank
SC	Supreme Court

SEC	Securities Exchange Commission
SOGA	Statutes of General Application
UK	United Kingdom
UKHL	United Kingdom House of Lords
US	United States

Part A

Background, Relationship, Theories, and Model

1 Introduction

1.1 Background

Corporate governance discourse has been a topical issue in the last two decades, particularly in the banking industry. These discussions emanated because of the global financial crisis of 2007–2009[1] and its intended effect, which devastated several banks and other financial institutions globally. The financial crisis negatively affected banks and other financial institutions because of their interconnectedness. The year 2008 saw some of the most significant bank failures in history.[2] This was evident in the collapse of Washington Mutual in September 2008, the acquisition of Bear Stearns by JP Morgan Chase in March 2008, and the collapse of Lehman Brothers in September 2008, which caused the global banking crisis.[3] That same year, Fortis and Dexia, the first European banks to experience a financial crisis, were rescued in September 2008.[4] This period marked the onset of a debt crisis in Eurozone countries, and several structural weaknesses in Member States' banking industries were exposed. In response to the financial crisis, governments worldwide bailed out, nationalised, and arranged mergers and acquisitions for several systematically important banks. For example, In 2008, the UK government invested £107.6 billion to acquire a controlling equity stake of 84% in the Royal Bank of Scotland and a 43% stake in Lloyds Banking Group to maintain financial stability, and in 2010, the UK government acquired the entirety of Northern Rock and Bradford & Bingley, using public funds to avert insolvencies in those banks and systemic breakdown of

1 Martin Conyon, William Judge, Michael Useem, 'Corporate governance and the 2008–09 financial crisis', *Corporate Governance: An International Review*, 19(5), 2011, pp. 399–404

2 Heather Stewart, 'We are in the worst financial crisis since depression, says IMF', *The Guardian*, Thursday 10 April 2008, available at: <www.theguardian.com/business/2008/apr/10/useconomy.subprimecrisis> accessed 12 January 2024

3 Rao-Nicholson Rekha, Salaber Julie, 'Impact of the financial crisis on cross-border mergers and acquisitions and concentration in the global banking sector', *Thunderbird International Business Review*, 58(2), 2016, pp. 161–173

4 Rao-Nicholson Rekha, Salaber Julie, 'Impact of the financial crisis on cross-border mergers and acquisitions and concentration in the global banking sector', *Thunderbird International Business Review*, 58(2), 2016

DOI: 10.4324/9781003474418-2

the entire financial system.[5] Some banks also engaged in merger and acquisition activities, as indicated earlier;[6] these mergers and acquisitions arguably were carried out to avert insolvencies in those banks and prevent a systemic failure of the entire financial system.[7] As also indicated earlier, besides the mergers and acquisitions, various governments have injected public funds into the different systematically important banks globally at one point or another. From September 2007 to December 2009, the UK Labour Government made several interventions to support the banking industry; it invested £137 billion of public funds in loans and capital to stabilise the financial system.[8] It could be argued that governments of countries involved in the bailouts viewed certain banks, particularly the systematically important ones, as 'too big to fail' due to their interconnectedness.[9] The waves of the financial crisis quickly spread across countries, and its effect was tough on those affected countries.[10] The impact of the financial crisis on the Nigerian banking industry was enormous because of its exposure to the capital market. Share prices plummeted, and foreign portfolio investors sold off their investments and repatriated all their funds, leading to a drop in banks' liquidity ratios.[11]

On the other hand, the global financial crisis of 2007–2009 also severely impacted South Africa. The South African economy went into recession in 2008–2009 for the first time in 19 years.[12] In 2009, approximately a million jobs were lost, and the unemployment rate remained high at 25%.[13] However, following the end of apartheid in South Africa in 1994, before the global financial crisis, the first banking crisis witnessed in South Africa was the banking crisis of 2002–2003.[14] The collapse of Saambou Bank in February 2002 negatively impacted some of the significant

5 Federico Mor, 'Bank rescues of 2007–09: Outcomes and cost', House of Commons Library, Briefing Paper 5748, available at: <https://commonslibrary.parliament.uk/research-briefings/sn05748/>

6 See note 3 earlier

7 Van Deventer Donald, 'Case studies in liquidity risk: Royal bank of Scotland PLC New York branch', Kamakura Corporation Working Paper, 4 August 2011

8 Federico Mor, 'Bank rescues of 2007–09: Outcomes and cost', House of Commons Library, Briefing Paper 5748, available at: <https://commonslibrary.parliament.uk/research-briefings/sn05748/>

9 Stefanos Ioannou, Dariusz Wójcik, Gary Dymski, 'Too-big-to-fail: Why megabanks have not become smaller since the global financial crisis?', *Review of Political Economy*, 31(3), 2019, pp. 356–381

10 Tony Dolphin, Laura Chappell, 'The effect of the global financial crisis on emerging and developing economies', The Institute for Public Policy Research Report, 2010, available at: <www.ippr.org/files/images/media/files/publication/2011/05/Financial%20crisis%20and%20developing%20economies%20Sep%202010_1798.pdf> accessed 13 January2024

11 Chuke Nwude, 'The crash of the Nigerian stock market, what went wrong, the consequences and the Panacea', *Journal of Developing Countries Studies*, 2(9), 2012, pp. 105–117

12 Ravinder Rena, Malindi Msoni, 'Global financial crises and its impact on the South African economy: A further update', *Journal of Economics*, 5(1), 2014, pp. 17–25, available at: <https://doi.org/10.1080/09765239.2014.11884980>

13 Ravinder Rena, Malindi Msoni, 'Global financial crises and its impact on the South African economy: A further update', *Journal of Economics*, 5(1), 2014, pp. 17–25, available at: <https://doi.org/10.1080/09765239.2014.11884980>

14 Roy Havemann, 'The South African small banks' crisis of 2002/3', *Economic History of Developing Regions*, 36(2), 2021, pp. 313–338, available at: <https://doi.org/10.1080/20780389.2021.1943348>

small- and medium-sized South Africa's banks, leading to the deregistration of half of the country's banks by the end of 2003.[15]

Before the global financial crisis of 2007–2009, the Nigerian banking industry witnessed numerous failures between the late 1990s and early 2000s.[16] Most Nigerian banks were owned either by the state governments or private individuals, and in most cases, directors and senior management appointments are based on political or tribal sentiments and not on merit as expected. Those directors and senior management staff awarded loans to themselves and their cronies, putting their banks, the banking industry, and the entire financial system in a difficult situation.

The consequence of banking failure is enormous; stakeholders like employees and customers suffer the most, and the institutional environment in most developing and emerging countries like Nigeria and South Africa does not offer adequate protection.[17] Customers cannot access their funds; their savings disappear when the banks fail because they will lose some, if not all, of their money. Although deposit guarantee schemes may cover some of the customers' money, it could take several years to get reimbursed because of the institutional environment in these countries. Similarly, employees suffer from banking failures; their salaries are unpaid for several months. In some cases, they could be owed salaries for several years, and in certain instances, they are made redundant without adequate compensation. The reasons for those banking failures were as a result of poor corporate governance.[18]

1.2 Legal Transplants in Africa

The corporate governance frameworks applicable in Nigeria and South Africa are based on the Anglo-Saxon corporate governance model.[19] The Anglo-Saxon corporate governance model, which originated from the United Kingdom (UK) and the United States (US), is premised on the availability of functioning institutions, such as an active external market for corporate control and an efficient legal system comprising the state's machinery for making, interpreting and enforcing the law.[20] Its primary focus is profit maximisation for shareholders' benefit, thus at the

15 Roy Havemann, 'The South African small banks' crisis of 2002/3', *Economic History of Developing Regions*, 36(2), 2021, pp. 313–338, available at: <https://doi.org/10.1080/20780389.2021.1943348>

16 NDIC, 'Closed financial institutions', available at: <https://ndic.gov.ng/failure-resolution/closed-financial-institutions/> accessed 15 January 2024

17 Institutional environment refers to legal systems, economic, social, and political factors influencing a country's formal and informal institutions

18 Lisa Cook, 'Were the Nigerian banking reforms of 2005 a success . . . and for the poor?', in Sebastian Edwards, Simon Johnson, David Weil (eds), *African Successes, Volume III: Modernization and Development* (University of Chicago Press, Chicago, 2016), pp. 157–182

19 Navajyoti Samanta, 'Transplantation of Anglo-American corporate governance and its impact on financial market growth: A comparative analysis of nineteen developing countries 1995–2014', *Corporate Governance*, 19(5), 2019, pp. 884–922, ISSN 1472-0701

20 Onyeka Osuji, Franklin Ngwu, Frank Stephen, *Corporate Governance in Developing and Emerging Markets* (Routledge, Abingdon and New York, 2017), p. 4

expense of other stakeholders, such as customers and employees. One would argue that despite the Anglo-Saxon model's relative success in the UK and the US, its implementation in Africa has failed to prevent banking failures.[21] The main reason behind this shortcoming of the transplantation of the Anglo-Saxon corporate governance model in Africa is its failure to acknowledge Africa's unique institutional arrangements; the weakness of institutions is prevalent in Africa, including an undeveloped market for corporate control and an inefficient legal/judicial system.[22] Arguably, the relative success of the Anglo-Saxon model in developed economies, such as the UK, is because of the availability of functional institutions, such as an efficient legal system which includes the state apparatus for making, interpreting, and enforcing the law. The UK Anglo-Saxon model depends on an active external market for corporate control and organised civil societies for its success. Nigeria and South Africa, the focus of this book, inherited the UK corporate governance model because of their historical past. Notwithstanding the differences in their institutional environments, Nigeria and South Africa have continued to model their corporate governance framework on that of the UK. This trend persists despite their inefficient legal system resulting from systemic corruption across the different tiers of government. Thus, implementing the UK's corporate governance model in both countries has deviated from what leading corporate governance theories have envisaged. This is due to Nigeria and South Africa's institutional environment, evidenced by its weak institutions, such as inadequate legal, regulatory, and supervisory systems, insiders' ownership concentration, an underdeveloped capital market, and systemic corruption across the different tiers of government. This has resulted in persistent banking failures in Nigeria and South Africa because of the weak corporate governance framework, evidenced by inaccurate reporting and non-compliance with regulatory requirements, gross insider abuses resulting in substantial non-performing loans, persistent illiquidity, and poor asset quality. Because of the institutional voids, when banks fail, stakeholders, mostly customers and employees, suffer because the current frameworks do not offer them any protection. Therefore, given the challenging institutional contexts in Nigeria and South Africa, this book proposes an alternative corporate governance framework in the banking industry in countries with challenging institutional contexts which would facilitate the recognition of stakeholders and protect stakeholders' interests.

In 1862, the British government introduced the Anglo-Saxon corporate law and regulations in Nigeria to regulate the British companies in the Nigerian business environment.[23] As a result, Nigeria inherited a system of corporate governance based on the Anglo-Saxon model. Even after independence, Nigeria had designed

21 Onyeka Osuji, Franklin Ngwu, Frank Stephen, *Corporate Governance in Developing and Emerging Markets* (Routledge, Abingdon and New York, 2017)

22 Emmanuel Adegbite, 'Good corporate governance in Nigeria: Antecedents, propositions and peculiarities', *International Business Review*, 24(2), 2015, pp. 319–330

23 Emmanuel Adegbite, Chizu Nakajima, 'Corporate governance and responsibility in Nigeria', *International Journal of Disclosure and Governance*, 8(3), 2011, pp. 252–271

her Companies Act 1968 based on the UK Companies Act 1948.[24] The subsequent Companies and Allied Matters Act (CAMA), the principal legislation presently governing corporate law in Nigeria, was introduced in 1990 and modelled on the English Companies Act 1985.[25] It is argued that there was no significant amendment to the law for 30 years until 2020, when the Act was repealed and re-enacted.[26] Notwithstanding the legislative attempt to repeal and re-enact CAMA, the newly enacted CAMA 2020 is in *pari materia* with the UK Companies Act 2006, premised on the Anglo-Saxon corporate law model, which failed to consider the challenging institutional context in Nigeria. In Nigeria, banks operate a system where ownership and management may be fused because Nigerian banks are owned by wealthy families and wealthy individuals, including few institutional ownerships, allowing them to control their businesses.[27]

South Africa's corporate governance framework has been derived from the United Kingdom due to its historical past and long-standing ties with Britain; thus, the country's corporate law and culture are deeply rooted in the British tradition.[28] In the late 19th and early 20th century, the mining finance houses established to exploit the Johannesburg gold deposits created pyramid structures prevalent in the 1990s.[29] These firms had ownership structures that led to unacceptable business practices characterised by elaborate control and conflicts of interest. Undoubtedly, the pyramid structures resulted from South Africa's historical background.[30] However, the Johannesburg Stock Exchange recently prohibited pyramid structures because they were profoundly unpopular with ordinary shareholders, amongst other reasons.[31]

As a result of the apartheid regime in South Africa, the country was isolated from the rest of the world, which resulted in corporate governance practices that were below par. Following the dissolution of the apartheid regime in South Africa in 1994, South Africa operate a corporate governance regime known as the King Code. It currently operates a corporate governance system, King Code IV, which is based on the traditional Anglo-Saxon corporate governance model.[32] Nevertheless, the Anglo-Saxon corporate governance model is alien to the peculiarity of the African institutional

24 Elewechi Okike, 'Corporate governance in Nigeria: The status quo', *Corporate Governance: An International Review*, 15(2), 2007, pp. 173–193

25 Udo Udoma, Belo-Osagie, 'The companies and allied matters act 2020 – what you need to know', *Part 9 Schemes of Arrangement, BusinessDay Newspaper*, Tuesday 8 September 2020, p. 14

26 CAMA 2020

27 Peterson Ozili, Olayinka Uadiale, 'Ownership concentration and bank profitability', *Future Business Journal*, 3(2), 2017, pp. 159–171

28 Andrew West, 'Theorising South Africa's corporate governance', *Journal of Business Ethics*, 68(4), 2006, pp. 433–448

29 Stephan Malherbe, Nick Segal, *Corporate Governance in South Africa* (OECD Development Center, Paris, 2001)

30 G.J. Rossouw, A. Van der Watt, D.P. Malan, 'Corporate governance in South Africa', *Journal of Business Ethics*, 37(3), May 2002, Corporate Governance Reforms in Developing Countries, pp. 289–302

31 G.J. Rossouw, A. Van der Watt, D.P. Malan, 'Corporate governance in South Africa', *Journal of Business Ethics*, 37(3), May 2002, Corporate Governance Reforms in Developing Countries

32 King IV Report on Corporate Governance for South Africa, 2016

context. The institutional context in any country is fundamental in determining the corporate law model that the country should implement for its corporate governance to be effective. This argument is supported by Osuji, Ngwu, and Stephen, who argued that the effectiveness of corporate governance models is context-dependent.[33]

The argument supporting the convergence of a global corporate governance model on the assumption of globalisation[34] is misleading and a total denial of the reality that every society is unique and has its institutional arrangement. The institutional arrangement is a core determinant for effective corporate governance,[35] so the corporate governance model for Nigeria and South Africa must factor in the challenging institutional context in these countries. The Anglo-Saxon corporate governance model is a shareholders-oriented model primarily designed to promote shareholders' interests, and shareholders' interest is to maximise profit for their benefit, which has been the traditional view of the corporation.[36] Given the various banking failures in Nigeria and South Africa occasioned by poor corporate governance, this book investigates the corporate governance framework of banks in challenging institutional contexts using the Nigerian and South African Deposit Money Banks (DMBs) as case studies.

1.3 Nature and Scope

The book examines the Anglo-Saxon corporate governance model employed by DMBs in Nigeria and South Africa to determine the extent to which it allows for recognising stakeholders and protecting stakeholders' interests. It addresses the limited stakeholders' recognition and protection under the Anglo-Saxon corporate governance model practised in most sub-Saharan African countries. The reason for choosing South Africa and Nigeria, amongst others, is that both are emerging countries in sub-Saharan Africa. There is a dearth of literature on the corporate governance of banks focusing on both countries. Nigeria and South Africa are amongst the largest economies in Africa based on their gross domestic product (GDP).[37] This

33 Onyeka Osuji, Franklin Ngwu, Frank Stephen, *Corporate Governance in Developing and Emerging Markets* (Routledge, Abingdon and New York, 2017), p. 3

34 Henry Hansmann, Reinier Kraakman, 'The end of history for corporate law', Yale Law School Working Paper No. 235; NYU Working Paper No. 013; Harvard Law School Discussion Paper No. 280; Yale SOM Working Paper No. ICF-00-09, January 2000

35 Emmanuel Adegbite, 'Good corporate governance in Nigeria: Antecedents, propositions and peculiarities', *International Business Review*, 24(2), 2015; Emmanuel Adegbite, Chizu Nakajima, 'Corporate governance and responsibility in Nigeria', *International Journal of Disclosure and Governance*, 8(3), 2011; Franklin Nakpodia, Emmanuel Adegbite, 'Corporate Governance and Elites', *Accounting Forum*, 42(1), 2018, pp. 17–31

36 Henry Hansmann, Reinier Kraakman, 'The end of history for corporate law', Yale Law School Working Paper No. 235; NYU Working Paper No. 013; Harvard Law School Discussion Paper No. 280; Yale SOM Working Paper No. ICF-00-09, January 2000

37 International Monetary Fund, 'World economic outlook – GDP 2024', available at: <https://www.imf.org/en/Publications/WEO/Issues/2024/07/16/world-economic-outlook-update-july-2024>; GDP (current US$), 'Nigeria, South Africa, Egypt, Arab Report, Data', available at: <www.worldbank.org> accessed 15 January 2024. By the end of 2022, South Africa's GDP was $405 bn, Nigeria's GDP was $473 bn, and Egypt was $477 bn

book explores ways of harnessing economic growth and national development in both countries and other developing and emerging countries, particularly those in Africa, through the involvement of multiple stakeholders in the corporate governance of banks.

The book examines banking regulation through the lens of corporate governance, focusing on the extent banks' current corporate governance frameworks allow for the recognition of stakeholders and protection of stakeholders' interests, especially in developing and emerging economies. This book provides a definitive answer to some essential issues concerning banking regulation and corporate governance in the African context. It unequivocally explores the criticality of corporate governance, the key factors that drive effective corporate governance in the banking industry, and the extent to which stakeholders are recognised and their interests protected under the corporate governance regulatory framework in Nigeria and South Africa. The book discusses the challenges of implementing an effective corporate governance framework in the banking industry of both countries. It proposes effective solutions for achieving desirable corporate governance in the banking industries of Nigeria and South Africa. Each chapter of the book unreservedly tackles a specific theme related to these issues raised.

1.4 Structure of the book

The book is organised into three parts, 'Part A,' 'Background, Relationship, Theories, and Model,' contains three chapters, each dealing with the conceptual and theoretical aspects of corporate governance and banking regulation. Chapter 1, 'Introduction,' provides a background for the book by exploring the problem of poor corporate governance frameworks in Africa, particularly concerning banks in Nigeria and South Africa. Chapter 2, titled 'Corporate Governance Concepts, Theories, and Models,' explores the theoretical issues that underpin corporate governance discourse in recent times. The chapter delves into the nature of corporate governance, why it is important, and the various theoretical perspectives on corporate governance. While several theories support corporate governance discourse, the chapter identifies the six most dominant theories: agency theory, stewardship theory, shareholder primacy theory, enlightened shareholder value theory (ESV), institutional theory, and stakeholder theory. The ESV theory, which is enshrined under s.172 of the UK Companies Act 2006, requires directors to consider the interests of employees and customers. However, the chapter argues that both the shareholder primacy and ESV theories amongst others are intended to maximise profits for the benefit of shareholders in the long run. The book adopts the stakeholder and institutional theories in its analysis and in designing the functional stakeholders' corporate governance model for developing and emerging markets. Chapter 3, titled 'Corporate Governance and Banking Regulation,' discusses the relationship between corporate governance and banking regulation. The chapter begins by exploring the two theories of banking regulation – the public interest theory and the private interest theory – that justify the need for banking regulation. Although both theories offer different justifications, the book favours the public interest theory because it serves all stakeholders. The chapter also examines the three types of banking regulation approaches: prudential, systemic, and conduct regulations. It argues that corporate governance is an essential part of prudential regulation. Additionally, the chapter explores two banking regulation strategies: command-and-control and self-regulatory strategies. The book prefers a hybrid strategy known as 'responsive regulation' that combines the advantages of both strategies to ensure that banks are adequately regulated.

Part B, titled 'Corporate Governance and Banking Regulation in Africa,' includes three chapters that analyse the effectiveness of corporate governance frameworks in Nigeria and South African banks. The aim is to determine if the existing corporate governance framework is sufficient and whether there is a correlation between corporate governance practices and banking failures. Chapter 4, titled 'Determinants of Effective Corporate Governance in the Banking Industry,' examines the corporate governance framework for banks. Considering banks' unique nature, this chapter aims to determine whether the corporate governance framework that applies to other non-financial institutions is suitable for banks. Banks face significant risks, including credit, operational, market, and liquidity risks. Therefore, an all-encompassing form of corporate governance framework is required in the banking industry. The chapter first examines the international standard for corporate governance, the OECD Principles of corporate governance, and the Basel Committee on Bank Supervision principles. It argues that these principles are not a one-size-fits-all solution. The institutional environment where the principles or guidelines should be implemented must be taken into account. Therefore, it argues that the issue of how to implement corporate governance in banks is context-dependent. Subsequently, the chapter examines the stakeholders in the banking industry and the various corporate governance models applicable to the banking industry. Furthermore, the chapter explores the Anglo-Saxon corporate governance model, underpinned by the shareholder theory, and the Continental European and the Japanese Keiretsu corporate governance models, underpinned by the stakeholder theory. The chapter argues that embedding corporate social responsibility (CSR) in the bank's corporate governance framework ensures that stakeholders are recognised and their interests are protected.

Chapter 5, titled 'Corporate Governance and Banking Regulation in Nigeria,' delves into the corporate governance model that applies to companies in Nigeria. The chapter starts by examining the history of corporate governance in Nigeria. It argues that the Nigerian corporate governance framework is similar to the English Company Law. The first companies that operated in Nigeria in 1862 were British companies registered in England and regulated under the English Companies Law after Lagos became a colony. However, after implementing the Statue of General Application (SOGA) on 1 January 1900, Nigeria inherited all the laws applicable in England. The chapter further argues that the Companies and Allied Matters Act (CAMA), which is the primary corporate law legislation in Nigeria, is founded on shareholder primacy.

Additionally, the chapter identifies and analyses the National Corporate Governance Code (NCGC) and other industry-specific codes that apply to companies operating in different industries in Nigeria. The findings show that although CAMA acknowledged the limited stakeholder recognition, it and other corporate governance codes in Nigeria are based on the Anglo-Saxon corporate governance framework that prioritises the interests of shareholders over key stakeholders such as employees and customers. The chapter also examines the corporate governance model in Nigerian DMBs by evaluating both the SEC and CBN codes. It argues that both codes have limited stakeholder recognition and protection of stakeholders' interests. Both codes are intended to promote shareholder primacy, which arguably has the potential to increase profits for shareholders' benefit. Furthermore, the findings reveal that several attempts were made to legislate a form of corporate social responsibility (CSR) to mitigate the limited stakeholder recognition and protection of stakeholders' interests; however, all attempts failed to materialise.

Chapter 6, 'Corporate Governance and Banking Regulation in South Africa,' examines the corporate governance framework that applies to companies in South Africa. The chapter explores the history of corporate governance in South Africa, including an overview of its development and a summary of the key provisions of South Africa's corporate governance codes. It also investigates the corporate governance framework in the South African banking industry to determine if it allows for the recognition of stakeholders and the protection of their interests. Additionally, the chapter addresses several issues related to the legal, regulatory, institutional, and supervisory corporate governance framework in banks in South Africa. It explores factors affecting corporate governance in the banking industry, such as political and socio-economic factors, and highlight the key challenges hindering effective corporate governance in the banking industry in South Africa. The chapter also analyses the principal legislation that applies to South African banks, including the Companies Act 71 of 2008, the King IV Corporate Governance Code, and the Johannesburg Stock Exchange Listing requirement. Furthermore, the chapter highlights the nature and scope of corporate social responsibility in the South African banking industry by exploring the current South African framework of corporate governance practices and aligning them with the principles of the African philosophy of Ubuntu.

The final part of this book, Part C, is titled 'Redefining Corporate Governance Model for Africa.' It comprises three chapters emphasising the importance of developing a corporate governance framework suitable for African banks. Thus, such a framework should consider the unique challenges the institutional context of developing and emerging markets poses. Chapter 7, entitled 'A Case for a More Efficient Corporate Governance for Banks in Africa,' argues that the current corporate governance framework in Nigeria and South Africa has failed to protect stakeholders' interests. This failure has resulted in poor corporate governance in the banking industries of both countries. The chapter further highlights the devastating challenges and effects that this poor governance has had due to the challenging institutional contexts in developing and emerging markets. Chapter 8, titled 'A Functional Stakeholder Model of Corporate Governance for Africa,' presents an alternative corporate governance framework for the banking industries of Nigeria and South Africa. The model is based on institutional and stakeholders' theoretical perspectives and addresses the insufficient recognition and protection of stakeholders' interests, leading to weaknesses in the corporate governance structure in developing and emerging markets. The chapter focuses on enhancing stakeholder engagement and protection, which are essential elements of effective corporate governance. Chapter 9, titled 'Conclusions, Recommendations, and Future Directions', summarises the book's mission, key arguments, and contributions. It discusses the practical and policy implications of the functional stakeholder model for different stakeholders, including regulators, politicians, and multinational banks. Furthermore, it identifies potential future research directions in the areas covered by the book. Lastly, the chapter emphasises how the book adds to the perspective of the Global South discourse and the debates surrounding the institutional environments of developing and emerging countries.

The synopsis of the chapters, together with their respective headings, is set out in the following.

Part A: Background, Relationship, Theories, and Model

Chapter 1: Introduction

This chapter serves as an introduction to the book, providing pertinent background information. It commences by examining the research background and the research problem within the corporate governance framework in the African banking industry to substantiate the need for this book. The chapter provides an introductory narration of the challenges confronting the African banking industry. It argues that the legal transplantation of corporate governance framework in Africa is influenced by corporate governance regulations from developed economies, like the UK, despite the differences in the institutional contexts between both countries. This corporate governance framework from developed economies transplanted into the African legal system fails to consider the peculiarity of African institutional arrangement, hence, a key factor contributing to banking failures. Furthermore, the chapter delves into the scope and nature of the book, exposing its perspective, which revolves around dissecting banking regulation in Africa through the prism of corporate governance. Finally, this chapter concludes by providing a summary of the chapters in this book.

Chapter 2: Corporate Governance Concepts, Theories, and Models

This chapter examines the theoretical concepts that form the basis of contemporary corporate governance discourse. It commences by investigating the fundamental aspects of corporate governance and its significance. The chapter proceeds to explore diverse theoretical perspectives on corporate governance, with a focus on the six most prevalent theories in corporate governance literature, namely, (i) agency theory, (ii) stewardship theory, (iii) shareholder primacy theory, (iv) enlightened shareholder value theory (ESV), (v) institutional theory, and (vi) stakeholder theory. The ESV theory, as enshrined in section 172 of the UK Companies Act 2006, mandates that company directors are obliged to act in a manner that they genuinely believe would most likely promote the company's overall success for the benefit of its members. This requirement includes consideration for the interests of the company's employees and the imperative to nurture the company's business relationships with customers, suppliers, and others. However, it is contended that both the shareholder primacy and the ESV theories aim to maximise long-term profits for the benefit of shareholders. The chapter adopts the stakeholders and institutional theories in its analysis and in designing the FSM framework for corporate governance in the African banking industry.

Chapter 3: Corporate Governance and Banking Regulation

This chapter provides an in-depth analysis of the correlation between corporate governance and banking regulation. It commences by examining the theories of banking regulation, specifically the public interest theory and the private interest theory, in order to demonstrate the justification for banking regulation. The chapter advocates for the public interest theory on the grounds that it best serves the interests of all stakeholders. Furthermore, it explores three distinct banking regulation approaches: prudential regulation, systemic regulation, and conduct regulation, emphasising the integral role of corporate governance within prudential regulation. The chapter also explores the different banking regulatory strategies, including command-and-control and self-regulatory strategies. Based on the advantages and disadvantages of these strategies, the book adopts a hybrid strategy called responsive regulation, which integrates both command-and-control and self-regulation strategies to ensure effective regulation of banks for the benefit of all stakeholders, which aligns with the public interest theory.

Part B: Corporate Governance and Banking Regulation in Africa

Chapter 4: Determinants of Effective Corporate Governance in the Banking Sector

This chapter explores the corporate governance frameworks formulated by international bodies to determine their suitability for the banking industry, given its distinctive characteristics. The chapter contends that a comprehensive corporate governance framework is imperative for the banking industry due to the notable risks inherent in banking operations, encompassing credit risk, operational risk, market risk, and liquidity risk. This chapter begins by examining international standards for corporate governance, such as the OECD Principles of Corporate Governance and the Basel Committee on Bank Supervision principles. The chapter emphasises the need to take into account the institutional environment of the country when attempting to implement these principles, as a one-size-fits-all approach may not be effective in most cases. This chapter also delves into the stakeholders in the banking industry and the different corporate governance models applicable to banks, such as the Anglo-Saxon, Continental European, and Japanese Keiretsu models. Lastly, this chapter concludes by advocating for the inclusion of corporate social responsibility in the bank's governance framework to ensure the recognition of stakeholders and protection of stakeholders' interests.

Chapter 5: Corporate Governance and Banking Regulation in Nigeria

This chapter explored the corporate governance model applicable in Nigeria and commenced by exploring the historical development of corporate governance in Nigeria. It argues that the Nigerian corporate governance framework is in *pari materia* with the United Kingdom corporate law as this has been the basis behind the historical development of corporate law in Nigeria. The chapter contended that the pioneer companies that operated in Nigeria in 1862, after Lagos became a colony, were British companies registered in England and regulated under the English Companies Law. However, following the implementation of the Statue of General Application (SOGA) on 1 January 1900, Nigeria inherited all the laws in force in England as of that day. The chapter also argued that the Companies and Allied Matters Act (CAMA), Nigeria's principal corporate law legislation, is premised on the shareholder primacy model practice in the United Kingdom. Furthermore, the National Corporate Governance Code (NCGC) and other industry-specific codes applicable to companies operating in different industries in Nigeria were identified and analysed. The findings revealed that although there is limited stakeholder recognition under CAMA, CAMA and other corporate governance codes in Nigeria are underpinned by the Anglo-Saxon corporate governance framework, which puts shareholders' interests over the interests of other key stakeholders such as employees and customers. This chapter also examined the corporate governance model in Nigerian DMBs. In addition to CAMA, which is the primary legislation that applies to banks as they are incorporated companies in Nigeria, the SEC and the CBN codes were also examined. The SEC code applies to banks listed on the Nigerian stock exchange, while the CBN code applies to all banks, irrespective of their listing status. The chapter argues that both the SEC and CBN codes exhibit limited recognition of stakeholders and do not adequately protect the interests of other stakeholders apart from shareholders. Furthermore, this chapter revealed several attempts to have a legislated form of CSR to help mitigate the limited stakeholders' recognition and protection of stakeholders' interests; however, all the attempts failed to materialise.

Chapter 6: Corporate Governance and Banking Regulation in South Africa

This chapter explores the corporate governance framework within the South African banking industry to determine the extent it allows for stakeholders' recognition and protection of stakeholder interests. The chapter begins by examining the historical development of corporate governance in South Africa and proceeds to discuss key legislation such as the Companies Act 71 of 2008, the King IV Corporate Governance Code, and the Johannesburg Stock Exchange listing requirements. It argues that the South African corporate governance framework is in *pari passu* with that of Nigeria due to both countries' historical ties with Britain. The chapter also highlights the dominance of shareholder interests in South African banks as practised in the UK, which raises concerns because of the difference in the institutional arrangements in the country. Additionally, the chapter explores the nature and extent of CSR in the South African banking sector. The overall aim of this chapter is to understand the current corporate governance practices in South African banks to have a holistic view of the institutional context in Africa and take into account the peculiarity of these countries in developing an alternative corporate governance model for sub-Saharan Africa.

Part C: Redefining Corporate Governance Model for Africa

Chapter 7: A Case for a More Efficient Corporate Governance for Banks in Africa

Based on the findings outlined in Chapters 5 and 6 concerning the corporate governance framework within Nigerian and South African banks respectively, this chapter advocates for a shift in the corporate governance for the banking industries in Africa. The chapter argues that the current corporate governance framework premised on the Anglo-Saxon corporate governance model practised in the UK, which primarily focuses on the maximisation of profit for the benefit of shareholders, has fallen short in adequately recognising other stakeholders and protecting the interests of stakeholders. This chapter further argues that the legal transplantation of corporate governance framework from developed economies without consideration for African countries' institutional context had occasioned several challenges leading to poor corporate governance in the banking industry in Africa. The chapter concludes that a new corporate governance model for banks in Africa, entitled the FSM, should be designed to take into account the challenging institutional contexts in developing and emerging markets.

Chapter 8: A Functional Stakeholder Model of Corporate Governance for Africa

This chapter proposes an alternative corporate governance model, the FSM, for the African banking industry. It addresses the challenges facing effective corporate governance in sub-Saharan Africa and aims to enhance the recognition of stakeholders and protection of stakeholders interests. The chapter is based on institutional and stakeholder's theoretical perspectives. Its main focus is to develop a corporate governance model that considers the unique characteristics of African institutional arrangements. The proposed FSM incorporates various recommendations to improve the limited recognition of stakeholders and protection of stakeholders' interests, which has undermined an effective corporate governance framework in developing and emerging markets. The chapter emphasises the importance of an effective board for corporate governance to thrive in Africa. It highlights ways to achieve this, such as including employees and debtholders as directors, increasing the number of non-executive directors and women on the board, establishing a mandatory CSR committee as well as redesigning the curriculum for those seeking to become bankers and continuous professional development for those already in the industry. This chapter argues that strengthening the enforcement framework under the proposed FSM is crucial to improving stakeholders' recognition and protecting stakeholders' interests. It recommends granting enforcement powers to third parties, such as the Attorney-General, professional bankers' associations, and lawyers. Finally, the chapter suggests establishing a specialised court to handle banking law and other ancillary matters; this would enhance the expertise of judges and address the preliminary objection relating to jurisdiction often exploited by some lawyers, which tends to delay the time it takes to deal with substantive matters.

Chapter 9: Conclusions, Recommendations, and Future Directions

This chapter provides the conclusion for this book. It begins with a concise overview of the objectives of this book, followed by an exposition of the theoretical and conceptual framework that underpins the research. The chapter offers a comprehensive summary of the key discussions in each chapter of the book. This chapter also recounted the recommendations made by the functional stakeholder model of corporate governance, which aims to address the current deficiencies of the Anglo-Saxon corporate governance model that have hindered the implementation of an effective corporate governance framework, particularly in the Nigerian banking industry and, by extension, across Africa. Additionally, this chapter highlights the original contributions of the research and elucidates the practical implications for various stakeholders, including DMBs, academia, auditors, governments, policymakers, and researchers. Lastly, this chapter discusses the limitations of the study and concludes by suggesting the directions for future research.

Reference List

Adegbite, Emmanuel, 'Good corporate governance in Nigeria: Antecedents, propositions and peculiarities', *International Business Review*, 24(2), 2015, pp. 319–330

Adegbite, Emmanuel, Chizu Nakajima, 'Corporate governance and responsibility in Nigeria', *International Journal of Disclosure and Governance*, 8(3), 2011, pp. 252–271

Companies and Allied Matters Act, 2020

Conyon, Martin, William Judge, Michael Useem, 'Corporate governance and the 2008–09 financial crisis', *Corporate Governance: An International Review*, 19(5), 2011, pp. 399–404

Cook, Lisa, 'Were the Nigerian banking reforms of 2005 a success . . . and for the poor?', in Sebastian Edwards, Simon Johnson, David Weil (eds), *African Successes, Volume III: Modernization and Development* (University of Chicago Press, Chicago, 2016), pp. 157–182

Dolphin, Tony, Laura Chappell, 'The effect of the global financial crisis on emerging and developing economies', The Institute for Public Policy Research Report, 2010, available at: <www.ippr.org/files/images/media/files/publication/2011/05/Financial%20crisis%20and%20developing%20economies%20Sep%202010_1798.pdf>

Hansmann, Henry, Reinier Kraakman, 'The end of history for corporate law', Yale Law School Working Paper No. 235; NYU Working Paper No. 013; Harvard Law School Discussion Paper No. 280; Yale SOM Working Paper No. ICF-00-09, January 2000

Havemann, Roy, 'The South African small banks' crisis of 2002/3', *Economic History of Developing Regions*, 36(2), 2021, pp. 313–338, available at: <https://doi.org/10.1080/20780389.2021.1943348>

International Monetary Fund, 'World economic outlook – GDP', 2024, available at: <https://www.imf.org/en/Publications/WEO/Issues/2024/07/16/world-economic-outlook-update-july-2024>

Ioannou, Stefanos, Dariusz Wójcik, Gary Dymski, 'Too-big-to-fail: Why megabanks have not become smaller since the global financial crisis?', *Review of Political Economy*, 31(3), 2019, pp. 356–381

King IV Report on Corporate Governance for South Africa, 2016

Malherbe, Stephan, Nick Segal, *Corporate Governance in South Africa* (OECD Development Center, Paris, 2001)

Mor, Federico, 'Bank rescues of 2007–09: Outcomes and cost', House of Commons Library, Briefing Paper 5748, available at: <https://commonslibrary.parliament.uk/research-briefings/sn05748/>

Nakpodia, Franklin, Emmanuel Adegbite, 'Corporate governance and elites', *Accounting Forum*, 42(1), 2018, pp. 17–31

NDIC, 'Closed financial institutions', available at: <https://ndic.gov.ng/failure-resolution/closed-financial-institutions/> accessed 15 January 2024

Nwude, Chuke, 'The crash of the Nigerian stock market, what went wrong, the consequences and the Panacea', *Journal of Developing Countries Studies*, 2(9), 2012, pp. 105–117

Okike, Elewechi, 'Corporate governance in Nigeria: The status quo', *Corporate Governance: An International Review*, 15(2), 2007, pp. 173–193

Osuji, Onyeka, Franklin Ngwu, Frank Stephen, *Corporate Governance in Developing and Emerging Markets* (Routledge, Abingdon and New York, 2017)

Ozili, Peterson, Olayinka Uadiale, 'Ownership concentration and bank profitability', *Future Business Journal*, 3(2), 2017, pp. 159–171

Rekha, Rao-Nicholson, Salaber Julie, 'Impact of the financial crisis on cross-border mergers and acquisitions and concentration in the global banking sector', *Thunderbird International Business Review*, 58(2), 2016, pp. 161–173

Rena, Ravinder, Malindi Msoni, 'Global financial crises and its impact on the South African economy: A further update', *Journal of Economics*, 5(1), 2014, pp. 17–25, available at: <https://doi.org/10.1080/09765239.2014.11884980>

Rossouw, G.J., A. Van der Watt, D.P. Malan, 'Corporate governance in South Africa', *Journal of Business Ethics*, 37(3), May 2002, Corporate Governance Reforms in Developing Countries, pp. 289–302

Samanta, Navajyoti, 'Transplantation of Anglo-American corporate governance and its impact on financial market growth: A comparative analysis of nineteen developing countries 1995–2014', *Corporate Governance*, 19(5), 2019, pp. 884–922, ISSN 1472-0701

Stewart, Heather, 'We are in the worst financial crisis since depression, says IMF', *The Guardian*, Thursday 10 April 2008, available at: <www.theguardian.com/business/2008/apr/10/useconomy.subprimecrisis>

Udo Udoma & Belo-Osagie, 'The companies and allied matters act 2020 – what you need to know', *Part 9 Schemes of Arrangement, BusinessDay Newspaper*, Tuesday 8 September 2020

Van Deventer, Donald, 'Case studies in liquidity risk: Royal bank of Scotland PLC New York branch', Kamakura Corporation Working Paper, 4 August 2011

West, Andrew, 'Theorising South Africa's corporate governance', *Journal of Business Ethics*, 68(4), 2006, pp. 433–448

2 Corporate Governance Concepts, Theories, and Models

2.1 Introduction

Corporate governance has recently become a significant point of discussion in the banking industry. One of the most pertinent questions underlying this discourse is 'What is the significance of corporate governance?' This chapter aims to answer this question, as it is essential to understanding corporate governance and its relevance to the banking industry. The chapter commences by exploring the different definitions of corporate governance. Although there is no consensus on the concept, a definition that attempts to recognise stakeholders and protect their interests was proposed in this chapter. Furthermore, the chapter delves into modern theories of corporate governance, such as agency, stewardship, shareholder primacy, and enlightened shareholder value (ESV) theories. It is argued that shareholder primacy and the ESV models that underlie the Anglo-Saxon corporate governance model are structured to advance shareholders' private interests. The fundamental objective of both models is to maximise profits for the benefit of shareholders. Additionally, the chapter examines institutional and stakeholder theories as alternative theories of corporate governance. Both institutional and stakeholder theories are utilised to investigate corporate governance issues in the banking industries of Nigeria and South Africa.

2.2 Defining Corporate Governance

'Corporate governance' comes from the Latin words '*corpus*,' meaning a body or an organisation, and '*gubernare*,' which means to steer, direct, or control.[1] Corporate governance has been an essential concept since the financial crisis of 2007–2009, but there is no consensus on its definition. The following definitions provide some insights into the various dimensions of the concept. Cadbury defined corporate governance as follows:

1 Jill Solomon, *Corporate Governance and Accountability* (John Wiley and Sons, The Atrium Southern Gate, Chichester, 2007), p. 1

DOI: 10.4324/9781003474418-3

> A system by which companies are directed and controlled. Boards of directors are responsible for the governance of their companies. The shareholders' role in governance is to appoint the directors and the auditors and satisfy themselves with an appropriate governance structure. The responsibilities of the board include setting the company's strategic aims, providing the leadership to put them into effect, supervising the management of the business, and reporting to shareholders on their stewardship. The board's actions are subject to laws, regulations and the shareholders in general meeting.[2]

According to Cadbury's definition, corporate governance encompasses the organisation and operation of a company's board of directors. The board of directors is responsible for reporting on its stewardship to the shareholders and is, therefore, accountable to them. However, it is worth noting that this definition of corporate governance prioritises the private interests of shareholders. One would argue that Cadbury's definition aligns with the definition offered by Shleifer and Vishny,[3] who viewed corporate governance as the mechanism through which investors secure a return on their investment. The primary concern here is how to maximise profits for shareholders by ensuring that managers generate adequate investment returns.

Another definition of corporate governance worthy of consideration is that offered by the Organisation for Economic Co-operation and Development (OECD), which defines corporate governance as follows:

> a set of relationships between a company's management, its board, its shareholders and other stakeholders. Corporate governance also provides the structure through which the objectives of the company are set, and the means of attaining those objectives and monitoring performance are determined.[4]

The definition of corporate governance provided by the OECD is broader in scope compared to Cadbury's definition. The key distinction between the two definitions is that the OECD's definition takes into account all stakeholders involved in corporate governance. This encompasses the board, managers, shareholders, auditors, customers, employees, and creditors. The OECD's definition also aligns with the definition given by Monk and Minow, who defined corporate governance as a set of relationships amongst various stakeholders in the corporation in determining its direction and performance.[5] Both definitions emphasise the importance of the rela-

2 Adrian Cadbury, *Report of the Committee on the Financial Aspects of Corporate Governance* (Gee, London, 1992), available at: <www.ecgi.org/codes/documents/cadbury.pdf> accessed 10 February 2024

3 Shleifer Andrei, Robert Vishny, 'A survey of corporate governance', *The Journal of Finance*, 52(2), 1997, p. 737

4 OECD, *G20/OECD, Principles of Corporate Governance* (OECD Publishing, Paris, 2015), p. 9

5 Robert Monk, Nell Minow, *Corporate Governance* (1st ed., Blackwell Publishing Ltd., Cambridge, MA, 1995), p. 1

tionships among various stakeholders in the corporation to determine its direction, structure, and the means for monitoring performance.

Preston defined corporate governance as 'the set of institutional arrangements that legitimates and directs the corporation in performing its functions.'[6] Based on Preston's definition, it is argued that corporate governance is a system of institutional arrangement aimed at various stakeholders within the corporation, each having a distinct role to play. For the purposes of this book, corporate governance refers to the institutional arrangements that shape the interconnected relationships between various stakeholders in a corporation. This creates checks and balances to promote the interests of all stakeholders. The definition has two parts. Firstly, it acknowledges the interlinked relationship between key stakeholders such as shareholders, creditors, employees, customers, regulators, directors, and auditors in the governance of banks. Secondly, the definition acknowledges the role of institutional arrangements in shaping the corporate governance framework. It could be argued that the framework for corporate governance should be tailored to each country,[7] as the issues pertaining to corporate governance are inherently socially, politically, culturally, and economically grounded in each jurisdiction, which may differentiate from one country to another. Given the unique challenges that each country faces, it is crucial to design a corporate governance framework that is adapted to its specific circumstances in order to address these issues effectively. Therefore, understanding corporate governance within the country's scope allows one to identify and analyse the peculiar problems inherent in such a country and propose a comprehensive corporate governance framework which considers the specific country's institutional voids. The lack of attention to the context that the institutional theory strives to fill forms a basis for institutional voids. These are intermediaries that allow banks to operate effectively. The absence or poor functioning of such intermediaries amounts to an institutional void.

Palepu and Khanna coined the term 'institutional voids' in 1997.[8] They describe these voids as the underdevelopment or the absence of formal institutions that support commercial activities in any country.[9] For a country's economy to function properly, there is a need for functioning institutions.[10] Institutions play a crucial role in any society as intermediaries between businesses and individuals. They come in various forms, and their nonexistence or non-functionality can lead to severe problems in corporate governance. An ineffective legal system/judiciary can pose

6 James Post, Lee Perston, Sybille Sach, *Redefining the Corporation: Stakeholder Management and Organisational Wealth* (Stanford University Press, Stanford, CA, 2002), p. 18

7 Onyeka Osuji, Franklin Ngwu, Frank Stephen, *Corporate Governance in Developing and Emerging Markets* (Routledge, Abingdon and New York, 2017), p. 3

8 Krishna Palepu, Turan Khanna, 'Why focused strategies may be wrong for emerging markets', *Harvard Business Review*, July–August 1997, pp. 41–51

9 Krishna Palepu, Turan Khanna, 'Why focused strategies may be wrong for emerging markets', *Harvard Business Review*, July–August 1997, pp. 41–51

10 Krishna Palepu, Turan Khanna, 'The nature of institutional voids in emerging markets', in Krishna Palepu, Turan Khanna (eds), *Winning in Emerging Markets: A Road Map for Strategy and Execution* (Harvard Business Press, Boston, 2010), pp. 13–26

considerable challenges in safeguarding the interests of customers and employees, especially where there are institutional voids in those countries.[11] Inadequate protection for banks' customers and employees directly results from institutional voids characterised by the weak legal system and the underdeveloped capital market. The legal system may not have adequately provided for the rights of both employees and customers, which could lead to their inability to exercise these rights in court. This is often due to the failure of the transplanted legal and regulatory framework to recognise the institutional voids present in these countries. As a result, employees and customers may find themselves unable to assert their rights in situations where they would otherwise be entitled to do so. The corporate governance framework in these countries must be designed to take into account the institutional voids present in these countries to ensure that the rights of all stakeholders are adequately protected.

2.3 Theoretical Perspectives on Corporate Governance

Corporate governance theories provide the basis for analysing, describing, interpreting, and predicting the interlinked relationship among stakeholders in the corporation. While several corporate governance theories exist, only a few dominate corporate governance discourse and literature, and these theories are the agency theory, stewardship theory, shareholder primacy theory, ESV theory, institutional theory, and stakeholder theory.[12] Exploring these corporate governance theories is essential for understanding the theoretical basis which underpins the different corporate governance models and mechanisms.

2.3.1 Agency Theory

The concept of agency theory is the oldest theory in management science and economics.[13] The origin of the agency theory dates back to the work of Jensen and Meckling, titled '*The Theory of the Firm: Managerial Behaviour, Agency Costs, and Ownership Structure.*'[14] Jensen and Meckling argued that the agency theory is a contractual relationship between the shareholders (principal) who engage the board of directors and senior management (agent) by delegating the management and control of its affairs to its agent because of the information at the agent's disposal. Suppose the agents are utility seekers; they will pursue their private interest, thereby disregarding the principal's interest, except the agent is monitored or/and

11 Krishna Palepu, Turan Khanna, 'The nature of institutional voids in emerging markets', in Krishna Palepu, Turan Khanna (eds), *Winning in Emerging Markets: A Road Map for Strategy and Execution* (Harvard Business Press, Boston, 2010), pp. 13–26

12 Christine Mallin, *Corporate Governance* (6th ed., Oxford University Press, Oxford, 2019), p. 80

13 Catherine Daily, Dan Dalton, Nandini Rajagopalan, 'Governance through ownership: Centuries of practice, decades of research', *Academy of Management Journal*, 46(2), 2003, pp. 151–158

14 Michael Jensen, William Meckling, 'Theory of the firm: Managerial behaviour, agency costs, and ownership structure', *Journal of Financial Economics*, 3, 1976, pp. 305–360, 308

incentivised, which is a cost to the corporation.[15] The cost of monitoring the agent is what is known as the agency cost. Alchian and Demsetz were the first to argue that monitoring employee performance is always at the cost of any corporation.[16]

Jensen and Meckling's primary concern is how to draft the contracts between the principal and the agent. They suggested that the principal concern in drafting the contract between them and the agent is incorporating the procedures for evaluating the agent's performance and rewarding such performance. Such a step will help minimise, if not eradicate, the conflict of interest between the shareholders and managers. If the agent is aware they are being monitored, they will strive to promote the company's objective, and through profit maximisation, shareholders can measure the agent's performance. It is argued that if the principal does not take the necessary steps to check the agent, there is the possibility that the agent will breach its fiduciary duty to the bank.

The modalities of drafting the contracts between the principal and the agent suggested by Jensen and Meckling will not eradicate the agency problem as they suggested. Just because an agreement contains modalities for monitoring and rewarding the agent does not necessarily mean ending the conflict of interest between the principal and the agent. The real solution goes beyond what the contract contains. What is crucial is the implementation and enforcement of the agreement between them. The contract must include effective sanctions for irresponsible behaviour and poor performance. Even though the agency theory is a core theory for understanding corporate governance, it has some fundamental flaws. The theory is narrowly conceived because it does not reflect corporate governance complexities if it is confined to a mere contractual relationship between two individuals, the principal (shareholders) and the agent (directors).[17] The theory fails to recognise other stakeholders' interests in the corporation. Perrow argues that the agency theory research is lopsided because researchers have mainly focused on the agent aspect of the 'principal and agent problem,' thereby presenting the agent as the cause of the problem.[18] The principal could be the problem in this relationship because when the principal fails to compensate the agent for the work done adequately, there is bound to be a problem.[19] Perrow further argued that another crucial flaw of the agency theory is that the proponents failed to acknowledge the principals' exploitative behaviours; this is evident when the principal regularly exploits, shuns, and deceives the agents.[20] The self-regulatory approach aligns with the agency theory

15 Michael Jensen, William Meckling, 'Theory of the firm: Managerial behaviour, agency costs, and ownership structure', *Journal of Financial Economics*, 3, 1976, pp. 305–360, 308

16 Armen Alchian, Harold Demsetz, 'Production, information costs, and economic organisation', *The American Economic Review*, p. 780, available at: <www.business.illinois.edu/josephm/BA545_Fall%202015/Alchian%20and%20Demsetz%20(1972).pdf>

17 Bob Tricker, *Corporate Governance: Principles, Policies, and Practices* (3rd ed., Oxford University Press, Oxford, 2015), p. 63

18 Charles Perrow, *Complex Organizations* (4th ed., Echo Point Books & Media, 2014), p. 224

19 Charles Perrow, *Complex Organizations* (4th ed., Echo Point Books & Media, 2014), p. 224

20 Charles Perrow, *Complex Organizations* (4th ed., Echo Point Books & Media, 2014), p. 224

because the board of directors acting on behalf of shareholders monitors the bank management against deviating from promoting shareholders' interests. Preventing the misalignment of the interests comes at a price to the bank, known as the agency cost. Several corporate governance mechanisms are put in place to mitigate agency costs; these mechanisms are explored in the later chapter of this book

2.3.2 Stewardship Theory

The stewardship theory is the alternative to the agency theory, even though it is also about the relationship between two individuals, the principal (shareholders) and the managers (stewards). The distinction between the stewardship and agency theories is based on two fundamental assumptions. The first is that managers are good stewards who ordinarily act in the shareholders' best interest, thereby reducing the agency costs of monitoring the directors.[21] The second assumption is that the steward directors are unlikely to act in any way that will be detrimental to the shareholders for fear of causing harm to their reputations.[22]

The stewardship theorists argue that, unlike agency theory, which sees the directors as economic beings and tends to suppress their aspirations, the stewardship theory recognises the importance of structures that empower the steward and offer maximum autonomy built on trust.[23] The stewardship theorist further argued that executive directors do not pursue their interests under the stewardship theory but act with integrity and independence.[24] Consequently, the cost of monitoring or assessing the directors is dispensed with because monitoring or evaluating the directors' actions is unnecessary as both parties' interests are aligned, so there is no need for non-executive directors. The stewardship theorists further assert that the bank's performance is linked to the executive directors' decision to maximise shareholder returns.[25] According to stewardship theorists, many non-financial motives are responsible for managerial behaviours, such as the need for achievement, recognition, the intrinsic satisfaction of successful performance, work ethic, and respect for constituted authority.[26] Unlike the executive directors under the agency theory, who may pursue their interests at the expense of the shareholder's interests, the executive directors under the stewardship theory are motivated by the

21 James Davis, David Schoorman, Lex Donaldson, 'Towards a stewardship theory of management', *Academy of Management Review*, 22(1), January 1997, pp. 20–47
22 James Davis, David Schoorman, Lex Donaldson, 'Towards a stewardship theory of management', *Academy of Management Review*, 22(1), January 1997, pp. 20–47
23 James Davis, David Schoorman, Lex Donaldson, 'Towards a stewardship theory of management', *Academy of Management Review*, 22(1), January 1997, pp. 20–47
24 James Davis, David Schoorman, Lex Donaldson, 'Towards a stewardship theory of management', *Academy of Management Review*, 22(1), January 1997, pp. 20–47
25 James Davis, David Schoorman, Lex Donaldson, 'Towards a stewardship theory of management', *Academy of Management Review*, 22(1), January 1997, pp. 20–47
26 Melinda Muth, Lex Donaldson, 'Stewardship theory and board structure: A contingency approach', *Corporate Governance: An International Review*, 6(1), January 1998, pp. 5–28, 6

non-financial benefits they will derive from being a good steward to the shareholders rather than pursuing their interests.

One major criticism against stewardship theory is that no empirical evidence supports the claim that a board mainly constituted of executive directors performs better. There is no linkage between board composition or leadership structure and corporate performance or behaviours in light of the existing literature on stewardship theory.[27] Stewardship theory supports unifying the Chieh Executive Officers' (CEOs) and the Chairman of the Boards' (COB) roles to reduce agency costs, thereby giving the stewards a greater responsibility in the bank.[28] One would argue that such fusion of the CEO's and COB's positions hinders adequate monitoring because having the same person as the CEO and COB means putting too much power in one individual's hands.

2.3.3 Shareholder Primacy Theory

The concept of shareholder primacy is premised on the traditional view that endows shareholders with the status of owners of corporations. As such, directors of these entities are obliged to act in the best interests of the shareholders. This notion holds that the ultimate goal of a corporation is to maximise shareholder value, which is often achieved through the payment of dividends, share buybacks, and the pursuit of profitable investments.[29] The Michigan State Supreme Court in *Dodge v Ford Motor Co* supported this position when it held that a business corporation is organised and carried on primarily for the shareholders' profit; hence, the directors' powers are to be directed towards that end.[30] However, later decisions, including *Shlensky v. Wrigley*[31] and *A. P. Smith Manufacturing Co. v. Barlow*,[32] rejected this line of reasoning, emphasising that directors need not treat shareholder wealth maximisation as their sole duty. Though the pronouncement might have given directors some authority or discretion in carrying out their duties, the decision in *Katz v Oak Industries, Inc.*[33] proved otherwise. In that case, the Delaware chancery court reaffirmed the reasoning in *Dodge v Ford Motor Co, holding* that directors must attempt within the law to maximise shareholders' interests in the long run. Milton Friedman once canvased this view when he argued that businesses' sole purpose is to utilise their resources and engage in activities designed to increase

27 Gavin Nicholson, Geoffrey Kiel, 'Can directors impact performance? A case-based test of three theories of corporate governance', *Corporate Governance: An International Review*, 15(4), July 2007, pp. 585–608, 588

28 James Davis, David Schoorman, Lex Donaldson, 'Towards a stewardship theory of management', *Academy of Management Review*, 22(1), January 1997, pp. 20–47

29 Elaine Sternberg, *Corporate Governance: Accountability in the Marketplace* (2nd ed., The Institute of Economic Affairs (IEA), London, 2004), p. 36

30 *Dodge v. Ford Motor Co.*, 170 N.W. 668, 684 (Mich. 1919)

31 *Shlensky v. Wrigley, 237 NE 2d 776 (Ill. App. 1968)*

32 *A.P. Smith Manufacturing Co. v. Barlow*, 13 N.J. 145, 98 A.2d 581 (1953)

33 *Katz v. Oak Industries, Inc.*, 508 A.2d 873, 1986 Del. Ch. LEXIS 379 (Del. Ch., 10 March 1986)

profits for shareholders' benefit, so long as they abide by the rules, engage in free competitions, and do not act with fraud or deception.[34]

Friedman's capitalist view of the corporation is premised on the agency theory. As earlier stated, the purpose of corporations is to make profits for the benefit of shareholders because the managers are agents appointed by the shareholders to serve their interests by judiciously using the available resources to generate the needed profits. Friedman's concern is for the managers to maximise profit for the shareholders within the confine of the law. Based on this, one could argue that using available resources judiciously for wealth maximisation includes using some key stakeholders to achieve this task. For example, company employees are viewed as part of the human resources used to achieve the organisation's corporate purpose, which is maximising profits for shareholders' benefit. Therefore, the primary argument of shareholder theorists is that corporations should be managed to benefit shareholders who own the corporations.[35]

To suggest that the shareholders are the owners of corporations is to conceive a corporation in the narrowest sense.[36] Corporations are businesses created by law with separate legal identities from their shareholders. One would argue that, at best, shareholders only have proprietary interests in the company, which is different from being the owner.[37] However, the court in *Multinational Gas and Petrochemical Co. Ltd v Multinational Gas and Petrochemical Services Ltd* held that the shareholders are in substance the company so long as the company is solvent.[38] The primary corporate objective of businesses focuses on shareholders' interest, and shareholders' interest equals profit maximisation. If directors claim to act in furtherance of the corporate objective of the banks, they are inadvertently acting in the interest of the shareholders.[39] This view has been supported by Sternberg, who asserted that the corporation is still a slave of the shareholders despite the doctrine of separate corporate personality.[40] Shareholders determine the corporate

34 Milton Friedman, Rose Friedman, *Capitalism and Freedom* (The University of Chicago Press, Chicago and London, 1962), p. 133

35 Milton Friedman, 'A Friedman doctrine', *The New York Times*, 13 September 1970, available at: <www.nytimes.com/1970/09/13/archives/a-friedman-doctrine-the-social-responsibility-of-business-is-to.html> accessed 18 February 2024

36 Elaine Sternberg, *Corporate Governance: Accountability in the Marketplace* (2nd ed., The Institute of Economic Affairs (IEA), London, 2004), p. 36

37 *Short v. Treasury Commissioners* (1948) 1 KB 116, 122, CA; *Her Majesty's Commissioners of Inland Revenue v. Laird Group Plc* [2003] UKHL 54, para 35; David Chandler, *Strategic Corporate Social Responsibility: Sustainable Value Creation* (4th ed., Sage, London, 2017), p. 119; David Chandler, *Corporate Social Responsibility: A Strategic Perspective* (Business Expert Press LLC, New York, 2015), pp. 11–13; John Kay, 'Shareholders think they own the company – they are wrong', *Financial Times*, 10 November 2015, available at: <www.ft.com/content/7bd1b20a-879b-11e5-90de-f44762bf9896> accessed 18 February 2024

38 *Multinational Gas and Petrochemical Co v. Multinational Gas and Petrochemical Services Ltd and Others* (1983) Ch 258, para 288, per Dillion LJ

39 *Foss v. Harbottle* (1843) 2 Hare 461, 67 ER 189

40 Elaine Sternberg, *Corporate Governance: Accountability in the Marketplace* (2nd ed., The Institute of Economic Affairs (IEA), London, 2004), p. 37

objective to maximise profit for their benefit. Directors, as agents of shareholders, must act to achieve this corporate objective; therefore, in pursuit of the corporate objective, directors engage in excessive risk-taking, which is detrimental to other banks' stakeholders.[41]

The proponents of the shareholder primacy theory justify their assertion that the company must be managed to maximise profit for the shareholders' benefit because they own the company and bear the risk of losses the company may incur. Sternberg believes that 'although the corporation has a separate legal personality in law, the corporation is a slave to the shareholders. She argued that the shareholders own the corporation; they must determine its purpose and are ultimately entitled to enslave it.'[42] Such a proposition is inaccurate and unfounded because Sternberg and other shareholder primacy theorists have deliberately ignored the corporation's status under corporate law, as held in the case of *Solomon v Solomon*.[43] Based on the doctrine of a separate legal entity, the company is an artificial person in law who can sue and be sued in its name. Therefore, it is misleading for shareholder primacy theorists like Sternberg to suggest that a group of persons (shareholders) can own another (company).[44]

One of the most significant criticisms of the shareholder primacy theory is its assumption that the government has increased social welfare; therefore, businesses should only focus on profit maximisation for the benefit of their shareholders. Empirical evidence does not support the increased welfare proposition. For example, in the US, where shareholder primacy has been practised for several years, there is still a high level of inequality between the rich and the poor.[45] Shareholders have continued to derive significant benefits from the increased corporate profit but failed to remunerate workers adequately, as evidence suggests that employees' wages have declined significantly in recent years.[46]

The shareholder primacy theory is premised on a false assumption that the company owners (shareholders) should be the sole beneficiary in the corporation so long as the company is solvent. It is misleading to suggest that only the

41 Grant Kirkpatrick, 'The corporate governance lessons from the financial crisis', *OECD Journal: Financial Market Trends*, 1, 2009, available at: <https://doi.org/10.1787/fmt-v2009-art3-en.> accessed 19 February 2024

42 Elaine Sternberg, *Corporate Governance: Accountability in the Market Place* (2nd ed., The Institute of Economic Affairs (IEA), London, 2004), p. 37

43 *Solomon v. Solomon* [1896] UKHL 1 [1897] AC 22

44 *Short v. Treasury Commissioners* (1948) 1 KB 116, 122, CA; *Her Majesty's Commissioners of Inland Revenue v. Laird Group Plc* [2003] UKHL 54 para 35, David Chandler, *Strategic Corporate Social Responsibility: Sustainable Value Creation* (4th ed., Sage, London, 2017), p. 119; David Chandler, *Corporate Social Responsibility: A Strategic Perspective* (Business Expert Press LLC, New York, 2015), pp. 11–13; John Kay, 'Shareholders think they own the company – they are wrong', *Financial Times*, 10 November 2015, available at: <www.ft.com/content/7bd1b20a-879b-11e5-90de-f44762bf9896> accessed 2 March 2024

45 Nicholas Heiserman, Brent Simpson, 'Higher inequality increases the gap in the perceived merit of the rich and poor', *Social Psychology Quarterly*, 80(3), 2017, pp. 243–253, available at: <https://doi.org/10.1177%2F0190272517711919>

46 Benedict Sheehy, 'Scrooge-the Reluctant Stakeholder: Theoretical problems in the shareholder-stakeholder debate', *University of Miami Business Law Review*, 14, 2005, pp. 193, 215

shareholders' investments are at stake compared to other stakeholder groups; thus, the company should be managed for their benefit alone because of their risk. However, in the banking industry, non-shareholder stakeholders, such as employees, customers like depositors, and debtholders, contribute to the bank's capital and long-term success and bear the risk of banking failures. Consequently, a reformed shareholder theory was postulated to mitigate the inherent flaws in the shareholder primacy theory. This new theory supposedly incorporates other stakeholders' interests in the corporation. The theory is known as the ESV theory and is explored in the next subsection.

2.3.4 Enlightened Shareholder Value Theory

The ESV is the rebranded form of shareholder theory that purports to consider the interests of non-shareholders in the corporation, such as customers and employees. However, it is argued that the ESV theory and the shareholder primacy theory are similar in scope because, in the ESV theory, the corporate objective is also to maximise profit for shareholders' benefit. The fundamental difference between both theories is the ESV's theory's longer-term approach to profit maximisation, which may include consideration of the interests of other stakeholders, such as customers and employees, that might affect profits. The ESV puts an obligation on directors when promoting the company's objective for the benefit of the shareholders to consider the interest of other stakeholders, such as employees,[47] customers, and suppliers,[48] and consider the impact of its operations on the community and the environment.[49]

The ESV theory has received a mixed reception amongst legal academics and corporate law practitioners who spent time evaluating how the principle operates in practice.[50] Some argued that it gives directors too much discretion; it is a shield for directors rather than a duty owed to the company.[51] s.172 CA 2006 protects the company's directors because they are not obligated to promote the interests of any other stakeholders except those of the shareholders.

s.172 CA 2006 requires directors to have regard to the constituents listed therein; however, this does not translate into promoting those stakeholders' interests.

Another problem with s.172 CA 2006 is that although it might seem to have provided a standard against which the directors' conduct can be assessed[52] by requiring them to act in good faith when exercising their independent judgment, it does not

47 S.172 (b) Companies Act 2006

48 S.172 (c) Companies Act 2006

49 S.172 (d) Companies Act 2006

50 Andrew Keay, 'The Enlightened Shareholder Value and Corporate Governance', *Modern Law Review*, 76(5), 2013, p. 940

51 Andrew Keay, 'The Enlightened Shareholder Value and Corporate Governance', *Modern Law Review*, 76(5), 2013, p. 940

52 Andrew Keay, 'The Enlightened Shareholder Value and Corporate Governance', *Modern Law Review*, 76(5), 2013, p. 940

clearly define what constitutes 'good faith.'[53] However, it is argued that the duty to act in good faith is subjective because it is for the director to decide in good faith what is in the best interest of the company. There is no mechanism to deter short-term profit drive by the directors on behalf of shareholders. To maximise the profit and promote the company's success, directors may engage in activities that undermine other stakeholders' interests. The UK Companies Act 2006 did not attempt to define the term 'success of the company' nor did the Act provide any parameter for measuring success. According to Andrew Keay, directors' actions do not necessarily need to lead to success in objective terms so long as they act in good faith, believing that their action was likely to promote the company's success.[54]

If directors breach s.172 CA 2006, only shareholders can bring a derivative claim against them.[55] Non-shareholder stakeholders, including those listed in s.172 CA 2006, are not entitled to take action against the directors for contravening the section or any other part of the Act.[56] So directors in promoting the 'success of the company' are to maximise profits, which is the corporate objective for the shareholders' benefit. As Lord Avebury puts it, 'in many, if not most, cases, the company's success depends on its ability to continue damaging the environment.'[57] So directors may not have regard to the environment and other constituents listed in s.172 CA 2006. There is no legal basis for those affected to enforce against the directors because only shareholders can enforce against directors on behalf of the company.

Based on the limited cases dealing with s.172 CA 2006, particularly related to its breach, it is argued that the ESV theory is not different from the shareholder primacy theory, although it purports to incorporate the recognition of some specific stakeholders in the corporation by requiring directors to have regard to them while endorsing the traditional objectives of the corporate law, which is profit maximisation for the benefit of shareholders. Consequently, in 2021, a coalition of over 1000 businesses and organisations launched the Better Business Act (BBA) campaign proposing reforms to s.172 CA 2006.[58] The number of companies in the coalition seeking an amendment to section 172 of the Companies Act 2006 has now increased to over 2500. The proposed reforms aim to foster an inclusive and equitable boardroom decision-making process premised on the notion of a triple-bottom-line approach to business, which takes into account the interests of people, the planet, and profitability in equal

53 S.173 Companies Act 2006

54 Andrew Keay, 'The Enlightened Shareholder Value and Corporate Governance', *Modern Law Review*, 76(5), 2013, p. 940

55 Section 260(1) Company Act 2006

56 Section 170(1) Company Act 2006

57 Lord Avebury of UK House of Lords Parliamentary Debates, 2006, available at: <https://publications.parliament.uk/pa/ld200506/ldhansrd/vo060206/text/60206-32.htm> accessed 5 March 2024

58 Julie Pybus, 'Better business act campaigners urge UK parliament to halt relentless pursuit of shareholder profits', *Pioneers Post*, 21 April 2022, available at: <www.pioneerspost.com/news-views/20220421/better-business-act-campaigners-urge-uk-parliament-halt-relentless-pursuit-of?utm_content=buffer9356d&utm_medium=social&utm_source=twitter.com&utm_campaign=buffer> accessed 5 March 2024

measure.[59] The BBA is based on the assertion that the triple-bottom-line approach to business is the only solid foundation for a sustainable economy.[60] Thus, the intended result of the reforms is to promote a corporate culture that is both sustainable and socially responsible while also ensuring that the organisation remains financially viable.[61] This approach is grounded in the understanding that a business's success is not solely measured by its profitability but also by its ability to manage its environmental and social impact effectively and to foster a positive relationship with its stakeholders.[62] If the BBA is enacted, it will displace the doctrine of shareholder primacy as the guiding principle of boardroom decision-making, thus amending the wording of s.172 CA 2006 to state that directors have a duty to 'advance the purpose' of the company instead of 'promote the success' of it.'[63] These proposed reforms give credence to the argument made in this book that there is a need for a more stakeholder approach to businesses. However, as it stands presently, the ESV theory embedded in s.172 CA 2006 further reaffirms the existing shareholder primacy approach to corporate law and corporate governance.

2.3.5 Institutional Theory

The institutional theory argues that the institutional environment influences the development of formal structures in a corporation.[64] The theory deals with how structures such as rules, values, norms, routines, regulatory systems, and beliefs become established as authoritative social behaviour guidelines.[65] An institutional void arises when these structures become deficient or underdeveloped. The institutional theory explains why corporations adopt similar characteristics and forms. The institutional theorists argued that 'organisations conform because they are rewarded

59 Bates Wells, 'The better business act', available at: <https://bateswells.co.uk/about/being-a-better-business/better-business-act/> accessed 5 March 2024

60 Christopher Marquis, 'Advocating for better business: U.K. coalition aligns to advance benefit corporation requirement', *Forbes*, 3 February 2022, available at: <www.forbes.com/sites/christophermarquis/2022/02/03/advocating-for-better-business-uk-coalition-aligns-to-advance-benefit-corporation-requirement/?sh=120648e055f4> accessed 5 March 2024

61 Christopher Marquis, 'Advocating for better business: U.K. coalition aligns to advance benefit corporation requirement', *Forbes*, 3 February 2022, available at: <www.forbes.com/sites/christophermarquis/2022/02/03/advocating-for-better-business-uk-coalition-aligns-to-advance-benefit-corporation-requirement/?sh=120648e055f4> accessed 5 March 2024

62 Christopher Marquis, 'Advocating for better business: U.K. coalition aligns to advance benefit corporation requirement', *Forbes*, 3 February 2022, available at: <www.forbes.com/sites/christophermarquis/2022/02/03/advocating-for-better-business-uk-coalition-aligns-to-advance-benefit-corporation-requirement/?sh=120648e055f4> accessed 5 March 2024

63 Social Good Connect, 'What is the better business act?', 23 June 2021, available at: <https://socialgoodconnect.org/better-business-act/> accessed 5 March 2024

64 Sheila Puffer, Daniel McCarthy, 'Institutional Theory' in *Wiley Encyclopedia of Management: Vol. 6, International Management* (John Wiley, New York, January 2015)

65 Sheila Puffer, Daniel McCarthy, 'Institutional Theory' in *Wiley Encyclopedia of Management: Vol. 6, International Management* (John Wiley, New York, January 2015)

for doing so through increased legitimacy, resources and survival capabilities,'[66] a view supported by renowned institutional theorists like Dimaggio and Powell. They argued that behaviours are regulated through coercive, normative, and mimetic isomorphisms.[67] These three forms of isomorphisms require further explanation.

Coercive isomorphism refers to the formal or informal pressures that regulatory authorities impose on regulated firms. For instance, the government can introduce a specific procedure through its regulatory agencies to ensure that the practices in the banking industry are legitimate. Coercive isomorphism can also include external pressures from other industries of the economy, such as non-governmental organisations and the government. These external pressures may require the banks to conform to socio-cultural expectations. An excellent example of such restrictive pressure could originate from governmental mandates, regulated forms of CSR, contractual relationships, and financial reporting requirements.[68] Coercive isomorphism arises when prudential regulators mandate banks to hold adequate financial resources such as minimum capital and liquidity ratio requirements and also to put comprehensive risk control measures in place. The banks must comply with such mandates, as failure to do so will attract appropriate sanctions.

Normative isomorphism is the pressures of social or professional norms or standards.[69] This results from people influenced by their similar educational backgrounds. Since people have had the same training, particularly within a particular profession, they tend to approach specific problems using the same method. Membership in a particular profession can significantly influence what is considered appropriate in the context of corporate governance. Auditors, for instance, commonly adopt a uniform auditing methodology based on best practices listed in audit tenders within the United Kingdom.

Companies have the ability to observe how auditing firms perform their operations. Suppose a firm of auditors does not follow the same method as others in the field to solve related accounting problems. In that case, it means that such a firm has deviated from the acceptable norm within that profession. The phenomenon of auditing firms adhering to the established norms of the profession is commonly referred to as 'normative isomorphism.' This practice is motivated by the perceived risk that deviation from accepted norms might negatively impact the likelihood of future appointments. Consequently, auditing firms tend to conform to established norms in order to avoid jeopardising their professional standing and future opportunities for engagement.

Mimetic isomorphism is a concept that pertains to the emulation of best practices within successful organisations. This is often pursued in the face of uncertainty within a given corporation. In striving for success or reaching a particular standard,

66 Richard Scott, 'The adolescence of institutional theory', *Administrative Science Quarterly*, 32(4), December 1987, pp. 493–511, 498

67 Paul Dimaggio, Walter Powell, 'The iron cage revisited: Institutional isomorphism and collective rationality in organisational fields', *America Sociological Review*, 48, April 1983, pp. 147–160

68 Paul Dimaggio, Walter Powell, 'The iron cage revisited: Institutional isomorphism and collective rationality in organisational fields', *America Sociological Review*, 48, April 1983, pp. 147–160

69 Paul Dimaggio, Walter Powell, 'The iron cage revisited: Institutional isomorphism and collective rationality in organisational fields', *America Sociological Review*, 48, April 1983, pp. 147–160

companies are frequently tempted to adopt the policies, practices, and procedures of prosperous companies within their industry. This practice is prevalent among small, medium, and start-up companies that seek to emulate established organisations, believing that their success is attributable to their organisational structure. Consequently, mimetic isomorphism is characterised by adopting established companies' policies, procedures, and practices as the norm, setting the standard for smaller firms and start-ups to follow.

Institutional theory has been criticised for its non-convergence. Lex Donaldson[70] argued that Lynne Zucker used the plural 'theories' in her article entitled *'Institutional Theories of Organisation'*[71] to suggest more than one institutional theory. There is also the argument that institutional theorists treat all organisations as one, thereby neglecting organisations' heterogeneousness.[72] They further argued that even though the institutional theorists acknowledge that differences exist in organisations, they see those differences as irrelevant to the institutional theory.[73] It is argued that this criticism is flawed to a certain extent. While it is true that organisations differ from one another, it is still possible for them to act in a similar manner. The differences between these organisations may be so insignificant that they would not alter the way organisations are influenced. This book utilises institutional theory to examine the Nigerian and South African institutional environments and its effect on corporate governance in the banking industry. The institutional theory helps to understand the challenges of implementing effective corporate governance in the Nigerian and South African banking industry by exploring the institutional voids in Nigeria and South Africa.

2.3.6 Stakeholder Theory

The term stakeholder has recently become a buzzword in corporate governance discourse. Despite its popularity, there seems to be a lack of clarity about the conceptualisation.[74] Various scholars have offered many definitions of stakeholders in corporate governance; however, the difference in these definitions centres on who may or may not qualify as a stakeholder.[75] Eden and Ackermann defined stakeholders as those 'people or small groups with the power to respond to, negotiate with,

70 Lex Donaldson, *American Anti-Management Theories of Organisation: A Critique of Paradigm Proliferation* (Cambridge University Press, Cambridge, 1995), p. 121

71 *Lynne Zucker, 'Institutional Theories of Organisation', Annual Review of Sociology, 13, 1987, pp. 443–464, available at:* <*www.jstor.org/stable/2083256*>

72 Royston Greenwood, C.R. Hinings, Dave Whetten, 'Rethinking institutions and organizations', *Journal of Management Studies*, 51(7), 2014, pp. 1206–1220, 1206

73 Royston Greenwood, C.R. Hinings, Dave Whetten, 'Rethinking institutions and organizations', *Journal of Management Studies*, 51(7), 2014, pp. 1206–1220, 1206

74 Jeffrey Harrison, Edward Freeman, Monica Sa de Abreu, 'Stakeholder theory as an ethical approach to effective management: Applying the theory to multiple contexts', *Review of Business Management*, 17(55), 2015, pp. 858–869, 858

75 Fran Ackermann, Colin Eden, 'Strategic management of stakeholders: Theory and practice', *Long Range Planning*, 44, 2011, pp. 179–196, 180

and change the organisation's strategic future.'[76] From this definition, individuals without the power to engage with the corporation will not qualify as stakeholders. This definition is too narrow because it excludes those who may have been affected directly or indirectly by the corporation's actions but lack the means to engage the corporation. This argument is supported by Bryson when he suggested that the definition of stakeholder offered by Eden and Ackermann is too restrictive because it prevents those affected but lacking the power or means to respond to or negotiate with the corporation.[77]

Edward Freeman, who defined stakeholders as any group or individual who can affect or is affected by the achievement of the organisation's objectives, provides a more comprehensive definition of the stakeholders.[78] This definition is used to identify the key stakeholders in the Nigerian and South African banking industry; this includes individuals or groups who are directly or indirectly affected by the banks' actions.

Having defined stakeholders in the corporation, it is necessary to explore further the stakeholder theory. This is another fundamental theory of corporate governance. It is prominent in many discussions on business ethics, organisational effectiveness, and corporate governance. Its origin dates back to the work of Edwin Merrick Dodd Jr. entitled '*For Whom Are Corporate Managers Trustees?*'[79] The work is centred on a debate between Dodd and Adolph Berle regarding whom the corporation managers should be accountable to. Berle believed that the corporation must act for the benefit of the shareholders, while Dodd argued that although the law supports Berle's opinion, the interests of employees should also be taken into consideration.[80] This is why some stakeholder theorists, including James Post, Lee Preston, and Sybille Sach, have challenged the prevalent notion of shareholder primacy and the corresponding corporate objective of profit maximisation.[81] These scholars have expressed dissent towards the underlying ideology of shareholder primacy and the ESV theories. They suggest that the corporate objective should not be limited to serving the interests of shareholders alone.[82] They argued that corporations should consider all stakeholders' interests, including employees, customers, suppliers, and society at large. They further argued that the corporation is an organisation mobilising resources for productive users to create wealth and

76 Colin Eden, Frank Ackermann, *Making Strategy: The Journey of Strategic Management* (1st ed., Sage, London, 1998), p. 117

77 John Bryson, 'What to do when stakeholders matter', *Public Management Review*, 6(1), 2004, pp. 21–53, 22

78 Edward Freeman, *Strategic Management: A Stakeholder Approach* (Pitman, Boston, 1984), p. 34

79 E. Merrick Dodd, Jr., 'For whom are corporate managers trustees?', *Harvard Law Review*, 45(7), May 1932, pp. 1145–1163

80 E. Merrick Dodd, Jr., 'For whom are corporate managers trustees?', *Harvard Law Review*, 45(7), May 1932, p. 1151

81 James Post, Lee Preston, Sybille Sach, *Redefining the Corporation: Stakeholder Management and Organisational Wealth* (Stanford University Press, Stanford, CA, 2002), p. 17

82 James Post, Lee Preston, Sybille Sach, *Redefining the Corporation: Stakeholder Management and Organisational Wealth* (Stanford University Press, Stanford, CA, 2002), p. 17

other benefits and not destroy wealth, increase risk, or intentionally cause harm to its multiple stakeholders.[83]

Organisations must strive to achieve corporate goals beyond maximising profits for the benefit of shareholders. The corporation comprises various internal and external constituents, such as employees, creditors, and local communities, whose interests must be recognised and protected. Stakeholder theorists advocate for a more inclusive approach, where corporations protect the interests of all stakeholders rather than just those of their shareholders. It is argued that the corporation should pursue all its stakeholders' interests because of the various roles they play in promoting the company's success, as the shareholder primacy and the ESV are inadequate in promoting all stakeholders' interests. BBA campaigners advocate for legislation to align company practices and policies with long-term benefits for people and the planet and profit by requiring public companies and their directors to weigh and advance some key stakeholders' interests, not just shareholders.[84]

As noted in the introductory chapter, identifying stakeholder groups within a corporation is not straightforward and may vary across organisations. Given the challenge of achieving consensus on stakeholder groups, some scholars have contended that virtually any entity within the human environment qualifies as a stakeholder. In this regard, Sternberg has posited that stakeholders now encompass 'everyone, everything, everywhere, including terrorists, competitors, vegetation, nameless sea creatures, and generations yet unborn.'[85] It is clear that identifying stakeholders is a multifaceted process subject to varying perspectives and interpretations. Nonetheless, the notion that virtually any entity within the human environment can be considered a stakeholder represents a significant expansion of traditional stakeholder theory, which focuses on more narrowly defined groups. So the argument is exaggerated; for instance, identifying stakeholders in a corporation like the banks is not as complex as Sternberg purports to make it look.

Freeman's stakeholder definition provides a helpful framework in the banking industry for identifying individuals or groups that can affect or are affected by a bank's objectives. This definition is particularly relevant in the context of determining stakeholder groups in the banking industry,[86] which fall into two broad categories of stakeholders: internal and external.

Internal stakeholders are the people or groups within a company who are crucial for its survival as a business. On the other hand, external stakeholders are those who affect or are affected by the company's objectives. Regarding the banking

83 James Post, Lee Preston, Sybille Sach, *Redefining the Corporation: Stakeholder Management and Organisational Wealth* (Stanford University Press, Stanford, CA, 2002), p. 17

84 Christopher Marquis, 'Advocating for better business: U.K. coalition aligns to advance benefit corporation requirement', *Forbes*, 3 February 2022, available at: <www.forbes.com/sites/christophermarquis/2022/02/03/advocating-for-better-business-uk-coalition-aligns-to-advance-benefit-corporation-requirement/?sh=120648e055f4> accessed 20 March 2024

85 Elaine Sternberg, 'The defects of stakeholders theory', *Corporate Governance: An International Review*, 5(1), January 1997, p. 4

86 Edward Freeman, *Strategic Management: A Stakeholder Approach* (Pitman, Boston, 1984), p. 46

industry, internal stakeholders include shareholders, employees, directors, managers, depositors, and creditors. Meanwhile, external stakeholders consist of host communities, government, public interest groups, trade unions, clients, business partners, and corporate regulators.[87] Like other corporate governance theories discussed earlier, the stakeholder theory has also been subject to various criticisms. Proponents of shareholder primacy and enlightened shareholder value theories, such as Sternberg, contend that the stakeholder theory is incompatible with business objectives. While the stakeholder theory was designed to enhance strategic management planning, Sternberg posits that the proposal to manage the corporation for all stakeholders' benefit undermines its primary objective of the corporation, which is to maximise profits for shareholders.[88] Sternberg posited that the stakeholder theory is incompatible with corporate governance, contending that the latter pertains solely to the board of directors' obligation to answer to the shareholders and not to any other group.[89] Sternberg argued that the stakeholder theory, which requires companies to be accountable to all stakeholders, is impractical because being accountable to everyone means being accountable to no one; consequently, Sternberg believes that the stakeholder theory is not a suitable model for corporate governance, suggesting that the theory does more harm than good since conventional corporate accountability based on the stakeholder's accountability theory is unjustified. Although stakeholder theory has been criticised by some scholars, particularly the proponents of shareholder primacy and ESV theories, it remains the fundamental theory underpinning the discussions in this book, alongside institutional theory. Stakeholder theory is useful in identifying the key stakeholders in the banking industry, including customers and employees, and their various challenges. Additionally, it helps to ascertain how their interests can be protected.

2.4. Conclusion

This chapter has explored the theories that form the basis of corporate governance discourse. It begins by examining the different definitions of corporate governance. While acknowledging that there is no consensus on the definition of corporate governance, the chapter highlights that defining the concept from a narrow perspective, such as the shareholder-centric viewpoint, is inaccurate and undermines other stakeholders' contributions and interests. This chapter delves into corporate governance theories, including agency, stewardship, shareholder primacy, ESV, institutional, and stakeholder theories. It argues that the agency theory is founded on an erroneous premise, given that it solely considers the relationship between

87 Edward Freeman, *Strategic Management: A Stakeholder Approach* (Pitman, Boston, 1984), p. 46

88 Elaine Sternberg, 'The defects of stakeholders theory', *Corporate Governance: An International Review*, 5(1), January 1997, p. 4

89 Elaine Sternberg, 'The defects of stakeholders theory', *Corporate Governance: An International Review*, 5(1), January 1997, p. 5

shareholders and managers in a corporation at the expense of other stakeholders. In contrast, stewardship theory is similar to agency theory in that it also focuses on the relationship between shareholders and managers. However, the stewardship theory does not involve agency costs associated with monitoring managers, as with agency theory.

The chapter further examined the shareholder primacy and the ESV theories entrenched in s.172 CA 2006; it argues that while the latter mandates directors to have regard to some stakeholders listed in the section when promoting the company's success, it is nothing more than a mere codification of the existing shareholder primacy approach to corporate law and governance. Both types of shareholder theories share the same corporate objectives, as directors are expected to maximise profits for the benefit of the shareholders, and no other individual apart from them should benefit from the company.

The institutional and stakeholder theories were also examined in this chapter and were adopted as the fundamental theories on which the discussions in this book are centred. The institutional theory is germane in exploring the Nigerian and South African banking institutional environments and the ensuing corporate governance challenges. On the other hand, the stakeholder theory is pertinent in examining the primary stakeholders in the banking industry. It also helps in understanding how the corporate governance framework protects the interests of these stakeholders, especially customers and employees.

Reference List

Ackermann, Fran, Colin Eden, 'Strategic management of stakeholders: Theory and practice', *Long Range Planning*, 44, 2011, pp. 179–196

Alchian, Armen, Harold Demsetz, 'Production, information costs, and economic organisation', *The American Economic Review*, p. 780, available at: <www.business.illinois.edu/josephm/BA545_Fall%202015/Alchian%20and%20Demsetz%20(1972).pdf>

Andrei, Shleifer, Robert Vishny, 'A survey of corporate governance', *The Journal of Finance*, 52(2), 1997, p. 737

A.P. Smith Manufacturing Co. v. Barlow (1953) 13 N.J. 145, 98 A.2d 581

Bryson, John, 'What to do when stakeholders matter', *Public Management Review*, 6(1), 2004, pp. 21–53

Cadbury, Adrian, *Report of the Committee on the Financial Aspects of Corporate Governance* (Gee, London, 1992), available at: <www.ecgi.org/codes/documents/cadbury.pdf>

Chandler, David, *Corporate Social Responsibility: A Strategic Perspective* (Business Expert Press LLC, New York, 2015), pp. 11–13

Chandler, David, *Strategic Corporate Social Responsibility: Sustainable Value Creation* (4th ed., Sage, London, 2017)

Companies Act, 2006

Daily, Catherine, Dan Dalton, Nandini Rajagopalan, 'Governance through ownership: Centuries of practice, decades of research', *Academy of Management Journal*, 46(2), 2003, pp. 151–158

Davis, James, David Schoorman, Lex Donaldson, 'Towards a stewardship theory of management', *Academy of Management Review*, 22(1), January 1997, pp. 20–47

Dimaggio, Paul, Walter Powell, 'The iron cage revisited: Institutional isomorphism and collective rationality in organisational fields', *America Sociological Review*, 48, April 1983, pp. 147–160

Dodd, E. Merrick, Jr., 'For whom are corporate managers trustees?', *Harvard Law Review*, 45(7), May 1932, pp. 1145–1163
Dodge v. Ford Motor Co. (1919) 170 N.W. 668, 684 (Mich.)
Donaldson, Lex, *American Anti-Management Theories of Organisation: A Critique of Paradigm Proliferation* (Cambridge University Press, Cambridge, 1995)
Eden, Colin, Frank Ackermann, *Making Strategy: The Journey of Strategic Management* (1st ed., Sage, London, 1998)
Foss v. Harbottle (1843) 2 Hare 461, 67 ER 189
Freeman, Edward, *Strategic Management: A Stakeholder Approach* (Pitman, Boston, 1984)
Friedman, Milton, 'A Friedman doctrine', *The New York Times*, 13 September 1970, available at: <www.nytimes.com/1970/09/13/archives/a-friedman-doctrine-the-social-responsibility-of-business-is-to.html>
Friedman, Milton, Rose Friedman, *Capitalism and Freedom* (The University of Chicago Press, Chicago and London, 1962)
Greenwood, Royston, C.R. Hinings, Dave Whetten, 'Rethinking institutions and organizations', *Journal of Management Studies*, 51(7), 2014, pp. 1206–1220
Harrison, Jeffrey, Edward Freeman, Monica Sa de Abreu, 'Stakeholder theory as an ethical approach to effective management: Applying the theory to multiple contexts', *Review of Business Management*, 17(55), 2015, pp. 858–869
Heiserman, Nicholas, Brent Simpson, 'Higher inequality increases the gap in the perceived merit of the rich and poor', *Social Psychology Quarterly*, 80(3), 2017, pp. 243–253, available at: <https://doi.org/10.1177%2F0190272517711919>
Jensen, Michael, William Meckling, 'Theory of the firm: Managerial behaviour, agency costs, and ownership structure', *Journal of Financial Economics*, 3, 1976, pp. 305–360
Katz v. Oak Industries, Inc. (10 March 1986) 508 A.2d 873, 1986 Del. Ch. LEXIS 379 (Del. Ch.)
Kay, John, 'Shareholders think they own the company – they are wrong', *Financial Times*, 10 November 2015, available at: <www.ft.com/content/7bd1b20a-879b-11e5-90de-f44762bf9896>
Keay, Andrew, 'The enlightened shareholder value and corporate governance', *Modern Law Review*, 76(5), 2013, p. 940
Kirkpatrick, Grant, 'The corporate governance lessons from the financial crisis', *OECD Journal: Financial Market Trends*, 1, 2009, available at: <https://doi.org/10.1787/fmt-v2009-art3-en>
Lord Avebury of UK House of Lords Parliamentary Debates, 2006, available at: <https://publications.parliament.uk/pa/ld200506/ldhansrd/vo060206/text/60206-32.htm>
Mallin, Christine, *Corporate Governance* (6th ed., Oxford University Press, Oxford, 2019)
Marquis, Christopher, 'Advocating for better business: U.K. coalition aligns to advance benefit corporation requirement', *Forbes*, 3 February 2022, available at: <www.forbes.com/sites/christophermarquis/2022/02/03/advocating-for-better-business-uk-coalition-aligns-to-advance-benefit-corporation-requirement/?sh=120648e055f4>
Monk, Robert, Nell Minow, *Corporate Governance* (1st ed., Blackwell Publishing Ltd., Cambridge, MA, 1995)
Multinational Gas and Petrochemical Co. v. Multinational Gas and Petrochemical Services Ltd. and Others (1983) Ch 258, para 288, per Dillion LJ
Muth, Melinda, Lex Donaldson, 'Stewardship theory and board structure: A contingency approach', *Corporate Governance: An International Review*, 6(1), January 1998, pp. 5–28
Nicholson, Gavin, Geoffrey Kiel, 'Can directors impact performance? A case-based test of three theories of corporate governance', *Corporate Governance: An International Review*, 15(4), July 2007, pp. 585–608
OECD, *G20/OECD, Principles of Corporate Governance* (OECD Publishing, Paris, 2015)
Osuji, Onyeka, Franklin Ngwu, Frank Stephen, *Corporate Governance in Developing and Emerging Markets* (Routledge, Abingdon and New York, 2017)

Palepu, Krishna, Turan Khanna, 'Why focused strategies may be wrong for emerging markets', *Harvard Business Review*, July–August 1997, pp. 41–51

Palepu, Krishna, Turan Khanna, 'The nature of institutional voids in emerging markets', in Krishna Palepu, Turan Khanna (eds), *Winning in Emerging Markets: A Road Map for Strategy and Execution* (Harvard Business Press, Boston, 2010), pp. 13–26

Perrow, Charles, *Complex Organizations* (4th ed., Echo Point Books & Media, 2014)

Post, James, Lee Perston, Sybille Sach, *Redefining the Corporation: Stakeholder Management and Organisational Wealth* (Stanford University Press, Stanford, CA, 2002)

Puffer, Sheila, Daniel McCarthy, 'Institutional theory', in *Wiley Encyclopedia of Management: Vol. 6, International Management* (John Wiley, New York, January 2015)

Pybus, Julie, 'Better business act campaigners urge UK parliament to halt relentless pursuit of shareholder profits', *Pioneers Post*, 21 April 2022, available at: <www.pioneerspost.com/news-views/20220421/better-business-act-campaigners-urge-uk-parliament-halt-relentless-pursuit-of?utm_content=buffer9356d&utm_medium=social&utm_source=twitter.com&utm_campaign=buffer>

Scott, Richard, 'The adolescence of institutional theory', *Administrative Science Quarterly*, 32(4), December 1987, pp. 493–511

Sheehy, Benedict, 'Scrooge-the reluctant stakeholder: Theoretical problems in the shareholder-stakeholder debate', *University of Miami Business Law Review*, 14, 2005, pp. 193, 215

Shlensky v. Wrigley (1968) 237 NE 2d 776 (Ill. App.)

Short v. Treasury Commissioners (1948) 1 KB 116, 122, CA, *Her Majesty's Commissioners of Inland Revenue v. Laird Group Plc* [2003] UKHL 54

Social Good Connect, 'What is the better business act?', 23 June 2021, available at: <https://socialgoodconnect.org/better-business-act/>

Solomon, Jill, *Corporate Governance and Accountability* (John Wiley and Sons, The Atrium Southern Gate, Chichester, 2007)

Solomon v. Solomon [1896] UKHL 1 [1897] AC 22

Sternberg, Elaine, 'The defects of stakeholders theory', *Corporate Governance: An International Review*, 5(1), January 1997

Sternberg, Elaine, *Corporate Governance: Accountability in the Marketplace* (2nd ed., The Institute of Economic Affairs (IEA), London, 2004)

Tricker, Bob, *Corporate Governance: Principles, Policies, and Practices* (3rd ed., Oxford University Press, Oxford, 2015)

Wells, Bates, 'The better business act', available at: <https://bateswells.co.uk/about/being-a-better-business/better-business-act/>

Zucker, Lynne, 'Institutional theories of organisation', *Annual Review of Sociology*, 13, 1987, pp. 443–64, available at: <www.jstor.org/stable/2083256>

3 Corporate Governance and Banking Regulation

3.1 Introduction

This chapter examines the interrelation between corporate governance and banking regulations. The primary objective of this chapter is to explore the theories behind banking regulations to demonstrate the nexus between corporate governance and banking regulations. The chapter establishes that corporate governance is integral to prudential and conduct regulations. The chapter commences by exploring the role of banks and banking in society. It posits that banks are unique due to their significant role in society and should be subject to more rigorous regulation than other companies. It also justifies the need for government regulation of banks because of their functions. For instance, banks provide payment and portfolio services and transform illiquid assets into liquid liabilities, making them volatile and susceptible to runs when performing these and other related functions. Additionally, the chapter examines the two broad approaches to banking regulation: the command-and-control approach and the self-regulatory approach. It argues that the command-and-control approach is geared towards the public interest theory, while self-regulation is more aligned with the private interest theory. The theoretical and conceptual frameworks explored in this chapter, such as the definition of banks, banking regulation, the justification for banking regulation, and the measures of banking regulation, are fundamental to facilitating discussions in this book by applying them to the Nigerian and South African contexts.

3.2 Regulation of Banks and Banking in Society

The term 'bank' originated from the Italian word 'Banca' or the French word 'Banque,' which both meant bench in English.[1] In the past, bankers used to have benches in the market centre where they exchanged money with traders. However, just accepting or collecting money does not qualify as banking operations. Therefore, to understand what constitutes banking, it is important to distinguish between

1 History of Banking, available at: <http://dailytools.in/BankingKnowledge/BankingHistory> accessed 8 April 2024

DOI: 10.4324/9781003474418-4

accepting deposits and granting loans or bank credits to customers. For instance, merely accepting customer deposits does not usually qualify as banking, even if the collector uses such monies for trading. Such interactions merely transfer purchasing power from one person to another, regardless of whether the deposits attract interest.[2] However, banking begins when the collector (bank) grants loans from the collected deposits to customers (borrowers), and the granting of loans will usually depend on the borrowers' creditworthiness.[3] Banking began when merchants lent part of the deposits they collected to traders with the assumption that they would repay the principal sum and the interest accrued on the due date.[4] During the 14th century, banking was still emerging; depositors were somehow responsible for regulating the industry. When these depositors demanded their deposits back and the merchants defaulted, the depositors resorted to unconventional measures to deal with the situation. They would break the benches where those merchants sat, meaning they could no longer conduct business in the marketplace.[5] In Latin, the practice was called 'bancum est ruptum,' which means bankruptcy in English. Although the measures taken by depositors were unorthodox, they ensured that there were consequences for banking failure. This was an appropriate method of dealing with merchants experiencing financial crises. Since then, banking regulation has evolved as a reaction to banking failure[6] resulting from excessive risk-taking and interconnectedness between financial and non-financial institutions.

Banking regulation refers to laws, rules, and procedural requirements enacted by the government, regulatory authorities, or banks themselves to reduce or absorb the risks associated with the banking business.[7] Kenneth Spong provides a precise definition of banking regulation by positing that it is the framework of laws and rules under which banks operate. By this definition, banking regulation encompasses rules, processes, and procedures that govern banking operations. The cardinal objectives of banking regulation are to ensure the protection of depositors, promote economic growth, foster market integrity, and prevent systemic financial risk owing to the inherent fragility of the financial system.[8] In the past decade, there has been a considerable amount of discourse surrounding financial regulation,

2 Abbott Payson Usher, 'The origins of banking: The primitive bank of deposit, 1200–1600', *The Economic History Review*, A4(4), April 1934, p. 399

3 Abbott Payson Usher, 'The origins of banking: The primitive bank of deposit, 1200–1600', *The Economic History Review*, A4(4), April 1934, p. 399

4 Abbott Payson Usher, 'The origins of banking: The primitive bank of deposit, 1200–1600', *The Economic History Review*, A4(4), April 1934, p. 399

5 Bruce Davis, 'A brief history of banking: The link between money and society', *The Guardian*, London, 21 August 2013, available at: <www.theguardian.com/sustainable-business/history-banking-money-society> accessed 8 April 2024

6 Xavier Freixas, Santomero, Anthony, 'An overall perspective on banking regulation', UPF, Economics and Business Working Paper No. 664, 10 March 2003, p. 2

7 Oladapo Olanipekun, 'Banking regulation and supervision: Concept, theory and rationale', in Oladapo Olanipekun (ed), *Banking: Theory, Regulation, Law and Practice* (Au Courant, Lagos, Nigeria, 2016), p. 4

8 Kenneth Spong, *Banking Regulation: Its Purposes, Implementation and Effects* (5th ed., USA Division of Supervision and Risk Management, Federal Reserve Bank, Kansas City, 2000), p. 6

particularly within the banking industry, following the global financial crisis of 2007–2009, which profoundly impacted most of the world's economies. A central point of contention was whether the government failed to discharge its duties in overseeing the banking industry, thereby contributing to the financial crisis.[9]

3.3 Justifications for Banking Regulation

The discourse among academia, policymakers, politicians, and other key stakeholders regarding banking crises has necessitated the need to explore the justifications for banking regulation. The fundamental argument suggests that the justification for banking regulation is primarily economic in nature. Unregulated markets are prone to failure due to financial market imperfections, such as information asymmetry, which results in negative externalities.[10] Therefore, banking regulation can reduce negative externalities by providing adequate information disclosure frameworks. The economic justification for banking regulation falls into two broad categories, the public and private interests[11] theories, and this is explored further in the next subsections.

3.3.1 Public Interest Theory

The proponents of the public interest theory contend that regulatory interventions are necessary to prevent negative externalities arising from market distortion in the public interest.[12] They argued that government regulatory interventions allocate scarce resources for individuals and shared interests.[13] They argued that private law might not offer the required solution due to market failure.[14] However, government regulation can efficiently overcome the disadvantages of imperfect competition, unbalanced market operations, missing markets, and undesirable market results.[15] The proponents of the public interest theory further argued that government regulation occurs because of market failures and unhealthy practices.[16] This position

9 Philip Booth et al., *Verdict on the Crash: Causes and Policy Implications* (Institute of Economic Affairs, London, 2009), p. 37

10 Xavier Freixas, Santomero, Anthony, 'An overall perspective on banking regulation', UPF, Economics and Business Working Paper No. 664, 10 March 2003, p. 4

11 Anthony Ogus, *Regulation: Legal Form and Economic Theory* (Hart Publishing, Oxford, 2004), p. 3

12 Paul Joskow, Roger Noll, 'Regulation in theory and practice: An overview', Working Papers 213, California Institute of Technology, Division of the Humanities and Social Sciences

13 Johan den Hertog, *General Theories of Regulation* (Economic Institute, CLAV, Utrecht University, Utrecht, 1999), p. 225

14 Johan den Hertog, *General Theories of Regulation* (Economic Institute, CLAV, Utrecht University, Utrecht, 1999), p. 225

15 Johan den Hertog, *General Theories of Regulation* (Economic Institute, CLAV, Utrecht University, Utrecht, 1999), p. 225

16 Johan den Hertog, *General Theories of Regulation* (Economic Institute, CLAV, Utrecht University, Utrecht, 1999), p. 225

seems correct because, following the global financial crisis of 2007–2009, many economies undertook a comprehensive review of their banking laws to determine whether or not stricter regulations were necessary. In the United Kingdom, the United States, and the European Union, measures were taken to address the issues that precipitated the crisis. These efforts were intended to enhance the stability of the financial system and further guard against future economic downturns.[17] The UK, for example, made several regulatory interventions relating to executive compensation to mitigate the excessive risk-taking appetite of directors who were rewarded for short-term performance.[18] Most banks' directors took unreasonable risks because of what they stood to benefit based on their short-term performance. This unbridled risk-taking eventually made the banks susceptible to failure, which was one reason for the global financial crisis of 2007–2009.[19]

The proponents of the public interest theory believed that regulators possess adequate information on all aspects of organisational behaviour and have the requisite enforcement mechanisms to promote the public interest.[20] Johan den Hertog argued that government regulation is needed to help prevent market failure. Without active government involvement in controlling the activities of banks, they may not act in the interest of all stakeholders, which becomes evident after exploring the private interest theory in the next section. There is a conflict of interest between what the public wants from the banking industry and what the banks prioritise. The public wants banks to focus on providing Micro, Small, and Medium Enterprises (MSME) loans to help alleviate poverty. However, the banks may be more interested in providing loans to multinational oil companies as they stand to benefit more in the short term. Public interest theorists argue that government regulatory intervention is necessary to ensure banks provide MSME loans, as this will promote financial inclusion and alleviate poverty, which is in the public interest and thereby promotes national economic development in the long run.

When a bank's interests do not align with the public interest, it is the government's responsibility to intervene and establish an equitable balance. One possible intervention involves limiting the loan-to-deposit ratio that banks can offer to MSMEs and multinational companies. The public interest theory contends that banking regulations should prioritise the interests of the public by protecting the interests of individual depositors, like MSMEs, and corporate clients, like multinational oil corporations, when they transact with banks.

17 Stephen Bell, Andrew Hindmoor, 'Are the major global banks now safer? Structural continuities and change in banking and finance since the 2008 crisis', *Review of International Political Economy*, 25(1), 2018, pp. 1–27, available at: <https://doi.org/10.1080/09692290.2017.1414070>

18 Victor Ediagbonya, 'The various changes in the remuneration practices in banks and other financial institutions in the United Kingdom after the global financial crisis', *SSRN*, 28 March 2017, available at: <http://dx.doi.org/10.2139/ssrn.2942472>

19 William Forbes, Lynn Hodgkinson, *Corporate Governance in the UK: Past, Present and Future* (Palgrave Macmillan, Basingstoke, 2015), p. 34

20 William Forbes, Lynn Hodgkinson, *Corporate Governance in the UK: Past, Present and Future* (Palgrave Macmillan, Basingstoke, 2015), p. 34

The distribution of financial resources across all economic industries is believed to enhance the welfare of citizens, in line with the public interest theory, which aligns regulation with welfare economics.[21]

Regulation of banks in the public interest means that the government must intervene in directing banking regulation to ensure a fair allocation of its financial resources to various parts of its economy. This regulatory intervention is necessary, as banks are susceptible to failure because of the risky nature of the banking business. Banks are likely to take excessive risks without government intervention, eventually leading to the breakdown of the entire financial system.[22]

One of the primary criticisms levelled against the public interest theory is its assumption that government regulation is always effective and can be implemented without incurring the high costs associated with market imperfections. This assumption implies that government regulation is free from the information and transaction costs that underlie market failure. However, there is no empirical or theoretical evidence to support this claim.[23] The efficacy of government regulation in the banking industry lies in its ability to prevent individual bank crises and systemic failure that could involve the entire financial system. Several factors must be considered for government intervention to provide the desired outcome of preventing a total collapse of the financial system. For instance, the institutional environment where banking regulation is applied is crucial since public interest differs from one jurisdiction to another and could mean different things in different social systems. This inherent variation depends mostly on various countries' value systems. Despite these criticisms, government regulatory interventions in the banking industry serve the public interest by providing corrective measures against market imperfections, including imperfect competition, unbalanced market operations, negative externalities, and information asymmetry.[24]

3.3.2 Private Interest Theory

Posner asserts that the private interest theory assumes that a particular stakeholder group actively seeks to advance their self-interest by influencing regulation.[25] According to private interest theorists, the government may establish regulations to

21 Sophie Harnay, Laurence Scialom, 'The influence of the economic approaches to regulation on banking regulations: A short history of banking regulations', *Cambridge Journal of Economics*, 40, 2015:, pp. 401–426, 403

22 Sophie Harnay, Laurence Scialom, 'The influence of the economic approaches to regulation on banking regulations: A short history of banking regulations', *Cambridge Journal of Economics*, 40, 2015:, p. 413

23 Richard Posner, 'Theories of economic regulation', *The Bell Journal of Economics and Management Science*, 5(2), 1974, pp. 335–358

24 Sophie Harnay, Laurence Scialom, 'The influence of the economic approaches to regulation on banking regulations: A short history of banking regulations', *Cambridge Journal of Economics*, 40, 2015, pp. 401–426, 403

25 Richard Posner, 'Theories of economic regulation', *The Bell Journal of Economics and Management Science*, 5(2), Autumn 1974, pp. 335, 343

serve the interests of a specific stakeholder group rather than the public interest.[26] Furthermore, proponents of the private interest theory contend that the most influential stakeholder group determines regulation based on their lobbying power to persuade the government to enact laws that provide economic benefits for them.[27] It will depend on how well they can lobby for the government to implement laws that will benefit them economically.[28] The private interest theory asserts that institutions are composed of interest groups that lobby the government for legislation that favours their interests. These interest groups employ their resources and influence to protect their interests. However, conflicts may arise among these groups due to their divergent interests. In such cases, when the government enacts laws, it invariably favours the most influential interest group, often ignoring the interests of others. Politicians who seek to win elections require funding from interest groups, such as banks' shareholders' groups, before or after the elections, in addition to garnering votes from specific stakeholders. The private interest theory asserts that politicians constantly focus on obtaining votes, while bank shareholders focus on maximising profits. This theory asserts that the regulatory capacity of politicians may be significantly diminished due to the support and donations provided by shareholder groups. Shareholders of banks leverage their influence to lobby the government into enacting laws that further their profit-making agenda. It suggests that banks' shareholders drive regulation by lobbying the government to make laws that would promote their profit-making agenda.

Consequently, politicians may be motivated to create legislation that shields established banks from competition, promotes monopolies, and maximises profits. This exchange of donations and information could lead to a sharp decline in politicians' regulatory capacity.[29] For example, the government could enact laws that make it difficult for entrepreneurs to enter the banking industry by introducing stringent entry requirements for obtaining a banking licence.[30] It is argued that regulatory decisions are influenced by the most important stakeholders. Politicians may try to balance the interests of different stakeholders, but they usually prioritise the most pressing issue. Suppose a politician disregards the interests of a particular stakeholder group. In that case, it can harm their chances of getting re-elected, as they are unlikely to receive votes or donations from that group.

Like any other theoretical framework, the private interest theory has shortcomings. One of the most significant criticisms of the theory is that empirical research does not support the hypothesis underlying the capture theory, which asserts that

26 Anthony Ogus, *Regulation: Legal Form and Economic Theory* (Hart Publishing, Oxford, 2004), p. 72

27 Anthony Ogus, *Regulation: Legal Form and Economic Theory* (Hart Publishing, Oxford, 2004), p. 72

28 Anthony Ogus, *Regulation: Legal Form and Economic Theory* (Hart Publishing, Oxford, 2004), p. 71

29 Richard Posner, 'Theories of economic regulation', *The Bell Journal of Economics and Management Science*, 5(2), 1974, pp. 336, 335–358

30 Anthony Ogus, *Regulation: Legal Form and Economic Theory* (Hart Publishing, Oxford, 2004), p. 72

regulation only promotes private interests.[31] This hypothesis fails to account for how interest groups subsequently take over the law-making process. While interest groups can lobby legislators to create laws that favour their interests, such lobbying does not equate to the complete takeover of the law-making process. Consequently, the private interest theory is deficient, lacking essential details and analysis concerning the interactions between political actors and other actors in the regulatory process. It is crucial to note that these criticisms call into question the reliability and applicability of the theory, which necessitates further refinement and improvement.[32]

Despite receiving criticisms, the public interest theory in banking regulation remains essential, as the theory suggests that banking regulation should serve the public's interest rather than the private interest because the primary objectives of banking regulation are to protect stakeholders, prevent financial crime, ensure financial system stability, and maintain market integrity.[33] The private interest theory of banking regulation, which prioritises profit maximisation, can lead to significant negative externalities that undermine financial stability. Banks seeking to maximise profits are willing to take significant risks that may appear desirable to shareholders but can be excessive from other stakeholders' perspectives, especially given the systemic consequences of bank crises.[34] Profit maximisation as a short-term approach can lead to an unsafe banking environment in the long run. Therefore, the public interest theory must take precedence over banks' shareholders' interests in maximising profits for their benefit because a safe banking environment is crucial to ensure the financial system's overall stability.[35]

The regulatory design implemented by banking regulatory and supervisory agencies is firmly rooted in these banking regulation theories. The private and public interest theories significantly influence the strategies and approaches used for banking regulation. Based on this example, it is necessary to further explore the various strategies and approaches used by regulatory agencies for banking regulation.

3.4 Strategies for Banking Regulation

Banking regulation strategies can be classified into three primary categories: prudential, systematic, and conduct regulations.[36] Prudential regulation comprises a

31 Anthony Ogus, *Regulation: Legal Form and Economic Theory* (Hart Publishing, Oxford, 2004),, p. 74

32 Johan den Hertog, *General Theories of Regulation* (Economic Institute, CLAV, Utrecht University, Utrecht, 1999), p. 235

33 Stuart Greenbaum, Anjan Thakor, Arnoud Boot, *Contemporary Financial Intermediation* (4th ed., Academic Press, London, 2020), p. 356

34 Andreas Kokkinis, 'A primer on corporate governance in banks and financial institutions: Are banks special?', in Iris H.-Y. Chiu et al. (eds), *The Law on Corporate Governance in Banks* (Elgar Financial Law and Practice, Cheltenham, 2015), p. 2

35 Michael Jensen, 'Value maximisation and stakeholders theory', *Harvard Business School Working Knowledge, Business Research for Business Leaders*, 24 July 2000, available at: <https://hbswk.hbs.edu/item/value-maximization-and-stakeholder-theory> accessed 8 April 2024

36 Charles Goodhart, Philipp Hartmann, David T. Llewellyn, Liliana Rojas-Suarez, Steven Weisbrod, *Financial Regulation: Why, How and Where Now?* (Routledge, Abingdon, Oxon, 1998), p. 5

set of specific rules or agreed-upon behaviours imposed by regulatory and supervisory agencies, the government, or self-imposed by the banking industry through an explicit or implied agreement.[37] The primary purpose of prudential regulation is to limit the activities of the banking industry and ensure that they act prudently to achieve a defined goal. Llewelyn has classified prudential regulation into three types: preventive, protective, and supportive regulations. Preventive regulations aim to curtail incurred risk, protective regulations provide protection in the event of banking failure, and supportive regulations act as the lender of last resort.[38] According to Llewelyn, banking regulation and supervision may take the following form: providing a safety net for depositors, imposing restrictions on bank asset holdings, setting capital requirements, and implementing prompt corrective action.[39] This perspective aligns with the public interest theory, which supports government intervention in banking regulation and highlights the necessity of a regulatory approach to tackle corporate governance issues in banks.

Systemic regulation refers to the process of mitigating systemic risk, which has the potential to cripple the entire financial system. Given the interconnectedness of banks, any single bank failure can cause a ripple effect, leading to the failure of multiple other banks and ultimately resulting in the collapse of the entire financial system.[40] A prime example of this phenomenon is when a systemically significant bank fails and depositors cannot withdraw their funds due to insufficient liquidity. Such an event can trigger panic withdrawals by depositors of other solvent banks, leading to the complete collapse of the financial system except the government makes adequate bailout intervention to rescue the affected banks.

The UK government's bailout of Royal Bank of Scotland, Lloyds TSB, and HBOS with £37 billion during the global financial crisis of 2007–2009 is a noteworthy example of such intervention. The UK government's timely intervention prevented the collapse of the UK banking industry, mitigating the systemic risk that threatened the financial system.[41] It is argued that systemic risks are negative externalities that can only be addressed by implementing robust prudential regulation. Banks deemed systematically significant are interconnected through their interbank borrowings and syndicate lendings, resulting in the potential for a failure in one bank to precipitate the distress of several other banks, thereby leading to the collapse of the entire financial system. Banking regulatory frameworks must be designed to address systemic risks in order to promote financial stability.

37 David Llewellyn, *The Regulation and Supervision of Financial Institutions* (The Institute of Bankers, London, 1986)

38 David Llewellyn, *The Regulation and Supervision of Financial Institutions* (The Institute of Bankers, London, 1986)

39 David Llewellyn, *The Regulation and Supervision of Financial Institutions* (The Institute of Bankers, London, 1986)

40 Olivier Butzbach, 'Systemic risk, macro-prudential regulation and organizational diversity in banking', *Policy and Society*, 35, 2016, pp. 239–251, 241

41 Peter Thai Larsen, 'UK launches £37bn banking rescue', *The Financial Times*, 23 October 2008, available at: <www.ft.com/content/83bc2cea-98ef-11dd-9d48-000077b07658> accessed 8 April 2024

From the preceding, it is correct to suggest that systemic regulation is an integral part of prudential regulation, and differentiating between them is a mere academic exercise. There are two types of prudential regulation: micro-prudential regulation and macro-prudential regulation. Micro-prudential regulation aims to protect individual banks from excessive risk-taking. In contrast, macro-prudential regulation aims to mitigate systemic risk to the entire financial system.[42] The overall objective of macro-prudential regulation supports the argument that systemic regulation is a fundamental component of prudential regulation.

Conduct regulation focuses on the appropriate standards of conduct for banks to operate in the financial system. This regulatory technique primarily emphasises how the banks carry out their businesses; in other words, this means the banks' business rules.[43] The conduct of business rules focuses on how banks interact with customers or clients, especially when it comes to their advertising, marketing, and sales practices.[44] This aspect of conduct regulation ensures that customers or clients are provided with sufficient information to make informed decisions. Corporate governance plays a pivotal role in business conduct due to the manner in which each bank responds to risks. As such, an effective corporate governance framework for the banking industry should address negative externalities resulting from information asymmetries and market failure.[45] It is argued that a more inclusive corporate governance framework underpinned by the public interest theory will provide positive ways of mitigating, detecting, and dealing with risks associated with the banking business.[46] The role of corporate governance regulation in the banking industry cannot be underestimated, as it is a fundamental element of prudential and conduct regulations. An effective corporate governance framework can enhance the soundness of individual banks and the stability of the entire financial system.[47]

3.5 Approaches to Banking Regulation

There are two main approaches to banking regulation: the command-and-control approach and the self-regulatory approach. The command-and-control approach is characterised by direct government intervention in the banking industry through

42 Frederic Boissay, Lorenzo Cappiello, 'European central bank: Eurosystem', *Financial Stability Review*, May 2014, p. 135

43 John Armour et al., *Principle of Financial Regulation* (Oxford University Press, Oxford, 2016), p. 75

44 John Armour et al., *Principle of Financial Regulation* (Oxford University Press, Oxford, 2016), p. 75

45 Kern Alexander, Rahul Dhumale, John Eatwell, *Global Governance of Financial Systems: The International Regulation of Systemic Risk* (Oxford University Press, New York, 2005), p. 243

46 Kern Alexander, Rahul Dhumale, John Eatwell, *Global Governance of Financial Systems: The International Regulation of Systemic Risk* (Oxford University Press, New York, 2005), p. 243

47 Andreas Kokkinis, 'Rethinking banking prudential regulation: Why corporate governance rules matter', *Journal of Business Law*, 7, 2012, pp. 612–629

legislation to regulate and govern the banking system.[48] Conversely, self-regulation is an alternative approach that places the regulation responsibility on individual banks or third-party organisations such as professional banking associations.[49] It is important to note that the effectiveness of each approach may depend on the jurisdiction and the institutional environment in that country. There is no one-size-fits-all solution, and banking regulation cannot depend solely on one approach. Command-and-control and self-regulation have advantages and disadvantages, therefore, it is necessary to examine these banking regulatory approaches further in the next subsections.

3.5.1 Command and Control

The government uses a banking regulatory approach that involves creating a mandatory set of rules that banks must follow, and regulatory or supervisory agencies monitor compliance. If banks fail to comply with these rules, they may face sanctions.[50] In theory, using this approach is more effective because the government sets legal regulations and monitors banks to ensure compliance.[51] The command-and-control approach requires direct government intervention in licensing, monitoring behaviour, on-site regulatory inspection, and imposing severe sanctions on banks for non-compliance.[52] This approach assumes that all relevant banks will conform to the same legal standards, thereby making the outcome predictable and consistent. The government enacts laws through the legislature and regulatory or supervisory agencies to enforce them.[53]

One of the primary criticisms levelled against the command-and-control regulatory approach is the absence of incentives for banks to exceed government-mandated minimum standards.[54] Banks that comply with these regulations merely fulfil the minimum requirements, which may be insufficient to address the risks associated with individual banks' profiles and the dynamic nature of the financial market.[55] This perspective supports the argument that the command-and-control approach

48 Robert Baldwin, Martin Cave, Martin Lodge, *Understanding Regulation: Theory Strategy and Practice* (2nd ed., Oxford University Press, Oxford, 2012), pp. 612–629

49 Robert Baldwin, Martin Cave, Martin Lodge, *Understanding Regulation: Theory Strategy and Practice* (2nd ed., Oxford University Press, Oxford, 2012), pp. 612–629

50 Robert Baldwin, Martin Cave, Martin Lodge, *Understanding Regulation: Theory Strategy and Practice* (2nd ed., Oxford University Press, Oxford, 2012), pp. 612–629

51 Robert Baldwin, Martin Cave, Martin Lodge, *Understanding Regulation: Theory Strategy and Practice* (2nd ed., Oxford University Press, Oxford, 2012), pp. 612–629

52 Howard Latin, 'Ideal versus real regulatory efficiency: Implementation of uniform standards and fine-tuning regulatory reforms', *Stanford Law Review*, 37(5), May 1985, pp. 1267, 1271

53 Howard Latin, 'Ideal versus real regulatory efficiency: Implementation of uniform standards and fine-tuning regulatory reforms', *Stanford Law Review*, 37(5), May 1985, pp. 1267, 1271

54 Neil Gunningham, Peter Grabosky, Darren Sinclair, *Smart Regulation, Designing Environmental Policy* (Oxford University Press, Oxford, 1998), p. 45

55 Neil Gunningham, Peter Grabosky, Darren Sinclair, *Smart Regulation, Designing Environmental Policy* (Oxford University Press, Oxford, 1998), p. 45

is too inflexible and costly to accommodate innovations.[56] Making changes to the legal standards may require the legislature to amend the law, which is usually not a straightforward process. However, in some cases, existing laws empower banking regulators and supervisors to adapt banking rules, procedures, and policies in response to changing circumstances.[57] The criticism that the command-and-control regulatory approach is costly concerns having enough personnel to monitor compliance.[58] To achieve this, regulators need sufficient staff to conduct regular on-site and off-site supervision, which can be more expensive than self-regulation. Nonetheless, it is more economical than the cost of banking failure, which can result in the collapse of the entire financial system. Therefore, the cost associated with the command-and-control regulatory approach is justified in the public's interest.

3.5.2 Self-Regulation

Self-regulation can be considered as a regulatory approach that occupies a middle ground between conventional regulation and deregulation.[59] Coglianese and Mendelson defined self-regulation as a set of rules created and enforced by the regulated firms themselves.[60] A self-regulatory approach occurs when individuals or a group of organisations take control over their members' conduct.[61] According to Sinclair, self-regulation can only flourish in the face of absolute willingness and cooperation from the banks.[62]

Although self-regulation may involve the banks implementing voluntary codes, these can be combined with sanctions. For instance, those who fail to abide by the codes can be named and shamed, deterring others and encouraging them to step up to avoid negative publicity. Self-regulation may be the preferred approach when the government regulatory approach is inadequate, particularly when there is a shortage of government personnel.[63] Furthermore, self-regulation may be a bet-

56 Neil Gunningham, Peter Grabosky, Darren Sinclair, *Smart Regulation, Designing Environmental Policy* (Oxford University Press, Oxford, 1998), p. 45

57 S.13 Banks and Other Financial Institutions Act, 2020 (BOFIA 2020)

58 S.29 BOFIA, 2020

59 Darren Sinclair, 'Self-regulation versus command and control – beyond false dichotomies', *Law & Policy*, 19, 1997, p. 529

60 Cary Coglianese, Evan Mendelson, 'Meta-regulation and self-regulation', in Martin Cave, Robert Baldwin, Martin Lodge (eds), *The Oxford Handbook on Regulation* (Oxford University Press, Oxford, 2010), p. 147

61 Robert Baldwin, Martin Cave, Martin Lodge, *Understanding Regulation: Theory Strategy and Practice* (2nd ed., Oxford University Press, Oxford, 2012), p. 137

62 Darren Sinclair, 'Self-regulation versus command and control – beyond false dichotomies', *Law & Policy*, 19, 1997, p. 529

63 Cary Coglianese, Evan Mendelson, 'Meta-regulation and self-regulation', in Martin Cave, Robert Baldwin, Martin Lodge (eds), *The Oxford Handbook on Regulation* (Oxford University Press, Oxford, 2010), p. 147

ter option if there are inadequate resources to facilitate effective monitoring and enforcement of the command-and-control regulatory approach.[64]

The government can get involved in self-regulation through a system known as statutory self-regulation. Under this system, the government may legislate on the self-regulatory structure while it vests the powers to implement on banks or the regulatory and supervisory agencies. So government involvement may take the form of oversight functions carried out by its agencies. For example, banks may need to get their drafted self-regulation rules approved by government regulatory and supervisory agencies.[65]

Self-regulation has several advantages over the command-and-control regulatory approach. It allows the implementation of rules, policies, and procedures that would have been impossible using the command-and-control regulatory approach due to inadequate cost, lack of personnel, industrial expertise, and market awareness.[66] Self-regulation is a cheaper alternative to the command-and-control regulatory approach because the cost of self-regulation is usually internalised into the business cost.[67] One reason for market failure is information asymmetry; banks involved in self-regulation have privileged insider information that may be challenging for regulatory agencies to obtain.[68] Self-regulation is a faster and more flexible method of addressing businesses' concerns than the command-and-control regulatory approach. It is flexible as it can quickly adjust to changes, unlike command-and-control, which usually takes time to amend the existing law or make a new one.[69]

Despite the advantages of adopting a self-regulatory approach, it has been noted that this approach is not without its shortcomings. Self-regulation can give rise to contemporary corporatism, whereby a particular interest group, such as shareholders, can wield excessive power without being accountable to other stakeholders.[70] This can lead to an abuse of power, where regulations are designed solely to protect the bank shareholders' interests, which may conflict with the public interest.[71]

64 Cary Coglianese, Evan Mendelson, 'Meta-regulation and self-regulation', in Martin Cave, Robert Baldwin, Martin Lodge (eds), *The Oxford Handbook on Regulation* (Oxford University Press, Oxford, 2010), p. 149

65 Cary Coglianese, Evan Mendelson, 'Meta-regulation and self-regulation', in Martin Cave, Robert Baldwin, Martin Lodge (eds), *The Oxford Handbook on Regulation* (Oxford University Press, Oxford, 2010), p. 150

66 Margot Priest, 'The privatization of regulation: Five models of self-regulation', *Ottawa Law Review*, 29, 1997–1998, pp. 233–302

67 Margot Priest, 'The privatization of regulation: Five models of self-regulation', *Ottawa Law Review*, 29, 1997–1998

68 Margot Priest, 'The privatization of regulation: Five models of self-regulation', *Ottawa Law Review*, 29, 1997–1998

69 A. Ogu, 'Rethinking self-regulation', in Robert Baldwin, Colin Scott, Christopher Hood (eds), *A Reader on Regulation* (Oxford University Press, Oxford, 1998)

70 A. Ogu, 'Rethinking self-regulation', in Robert Baldwin, Colin Scott, Christopher Hood (eds), *A Reader on Regulation* (Oxford University Press, Oxford, 1998), p. 375

71 A. Ogu, 'Rethinking self-regulation', in Robert Baldwin, Colin Scott, Christopher Hood (eds), *A Reader on Regulation* (Oxford University Press, Oxford, 1998), p. 376

Therefore, it is evident that relying solely on self-regulation will not be adequate in preventing corporate governance issues in the banking industry.[72] While there is recognition of the importance of both the command and control and self-regulatory approaches, finding a middle ground between these two regulatory approaches is vital in ensuring that banking regulation is designed to serve the public interest[73]

3.5.3 Responsive Regulation

Responsive regulation is a regulatory approach that strikes a balance between command-and-control and self-regulatory methods. Unlike command-and-control regulation, which often fails to secure a commitment to compliance with the law, responsive regulation fosters a moral obligation to comply with regulations.[74] Command-and-control regulation does not consider the morality of regulated behaviour; instead, it relies on imposing sanctions to enforce compliance.[75] An example of responsive regulation is involving third-party entities in banking regulation. Rather than allowing the banks to self-regulate their risk management directly, banking associations could be entrusted with powers to monitor individual banks' risk management processes. Such a regulatory system can be achieved by granting banks the power to self-regulate their risk management processes while simultaneously authorising a third party, such as a bankers' association, to supervise and monitor them. This approach ensures that businesses operate within the bounds of the law while providing them with the necessary autonomy to manage their operations. Responsive regulation provides a valuable theoretical framework for analysing and addressing corporate governance challenges, particularly the limited stakeholders' recognition and the protection of stakeholders' interests in the Nigerian and South African banking industries.

3.6 Conclusion

The primary objective of this chapter was to investigate the relationship between corporate governance and banking regulation. The chapter delved into the regulatory theories underpinning banking regulation and put forward the argument that the justification for banking regulation is solely economic. In particular, two banking regulation theories:: public and private interest theories were explored. It was established that the economic rationale for banking regulation based on the public interest theory is to protect the interests of relevant stakeholders, such as

72 Ian Ayres, John Braithwaite, *Responsive Regulation: Transcending the Deregulation Debate* (Oxford University Press, Oxford, 1995), p. 20

73 Ian Ayres, John Braithwaite, *Responsive Regulation: Transcending the Deregulation Debate* (Oxford University Press, Oxford, 1995), p. 20

74 Christine Parker, 'The "compliance" trap: The moral message in responsive regulatory enforcement', *Law & Society Review*, 40, 2006, p. 591

75 Christine Parker, 'The "compliance" trap: The moral message in responsive regulatory enforcement', *Law & Society Review*, 40, 2006, p. 591

the interests of banks' shareholders. This chapter further examined the three techniques for banking regulation: prudential regulation, systemic regulation, and conduct regulation. It was argued that corporate governance regulation constitutes a critical component of both prudential and conduct regulations. Additionally, the two fundamental approaches to banking regulation, the command and control, and self-regulatory approaches were explored. The chapter analysed the merits and drawbacks of both regulatory approaches. It concluded that a hybrid regulatory approach, known as 'responsive regulation,' would better address corporate governance challenges, particularly the limited recognition of stakeholders and protection of stakeholders' interests in the Nigerian and South African banking industries.

Reference List

Alexander, Kern, Rahul Dhumale, John Eatwell, *Global Governance of Financial Systems: The International Regulation of Systemic Risk* (Oxford University Press, New York, 2005)

Armour, John et al., *Principle of Financial Regulation* (Oxford University Press, Oxford, 2016)

Ayres, Ian, John Braithwaite, *Responsive Regulation: Transcending the Deregulation Debate* (Oxford University Press, Oxford, 1995)

Baldwin, Robert, Martin Cave, Martin Lodge, *Understanding Regulation: Theory Strategy and Practice* (2nd ed., Oxford University Press, Oxford, 2012)

Banks and Other Financial Institutions Act, 2020

Bell, Stephen, Andrew Hindmoor, 'Are the major global banks now safer? Structural continuities and change in banking and finance since the 2008 crisis', *Review of International Political Economy*, 25(1), 2018, pp. 1–27, available at: <https://doi.org/10.1080/09692290.2017.1414070>

Boissay, Frederic, Lorenzo Cappiello, 'European central bank: Eurosystem', *Financial Stability Review*, 1, May 2014

Booth, Philip et al., *Verdict on the Crash: Causes and Policy Implications* (Institute of Economic Affairs, London, 2009)

Butzbach, Olivier, 'Systemic risk, macro-prudential regulation and organizational diversity in banking', *Policy and Society*, 35, 2016, pp. 239–251

Coglianese, Cary, Evan Mendelson, 'Meta-regulation and self-regulation', in Martin Cave, Robert Baldwin, Martin Lodge (eds), *The Oxford Handbook on Regulation* (Oxford University Press, Oxford, 2010)

Davis, Bruce, 'A brief history of banking: The link between money and society', *The Guardian*, London, 21 August 2013, available at: <www.theguardian.com/sustainable-business/history-banking-money-society>

den Hertog, Johan, *General Theories of Regulation* (Economic Institute, CLAV, Utrecht University, Utrecht, 1999), p. 235

Ediagbonya, Victor, 'The various changes in the remuneration practices in banks and other financial institutions in the United Kingdom after the global financial crisis', *SSRN*, 28 March 2017, available at: <http://dx.doi.org/10.2139/ssrn.2942472>

Forbes, William, Lynn Hodgkinson, *Corporate Governance in the UK: Past, Present and Future* (Palgrave Macmillan, Basingstoke, 2015)

Freixas, Xavier, Santomero, Anthony, 'An overall perspective on banking regulation', UPF, Economics and Business Working Paper No. 664, 10 March 2003

Goodhart, Charles, Philipp Hartmann, David T. Llewellyn, Liliana Rojas-Suarez, Steven Weisbrod, *Financial Regulation: Why, How and Where Now?* (Routledge, Abingdon, Oxon, 1998)

Greenbaum, Stuart, Anjan Thakor, Arnoud Boot, *Contemporary Financial Intermediation* (4th ed., Academic Press, London, 2020)

Gunningham, Neil, Peter Grabosky, Darren Sinclair, *Smart Regulation, Designing Environmental Policy* (Oxford University Press, Oxford, 1998)

Harnay, Sophie, Laurence Scialom, 'The influence of the economic approaches to regulation on banking regulations: A short history of banking regulations', *Cambridge Journal of Economics*, 40, 2015, pp. 401–426

History of Banking, available at: <http://dailytools.in/BankingKnowledge/BankingHistory>

Jensen, Michael, 'Value maximisation and stakeholders theory', *Harvard Business School Working Knowledge, Business Research for Business Leaders*, 24 July 2000, available at: <https://hbswk.hbs.edu/item/value-maximization-and-stakeholder-theory>

Joskow, Paul, Roger Noll, 'Regulation in theory and practice: An overview', in Gary Fromm (ed), *Studies in Public Regulation* (The MIT Press, Cambridge, MA, 1981) pp. 1–78

Kokkinis, Andreas, 'Rethinking banking prudential regulation: Why corporate governance rules matter', *Journal of Business Law*, 7, 2012, pp. 612–629

Kokkinis, Andreas, 'A primer on corporate governance in banks and financial institutions: Are banks special?', in Iris H.-Y. Chiu et al. (eds), *The Law on Corporate Governance in Banks* (Elgar Financial Law and Practice, Cheltenham, 2015)

Latin, Howard, 'Ideal versus real regulatory efficiency: Implementation of uniform standards and fine-tuning regulatory reforms', *Stanford Law Review*, 37(5), May 1985

Llewellyn, David, *The Regulation and Supervision of Financial Institutions* (The Institute of Bankers, London, 1986)

Ogus, Anthony, 'Rethinking self-regulation', in Robert Baldwin, Colin Scott, Christopher Hood (eds), *A Reader on Regulation* (Oxford University Press, Oxford 1998)

Ogus, Anthony, *Regulation: Legal Form and Economic Theory* (Hart Publishing, Oxford, 2004)

Olanipekun, Oladapo, 'Banking regulation and supervision: Concept, theory and rationale', in Oladapo Olanipekun (ed), *Banking: Theory, Regulation, Law and Practice* (Au Courant, Lagos, Nigeria, 2016)

Parker, Christine, 'The "compliance" trap: The moral message in responsive regulatory enforcement', *Law & Society Review*, 40, 2006

Posner, Richard, 'Theories of economic regulation', *Bell Journal of Economics and Management Science*, 5(2), 1974, pp. 336, 335–358

Priest, Margot, 'The privatization of regulation: Five models of self-regulation', *Ottawa Law Review*, 29, 1997–1998, pp. 233–302

Sinclair, Darren, 'Self-regulation versus command and control – beyond false dichotomies', *Law & Policy*, 19, 1997, p. 529

Spong, Kenneth, *Banking Regulation: Its Purposes, Implementation and Effects* (5th ed., USA Division of Supervision and Risk Management, Federal Reserve Bank, Kansas City, 2000)

Thai Larsen, Peter, 'UK launches £37bn banking rescue', *The Financial Times*, 23 October 2008, available at: <www.ft.com/content/83bc2cea-98ef-11dd-9d48-000077b07658>

Usher, Abbott Payson, 'The origins of banking: The primitive bank of deposit, 1200–1600', *The Economic History Review*, A4(4), April 1934

Part B

Corporate Governance and Banking Regulation in Africa

4 Determinants of Effective Corporate Governance in the Banking Industry

4.1 Introduction

This chapter examines the factors that contribute to effective corporate governance in the banking industry. It argues that a sound corporate governance framework is critical since the banking business is inherently risky. Such a corporate governance framework ensures that risks are appropriately managed and relevant stakeholders' interests, such as employees and customers, are promoted. The international frameworks for bank governance, such as the Basel Committee on Banking Supervision (BCBS) Corporate Governance Principles for Banks and the OECD Principles of Corporate Governance, were examined. Although these international instruments are not legally binding, they have significantly influenced corporate governance frameworks in many countries, highlighting their importance in promoting effective corporate governance in the banking industry. Since one of the criticisms of the stakeholder model discussed in Chapter 2 is the difficulty in identifying which individuals or groups fall under this category, it is necessary to explore the stakeholders in the banking industry. The chapter explored the dominant models of corporate governance in the banking industry: the Anglo-Saxon, Continental European, and Japanese models. It argues that shareholder primacy underpins the Anglo-Saxon model, while the Continental European and Japanese Keiretsu models are underpinned by stakeholder theory. Additionally, the various corporate governance mechanisms in the banking industry and the concept of corporate social responsibility were identified and discussed. It argues that incorporating corporate social responsibility into banks' corporate governance promotes the recognition of stakeholders and protection of stakeholders' interests. This chapter emphasises the need for an effective corporate governance framework in the banking industry that promotes the interests of all stakeholders, as such a framework is crucial for the stability and sustainability of the banking industry.

4.2 Notion of Effective Corporate Governance

Scholarships in corporate governance have attempted to re-conceptualise corporate governance in the wake of corporate scandals in recent times, particularly after

DOI: 10.4324/9781003474418-6

the global financial crisis of 2007–2009.[1] The re-conceptualisation is reflected in academic works as well as in corporate governance practices, as a new layer of concern has been added to the concept. It is noteworthy that academic literature, professionals in the field, and even corporate governance codes have now adopted the term 'effective corporate governance' to describe this new trend.[2] However, despite the widespread use of the term 'effective corporate governance,' no definition has been offered for this newly coined concept. The general perception among academics and corporate law practitioners is that effective corporate governance is synonymous with good corporate governance.[3]

According to Millstein et al., effective corporate governance is characterised by four fundamental principles: fairness, transparency, accountability, and responsibility.[4] The principle of fairness involves protecting shareholders through regulations that prohibit fraud, self-dealing by managerial or controlling shareholders, and other insider misconduct.[5] The accountability principle is achieved by clearly defining governance roles and responsibilities, which enables the board to monitor management and ensure that they act in the best interests of shareholders.[6] Transparency is achieved through regulations that mandate the timely dissemination of information to shareholders.[7] Responsibility ensures that corporations comply with acceptable societal standards in which they operate.[8] It can be argued that these principles,

1 Donald Nordberg, 'Edging toward "reasonably" good corporate governance', *Philosophy of Management*, 17, 2018, pp. 353–371, available at: <https://doi.org/10.1007/s40926-017-0083-9>

2 Melinda Timea Fülöp, 'Why do we need effective corporate governance?', *International Advances in Economic Research*, 20, 2014, pp. 227–228, available at: <https://doi.org/10.1007/s11294-013-9430-3> accessed 15 April 2024

3 Melinda Timea Fülöp, 'Why do we need effective corporate governance?', *International Advances in Economic Research*, 20, 2014, pp. 227–228, available at: <https://doi.org/10.1007/s11294-013-9430-3> accessed 15 April 2024

4 Ira Millstein, Michel Albert, Adrian Cadbury, Robert Denham, Dieter Fedddersen, Nobuo Tateisi, *Corporate Governance: Improving Competitiveness and Access to Capital in Global Markets: A Report to the OECD by the Business Sector Advisory Group on Corporate Governance* (OECD Publishing, Paris, 1998), available at: <https://doi.org/10.1787/9789264162709-en>

5 Ira Millstein, Michel Albert, Adrian Cadbury, Robert Denham, Dieter Fedddersen, Nobuo Tateisi, *Corporate Governance: Improving Competitiveness and Access to Capital in Global Markets: A Report to the OECD by the Business Sector Advisory Group on Corporate Governance* (OECD Publishing, Paris, 1998), available at: <https://doi.org/10.1787/9789264162709-en>, p. 40

6 Ira Millstein, Michel Albert, Adrian Cadbury, Robert Denham, Dieter Fedddersen, Nobuo Tateisi, *Corporate Governance: Improving Competitiveness and Access to Capital in Global Markets: A Report to the OECD by the Business Sector Advisory Group on Corporate Governance* (OECD Publishing, Paris, 1998), available at: <https://doi.org/10.1787/9789264162709-en>, p. 40

7 Ira Millstein, Michel Albert, Adrian Cadbury, Robert Denham, Dieter Fedddersen, Nobuo Tateisi, *Corporate Governance: Improving Competitiveness and Access to Capital in Global Markets: A Report to the OECD by the Business Sector Advisory Group on Corporate Governance* (OECD Publishing, Paris, 1998), available at: <https://doi.org/10.1787/9789264162709-en>, p. 40

8 Ira Millstein, Michel Albert, Adrian Cadbury, Robert Denham, Dieter Fedddersen, Nobuo Tateisi, *Corporate Governance: Improving Competitiveness and Access to Capital in Global Markets: A Report to the OECD by the Business Sector Advisory Group on Corporate Governance* (OECD Publishing, Paris, 1998), available at: <https://doi.org/10.1787/9789264162709-en>, p. 23

which constitute effective corporate governance, are underpinned by shareholder primacy. Fairness is a crucial element of effective corporate governance, designed to protect shareholder interests and ensure equal treatment of all shareholders, especially minority shareholders. Therefore, the board is accountable to the shareholders. The Financial Reporting Council supports this point by stating that effective corporate governance enables shareholders to hold directors accountable and access information needed to evaluate management's performance.[9] Thus, to be effective, corporate governance must be based on a combination of internal and external environments to maximise corporate performance, minimise risk, and protect all stakeholders' interests.[10] Effective corporate governance is essential to ensure that corporations operate with integrity, responsibility, transparency, accountability, and fairness towards all stakeholders. It also ensures that corporations contribute to the welfare of society. In a broader context, effective corporate governance is fundamental to banks' proper functioning within the national and global economy. Consequently, examining the international standards for effective corporate governance in the banking industry will help understand the global regulatory framework for the banking industry.

4.3 International Standards for Corporate Governance of Banks

The Basel Committee on Bank Supervision has released a series of guidelines addressing various corporate governance issues in the banking industry. Of these, the most salient are those pertaining to compliance and the compliance function within banks. The guidelines offer guidance on best practices intended to assist banks in designing, implementing, and maintaining an efficient compliance function.[11] It outlines directors' and senior management's roles and responsibilities in ensuring that their banks comply with relevant banking regulations.[12] The internal audit function guideline[13] aims to reinforce the internal audit function of banks by promoting compliance with national and international professional standards on internal auditing.[14] In the same vein, the Basel guidelines on the external audits of

9 Financial Reporting Council, 'Effective corporate governance', July 2011, available at: <www.frc.org.uk/getattachment/8d5dd29f-0630-4521-86b2-f41a75d9be6b/FRC-Effective-Corporate-Governance-July-2011.pdf> accessed 15 September 2021

10 Melinda Timea Fülöp, 'Why do we need effective corporate governance?', *International Advances in Economic Research*, 20, 2014, pp. 227–228, available at: <https://doi.org/10.1007/s11294-013-9430-3> accessed 15 April 2024

11 Melinda Timea Fülöp, 'Why do we need effective corporate governance?', *International Advances in Economic Research*, 20, 2014, pp. 227–228, available at: <https://doi.org/10.1007/s11294-013-9430-3> accessed 15 April 2024

12 Melinda Timea Fülöp, 'Why do we need effective corporate governance?', *International Advances in Economic Research*, 20, 2014, pp. 227–228, available at: <https://doi.org/10.1007/s11294-013-9430-3> accessed 15 April 2024

13 Basel Committee on Banking Supervision, 'The internal audit function in banks', Bank for International Settlement, June 2012, available at: <www.bis.org/publ/bcbs223.pdf> accessed 15 April 2024

14 Basel Committee on Banking Supervision, 'The internal audit function in banks', Bank for International Settlement, June 2012, available at: <www.bis.org/publ/bcbs223.pdf> accessed 15 April 2024

banks seek to provide a framework that supports audit committees in their governance and oversight of the external audit function.[15] The banks' corporate governance principles[16] provide a framework within which banks and supervisors can achieve comprehensive and transparent risk management and effective decision-making. This guideline underscores the importance of effective corporate governance for banks' safe and sound functioning.[17] It stressed the importance of risk governance as a fundamental component of the bank's corporate governance framework[18] and the importance of promoting the value of strong boards and board committees.[19]

Compared to the previous one, the recent corporate governance principles are unique because the 2015 principles introduced a new distinction between the board of directors and senior management's duties.[20] The BCBS Corporate Governance Principles for Banks focus on promoting effective corporate governance in the banking industry. The principles do not have the force of law. However, it is intended to set the international standards that the banks are expected to follow to promote public confidence and uphold the safety and soundness of the banking system.[21]

The OECD Principles of Corporate Governance is another international framework for effective corporate governance that applies to the banking industry.[22] They provide specific guidance to assist governments, policymakers, regulators, corporations, and stakeholders in the OECD and non-OECD countries to improve the legal, regulatory, supervisory, and institutional framework underpinning corporate governance in their jurisdictions.[23] The OECD Principles of Corporate Governance were issued initially in 1999, and since then, it has become the

15 Basel Committee on Banking Supervision, 'The internal audit function in banks', Bank for International Settlement, June 2012, available at: <www.bis.org/publ/bcbs223.pdf> accessed 15 April 2024
16 Basel Committee on Banking Supervision, 'Corporate governance principles for banks', Bank for International Settlement, July 2015, available at: <www.bis.org/bcbs/publ/d328.pdf> accessed 15 April 2024
17 Basel Committee on Banking Supervision, 'Corporate governance principles for banks', Bank for International Settlement, July 2015, available at: <www.bis.org/bcbs/publ/d328.pdf> accessed 15 April 2024
18 Basel Committee on Banking Supervision, 'Corporate governance principles for banks', Bank for International Settlement, July 2015, available at: <www.bis.org/bcbs/publ/d328.pdf> accessed 15 April 2024
19 Basel Committee on Banking Supervision, 'Guidelines on the corporate governance principles for banks', pp. 1–13, available at: <https://assets.kpmg.com/content/dam/kpmg/pdf/2016/05/Corporate-Governance-Principles.pdf>
20 Basel Committee on Banking Supervision, 'Guidelines on the corporate governance principles for banks', pp. 1–13, available at: <https://assets.kpmg.com/content/dam/kpmg/pdf/2016/05/Corporate-Governance-Principles.pdf>
21 Rym Ayadi, Sami Naceur, Barbara Casu, Barry Quinn, 'Does Basel compliance matter for bank performance?', *Journal of Financial Stability*, 23, April 2016, pp. 15–32
22 OECD, *G20/OECD Principles of Corporate Governance* (OECD Publishing, Paris, 2015), available at: <https://doi.org/10.1787/9789264236882-en.> accessed 15 April 2024
23 OECD, *G20/OECD Principles of Corporate Governance* (OECD Publishing, Paris, 2015), available at: <https://doi.org/10.1787/9789264236882-en.> accessed 15 April 2024

international benchmark for measuring corporate governance in publicly traded companies. It has undergone a series of reviews, with the most recent principles issued in 2015.[24] The OECD revised principles cover six primary areas of corporate governance: the establishment of an effective corporate governance framework, the safeguarding of shareholders' basic rights, the promotion of equitable treatment of shareholders, the recognition of stakeholders' roles in corporate governance, the promotion of transparency and disclosure, and the definition of the board's responsibilities.[25]

The Financial Stability Board Forum has endorsed the OECD Principles of Corporate Governance as one of the 12 significant standards for ensuring a stable financial system. Although these principles and the BCBS Corporate Governance Principles for Banks are not legally binding, they serve as a benchmark for measuring effective corporate governance in the banking industry. However, when implementing these international guidelines into a country's corporate governance framework, it is important to consider the country's legal, socio-economic, and cultural circumstances. This means that the guidelines must be tailored to align with the institutional environment of the recipient country. Before assessing how these international guidelines have influenced corporate governance in the Nigerian and South African banking industries, it is necessary first to identify the stakeholders in bank governance.

4.4 Stakeholders in Banks' Corporate Governance

The effective governance of a bank is essential for its growth and the overall economic development of any nation. According to Maher and Anderson, the relationship between stakeholders in a corporation affects corporate governance and economic performance.[26] Several stakeholders are involved in promoting effective corporate governance in the banking industry, including shareholders, employees, creditors, government, corporate regulators, customers, host communities, public interest groups, and trade unions. Their importance as stakeholders in banks' governance is examined further in the next subsections.

4.4.1 Shareholders

The term 'shareholder' refers to an individual who possesses shares in a company. Unfortunately, the definition of a 'share' provided by the UK Companies Act 2006 is insufficient, as it simply defines a share as a share in the company's share capital.[27]

24 OECD, *G20/OECD Principles of Corporate Governance* (OECD Publishing, Paris, 2015), available at: <https://doi.org/10.1787/9789264236882-en.> accessed 15 April 2024

25 OECD, *G20/OECD Principles of Corporate Governance* (OECD Publishing, Paris, 2015), available at: <https://doi.org/10.1787/9789264236882-en.> accessed 15 April 2024

26 Maria Maher, Thomas Anderson, *Corporate Governance: Effects on Firm Performance and Economic Growth* (OECD Publishing, Paris, 1999), p. 8

27 S.540(1) Companies Act, 2006

This definition does not provide a clear understanding of what a share is. Lord Russell, however, offered a more comprehensive definition, stating that 'a share in a limited company is a form of property that embodies an individual's interest in the company. This interest comprises rights and obligations established by the Companies Act and the company's memorandum and articles of association.'[28] A bank is typically a joint-stock company with its shares listed and traded on a stock exchange.[29] Those who purchase the bank's shares become the bank shareholders; the act of purchasing the shares comes with certain rights and responsibilities.[30] The rights arising from shareholders' investment in banks include the right to inspect the banks' accounting records, attend and vote at general and special meetings, and appoint directors.[31] As discussed earlier, the agency theory is unique because shareholders appoint directors to act on their behalf. Shareholders ensure that senior management and directors do not pursue their interests by implementing an adequate monitoring mechanism. Bank shareholders subject to the leave of court can bring a derivative action against a director, third party, or both for an actual or proposed act or omission involving negligence, default, breach of duty, or breach of trust by a bank director.[32] It does not matter if the cause of action arose before or after the shareholder seeking to bring or continue the derivative action became a bank shareholder.[33]

The bank's shareholders' entitlement to receive dividends depends on the profits earned; however, shareholders will not receive any dividends when the bank incurs losses. Their situation might be worse if the losses lead to insolvency. In such instances, shareholders will forfeit all their contributions to the bank if it is a limited liability company.[34] In certain circumstances, the scope of shareholders' liability may extend beyond their initial investment in the bank. Although the courts are reluctant to lift the corporate veil, there are instances where they are prepared to lift the veil of incorporation, which is pierced by the courts, for example, where there is evidence of impropriety,[35] agency,[36] façade,[37] and interest of justice.[38] This means that the individuals in control of the bank would be held accountable for their actions, and the shareholders would be personally liable for any damages incurred.[39]

28 *Commissioners of Inland Revenue v. Crossman* [1937] AC 26 (HL) 66
29 Kern Alexander, *Principles of Banking Regulation* (Cambridge University Press, Cambridge, 2019), p. 87
30 Kern Alexander, *Principles of Banking Regulation* (Cambridge University Press, Cambridge, 2019), p. 87
31 Kern Alexander, *Principles of Banking Regulation* (Cambridge University Press, Cambridge, 2019), p. 146
32 S.260 (3)(5) Companies Act, 2006
33 S.260 (3)(5) Companies Act, 2006 S260 (4)
34 Research and Market Development Department Securities and Exchange Commission, available at: <http://proshareng.com/admin/upload/reports/2625.pdf> accessed 15 April 2024
35 *Gilford Motor Co Ltd v. Horne* [1933] Ch 935
36 *Re FG (Films) Ltd.* (1953) 1 WLR 483
37 *Jones v. Lipman* (1962) 1 WLR 832; *Gilford Motor Co Ltd v. Horne* [1933] Ch 935
38 *Re A Company* [1985] BCLC 333; *Conway v. Ratiu* (2006) 1 All ER 571
39 Jonathan Macey, Geoffery Miller, 'Double liability of bank shareholders: History and implications', *Wake Forest Law Review*, 27, 1992, pp. 31–62

Banks' shareholders consist of individuals, institutions, and sometimes governments. While individuals and institutional investors acquire shares in banks to maximise their profits, the government may acquire shares in banks to stabilise the financial system in times of crisis, such as during the financial crisis of 2007–2009. It is worth noting that there is nothing wrong with governments acquiring bank shares to generate profits. However, recent events have shown that when the possibility of banks failing arises, governments intervene by acquiring shares to stabilise the financial system. The role of the government as a stakeholder in banks will be explored later in this chapter.

4.4.2 Employees

The banks' employees are another critical stakeholder in the banking industry because they also bear the residual risks in the bank, as the payment of their incomes depends on the banks remaining a going concern.[40] Unlike shareholders, who can reduce their financial risk through portfolio diversification, employees cannot diversify their risk.[41] They rely solely on the bank to provide them with income to meet their various financial needs. Like bank shareholders whose investment is mainly capital, bank employees invest their human resources to ensure the success of the bank's corporate objective. One would, therefore, argue that bank employees and shareholders are in a kind of symbiosis relationship because while employees rely on the management who act for the shareholders for their incomes, the shareholders rely on the employees to deliver on the corporate objective of the bank, which is profit maximisation for the benefit of shareholders. From a bank employee's perspective, the bank's long-term growth and prosperity are significant because their emoluments and other benefits are guaranteed if they are solvent and remain a going concern.

When a bank experiences losses, its employees are often significantly affected. In an attempt to recover its liquidity and cash flows, the bank may reduce or completely stop the employees' salaries, bonuses, and other benefits. In some cases, the bank may even lay off some of its employees. The impact of these losses on bank employees can be severe and may go beyond just financial consequences. Former employees of a failed bank may find it challenging to secure new employment opportunities, not due to high levels of unemployment in the country but due to their association with a failed financial institution. In *Malik v Bank of Credit and Commerce International SA*[42] and *Mahmud v Bank of Credit and Commerce International SA*,[43] the employees brought an action against the bank for loss of reputation and stigmatisation. They claimed that no one was willing to employ them because they were former employees of a particular bank involved in massive fraud, money laundering, and other financial crimes. The court held that there is

40 Robert Wearing, *Cases in Corporate Governance* (Sage, London, 2005), p. 10

41 Robert Wearing, *Cases in Corporate Governance* (Sage, London, 2005), p. 10

42 *Malik v. Bank of Credit and Commerce International SA (1997) 3 WLR 95; Mahmud v. Bank of Credit and Commerce International SA [1997] UKHL 23*

43 *Malik v. Bank of Credit and Commerce International SA (1997) 3 WLR 95; Mahmud v. Bank of Credit and Commerce International SA [1997] UKHL 23*

an implied term in employment contracts that the employer shall not conduct itself in a manner calculated or likely to destroy or seriously damage the relationship of confidence and trust between employer and employee.[44] Although employees may be entitled to damages in such circumstances, pursuing such remedies can be challenging and typically requires significant resources. The costs associated with litigation are often considerable and time-consuming, and those employees who have lost their jobs may lack the financial resources to engage the services of an experienced legal representative. It follows that bank employees are likely to prefer working in banks with a strong work ethic to ensure their salaries are paid continuously, enabling them to meet their financial obligations. Should they decide to terminate their employment with a particular bank, they can seek re-employment elsewhere without being stigmatised owing to their previous employer's involvement in unethical or fraudulent practices.

4.4.3 Creditors

Bank creditors play a crucial role in the functioning of banks. They contribute to the banks' capital by offering credit to them. Apart from selling their stocks in the stock market to raise capital, banks borrow amongst themselves through the interbank lending market. As providers of debt finance for other banks, they advance funds with the expectation of receiving repayment of the principal sum and interest on debts when due. The OECD corporate governance principles highlighted creditors' significant place in bank governance and how their interests should be protected by law if the banks become insolvent. It stated that creditors are key stakeholders, and the terms, volume, and type of credit extended to banks will depend significantly on their rights and enforceability.[45] Francis et al. strongly support the view that poor corporate governance is inimical to the bank's ability to secure finance on favourable terms from other banks, as most banks would advance loans with a low-interest rate and, for a more extended period, to banks with an excellent corporate governance record; however, banks with a poor corporate governance record may struggle to get loans from the other banks on favourable terms.[46]

Besides borrowing amongst themselves through the interbank lending market, banks may also secure credit through debtholders, which comprise depositors operating regular accounts, fixed accounts, and bondholders.[47] In most instances, these

44 *Malik v. Bank of Credit and Commerce International SA (1997) 3 WLR 95; Mahmud v. Bank of Credit and Commerce International SA [1997] UKHL 23*

45 OECD, *G20/OECD, Principles of Corporate Governance* (OECD Publishing, Paris, 2015), p. 36

46 Bill Francis, Iftekhar Hasan, Liang Song, *Corporate Governance, Creditor Protection, and Bank Loan Contracting in Emerging Markets* (Lally School of Management and Technology of Rensselaer Polytechnic Institute, New York, 2007), p. 6

47 Klaus Hopt, 'Better governance of financial institutions, corporate governance of banks and other financial institutions after the financial crisis', in Eddy Wymeersch, Klaus Hopt, Guido Ferrarini (eds), *Financial Regulation and Supervision, a Post-Crisis Analysis* (Oxford University Press, Oxford, 2012), p. 349

creditors provide unsecured credit for the banks, although such credits may attract interest at various times. Debtholders are concerned about directors' risk-taking appetites, unlike the shareholders who are eager to maximise profit and are less concerned about the risks involved; debtholders want the banks to remain solvent so that their monies are paid to them when demanded or as at when due.[48] If a bank is experiencing financial difficulty, bondholders may face difficulties when attempting to sell their debt, as the market price will reflect concerns about the bank's current situation. This may result in a loss of funds for bondholders who manage to sell their debt. Other debtholders, such as depositors with fixed and standard accounts, are also likely to be troubled by excessive risk-taking by banks. Although their accounts are theoretically covered by deposit insurance schemes, in many cases, the coverage is lower than the amount held in their bank accounts, particularly in the case of DMBs operating in challenging institutional environments. Incorporating debtholders into banks' corporate governance can assist in mitigating excessive risk-taking by bank directors.[49]

4.4.4 Government

Governments play a significant role in the governance of banks. There are multiple reasons why governments are interested in the corporate governance of banking institutions in various jurisdictions. Firstly, banks hold a fundamental position in the economic development of any nation. In addition to their traditional role of providing payment and portfolio services, they transform illiquid assets into liquid assets. Secondly, governments are interested in the sustainability of banks because profitable banks pay taxes, and these taxes can be used to provide basic infrastructure for individuals. Thirdly, governments are also concerned with banks' corporate governance and sustainability because solvent banks are more likely to create employment opportunities for the growing population.

The role of the government in the corporate governance of banks is not fixed. It can perform multiple functions, such as policymaking, monitoring, supervising, and enforcing banking regulations. While it may seem straightforward for the government to play these roles in public companies, regulating state-owned companies can be more challenging. In China, where most banks are state-owned, there are often conflicts of interest among those managing and controlling Chinese

48 Klaus Hopt, 'Better governance of financial institutions, corporate governance of banks and other financial institutions after the financial crisis', in Eddy Wymeersch, Klaus Hopt, Guido Ferrarini (eds), *Financial Regulation and Supervision, a Post-Crisis Analysis* (Oxford University Press, Oxford, 2012), p. 349

49 Klaus Hopt, 'Better governance of financial institutions, corporate governance of banks and other financial institutions after the financial crisis', in Eddy Wymeersch, Klaus Hopt, Guido Ferrarini (eds), *Financial Regulation and Supervision, a Post-Crisis Analysis* (Oxford University Press, Oxford, 2012), p. 349

state-owned banks.[50] Such conflicts may arise between shareholders and managers, particularly when shareholders are focused on profit maximisation while managers, on the other hand, strive to enhance the value of state-owned assets and promote national objectives.

The potential for conflicting interests among shareholders, government, and managers may hinder the government's ability to execute its policymaking, supervisory, and enforcement duties. For example, during the financial crisis, the governments of the United Kingdom, the United States, France, Ireland, Denmark, and Germany intervened by injecting public funds into several systemically important banks. This was due to the perceived insurmountable risk of their failure due to their size and importance to the entire financial system.[51] Sometimes, the intervention made the government own all the shares in those banks. However, the government's motivation to acquire majority shares or, in some cases, all the shares in those banks was not motivated by the desire to maximise profit but to prevent the breakdown of the entire financial system. This was seen during the financial crisis of 2007–2009 when the UK government injected over £955 billion into some systemically important banks like Lloyds TSB, Barclays, Northern Rock, HBOS, and Royal Bank of Scotland to avert the collapse of the entire financial system during the 2007–2009 financial crisis.[52] It is, therefore, argued that the government is a key contributor to the banking industry due to its commitment to ensuring the banks' soundness and the financial system's stability. Therefore, the core objective of financial stability justifies the establishment of various supervisory and regulatory agencies. Their role as stakeholders in the bank's governance is examined further in the next subsection.

4.4.5 Banking Regulators and Supervisors

Banking regulators and supervisors are crucial stakeholders in the banking industry, and their primary objective is to ensure a safe and sound banking system. Depending on the jurisdiction, banking regulators can be government agencies or professional associations. It is important to differentiate between a professional association and a public interest group. A public interest group is a pressure group, while professional associations work as regulators for banks operating within that particular profession. By law, banking regulatory and supervisory agencies have the authority to ensure that banks adhere to the rules and regulations governing the conduct of banking business. Banking regulators and supervisors are responsible for implementing, supervising, monitoring, and enforcing banking regulations to

50 Zhaofeng Wang, 'Corporate governance under state control: The Chinese experience', *Theoretical Inquiries in Law*, 13(2), 2012, p. 493

51 Pepper Culpepper, Raphael Reinke, 'Structural power and bank bailouts in the UK and the US', *Politics and Society*, 42(4), December 2014, pp. 427–454, available at: <https://doi.org/10.1177/0032329214547342>

52 National Audit Office, 'Maintaining the financial stability of UK banks: Update on the support schemes', available at: <www.nao.org.uk/report/maintaining-the-financial-stability-of-uk-banks-update-on-the-support-schemes/> accessed 15 April 2024

maintain the financial stability of the banking system.[53] The central bank is a government agency that operates as a regulator and supervisor across multiple jurisdictions, functioning as the bankers' bank and lender of last resort.[54] However, numerous stakeholders criticised central banks' performance as regulators in the aftermath of the global financial crisis of 2007–2009 for their inability to proactively regulate individual banks' excessive risk-taking. The contention is that the central banks have not been adequately proactive in addressing the issue of excessive risk-taking culture in various commercial banks under their watch; as a result, they disregarded one of their core supervisory responsibilities, which is to ensure the macro-prudential regulation of commercial banks.[55]

It is important to note that not all countries have central banks as the primary regulators responsible for micro- and macro-prudential regulation. For instance, in the UK, a 'twin peak' approach to banking regulation has been adopted, which involves two regulatory and supervisory agencies: the Prudential Regulation Authority (PRA) and the Financial Conduct Authority (FCA), both responsible for different regulatory and supervisory objectives. The PRA is responsible for ensuring banks' solvency and financial soundness through prudential objectives, while the FCA is responsible for the conduct of banking business. Both agencies possess significant law-making and enforcement powers to ensure compliance by the banks. Banking regulators and supervisors are pivotal stakeholders in bank governance.

4.4.6 Host Communities

The host communities have a significant role in the banking industry, particularly regarding banks operating within their vicinity. The reasons that prompt the host communities to take a keen interest in the banks operating within their area are manifold. Firstly, these communities anticipate banks operating in their area to provide employment opportunities for their residents, which would lead to economic development within these communities.[56] Host communities expect that the continued operation of banks guarantees job security for the residents. However, if the banks experience financial difficulties, the likelihood of staff layoffs increases, leading to high unemployment within the host communities.[57] A case in point is HSBC, which terminated the employment of over 10,000 staff members in 2019 due to the US interest rate cuts, Brexit uncertainty, the US-China trade war, and unrest in Hong Kong.[58]

53 Karen Yeung, 'Regulatory agencies', in Peter Cane, Joanne Conaghan (eds), *The New Oxford Companion* (Oxford University Press, Oxford, 2008), p. 998

54 Iris Chiu, Joanna Wilson, *Banking Law and Regulation* (Oxford University Press, Oxford, 2019), p. 241

55 Iris Chiu, Joanna Wilson, *Banking Law and Regulation* (Oxford University Press, Oxford, 2019) , p. 241

56 Christine Mallin, *Corporate Governance* (6th ed., Oxford University Press, Oxford, 2019), p. 82

57 Christine Mallin, *Corporate Governance* (6th ed., Oxford University Press, Oxford, 2019), p. 82

58 David Crow, 'HSBC to axe up to 10,000 jobs in cost-cutting drive', *The Financial Times*, 6 October 2019, available at: <www.ft.com/content/b43e7b3e-e6c7-11e9-b112-9624ec9edc59> accessed 15 April 2024

Another reason the host communities show interest in banks operating in their area is the role of the banks in promoting financial inclusion.[59] Financial inclusion refers to the banks' willingness and ability to offer loans on favourable terms to residents to engage in various businesses, thereby reducing the unemployment rate and boosting economic development in the communities.[60] Host communities also expect banks to help provide infrastructure that may be lacking in their area.[61] This reflects the societal expectation that banks, as responsible corporate citizens, should engage in social responsibility within their communities.[62] This gives rise to the concept of corporate social responsibility, which is examined later in this chapter.

4.5 Bank Stakeholders and Regulatory Approaches to Corporate Governance

The shareholder model and the stakeholder model are two types of corporate governance models practised worldwide.[63] However, these models have many variations in different countries due to various factors such as ownership structure, culture, history, legal system, institutional framework, and regulatory environment.[64] Distinct characteristics underpin these variations, and contrary to the argument by Weimer and Pape that the Anglo-Saxon model is the best corporate governance model to guarantee sustainable economic growth,[65] the corporate governance model adopted in any jurisdiction must be based on the institutional environment in that country. In order to provide some context to this argument, it is important to examine the Anglo-Saxon model, which is based on the shareholder theory, as well as the Continental European and the Japanese *Keiretsu* models, which are both based on the stakeholder theory.

59 The World Bank, 'Understanding poverty: Financial inclusion', available at: <www.worldbank.org/en/topic/financialinclusion/overview> accessed 15 April 2024

60 The World Bank, 'Understanding poverty: Financial inclusion', available at: <www.worldbank.org/en/topic/financialinclusion/overview> accessed 15 April 2024

61 Amaeshi Kenneth, Bongo Adi, Chris Ogbechie, Olufemi Amao, 'Corporate social responsibility in Nigeria: Western mimicry or indigenous influences?', *The Journal of Corporate Citizenship*, 24, Winter 2006, pp. 83–99

62 Amaeshi Kenneth, Bongo Adi, Chris Ogbechie, Olufemi Amao, 'Corporate social responsibility in Nigeria: Western mimicry or indigenous influences?', *The Journal of Corporate Citizenship*, 24, Winter 2006, pp. 83–99

63 Simon Deakin, 'Corporate governance and financial crisis in the long run', Working Papers WP417, Centre for Business Research, University of Cambridge, 2010, p. 2, available at: <www.cbr.cam.ac.uk/fileadmin/user_upload/centre-for-business-research/downloads/working-papers/wp417.pdf> accessed 15 April 2024

64 Gregory Francesco Maassen, *An International Comparison of Corporate Governance Models* (Spencer Stuart, Amsterdam, The Netherlands, 1999), p. 41

65 Jeroen Weimer, Joost Pape, 'A taxonomy of systems of corporate governance', *Corporate Governance: An International Review*, 7(2), April 1999, pp. 152–166, 152

4.5.1 Anglo-Saxon Model

The Anglo-Saxon corporate governance model is premised on shareholders theory; under this model, the shareholders are the most influential stakeholders to whom directors owe a fiduciary duty to act in their best interests.[66] Originating from the United Kingdom and the United States, this model has become the norm in most banks worldwide, particularly in Commonwealth countries.[67] Under this model, the influence of bank shareholders is institutionalised, so the board must act as an intermediary in maximising shareholders' wealth.[68] In the UK, bank shareholders typically appoint board members of the board of directors and retain the power to terminate their employment in case of wrongdoing or misconduct. The power to hire and fire directors is one mechanism banks' shareholders have at their disposal to minimise the agency problem.[69] Directors are more likely to pursue the banks' corporate objectives by maximising profit and limiting self-interest when informed that they may be dismissed for non-performance or any other corporate misconduct.

The Anglo-Saxon model is characterised by its unique external control mechanisms that are designed to reduce the agency problem. Shareholders of banks operating under this model may leverage discipline mechanisms such as hostile takeovers or proxy fights to remove ineffective and underperforming management teams.[70] However, this model varies slightly between countries in terms of its components. The board of directors in the Anglo-Saxon model is a one-tiered system composed of non-executive directors whom the bank's shareholders elect. However, there are deviations from this norm in some countries that, although practised in a one-tiered board system, the board comprises executive and non-executive directors. Another aspect of divergence in the Anglo-Saxon model between countries is the duality. The duality role means that one person simultaneously has a dual role as Chairman of the Board (COB) and Chief Executive Officer (CEO). Although having the same person serve as the COB and CEO is prohibited in the UK, it is acceptable in the US. Despite the ongoing debates about the US approach to duality and whether it compromises the board's independence in the wake of financial scandals, this variation of the Anglo-Saxon corporate governance model remains prevalent in the US.

The previous discussion on corporate governance theories is relevant to implementing the Anglo-Saxon model. The Anglo-Saxon model is built on the foundation of the shareholder theory. However, the board's composition is determined by either the agency or stewardship theories. In a one-tier board system shaped by the agency theory, the board will likely have more non-executive directors.

66 Jeroen Weimer, Joost Pape, 'A taxonomy of systems of corporate governance', *Corporate Governance: An International Review*, 7(2), April 1999, p. 153

67 Jeroen Weimer, Joost Pape, 'A taxonomy of systems of corporate governance', *Corporate Governance: An International Review*, 7(2), April 1999, p. 153

68 Jeroen Weimer, Joost Pape, 'A taxonomy of systems of corporate governance', *Corporate Governance: An International Review*, 7(2), April 1999, p. 153

69 S.168 (1) UK Companies Act 2006

70 James Walsh, James Seward, 'On the efficiency of internal and external corporate control mechanisms', *The Academy of Management Review*, 15(3), July 1990, 421–458, 434

Conversely, a one-tier board system based on stewardship theory is expected to consist of more executive directors.

Furthermore, the stewardship theory allows the same person to hold the position of the bank's COB and CEO.[71] This is because directors, as stewards, are less likely to pursue their self-interests in contrast to the agency theory, which creates a misalignment of interests.[72] Inadequate monitoring of directors under the agency theory leads to self-interests being pursued at the expense of the shareholders.

4.5.2 Continental European Model

In contrast to the Anglo-Saxon model, which prioritises the interests of shareholders above all others, the Continental European model seeks to promote the interests of all relevant stakeholders.[73] This model is practised in countries such as Germany, where the law prohibits banks from pursuing only the interests of shareholders.[74] Consequently, the Continental European model adopts a stakeholder-oriented approach, as opposed to the Anglo-Saxon model, which primarily focuses on maximising profits for the benefit of shareholders. The key stakeholders in the Continental European model are the same as those identified earlier in this chapter, including shareholders, employees, debtholders, regulators, government, and creditors.[75]

The board structure differs between the Continental European and Anglo-Saxon models. The Anglo-Saxon model has a one-tier board structure, whereas the Continental European model has a two-tier board system consisting of the executive and supervisory boards.[76] In Germany, the executive board is called *Vorstand*, while the supervisory board is called *Aufsichtsrat;* the supervisory board monitors the executive board.[77] The supervisory board's role is to oversee the activities of the executive board. The Anglo-Saxon model, on the other hand, merges the executive and supervisory roles into a single board system.

71 Giovanna Michelon, Antonio Parbonetti, 'The effect of corporate governance on sustainability disclosure', *Journal of Management and Governance*, 16, 2012, pp. 477–509, available at: <https://doi.org/10.1007/s10997-010-9160-3>

72 Zhong Tan, 'Stewardship in the interests of systemic stakeholders: Re-conceptualizing the means and ends of Anglo-American corporate governance in the wake of the global financial crisis', *Journal of Business and Technology Law*, 9(2), 2014, available at: <http://digitalcommons.law.umaryland.edu/jbtl/vol9/iss2/3> accessed 15 April 2024

73 Lucian Cernat, 'The emerging European corporate governance model: Anglo-Saxon, Continental, or still the century of diversity?', *Journal of European Public Policy*, 11(1), 2004, pp. 147–166

74 Franklin Allen, 'Corporate governance in emerging economies', *Oxford Review of Economic Policy*, 21(2), 2005, pp. 164–177, available at: <www.jstor.org/stable/23606977>

75 Jeroen Weimer, Joost Pape, 'A taxonomy of systems of corporate governance', *Corporate Governance: An International Review*, 7(2), April 1999, pp. 152–166, 157

76 Jeroen Weimer, Joost Pape, 'A taxonomy of systems of corporate governance', *Corporate Governance: An International Review*, 7(2), April 1999

77 Jeroen Weimer, Joost Pape, 'A taxonomy of systems of corporate governance', *Corporate Governance: An International Review*, 7(2), April 1999

The supervisory board is tasked with appointing and removing members of the executive board, particularly in cases of underperformance or gross misconduct. Despite the distinct roles of the two-tier board system, it could be that the autonomy of the board, particularly the executive board, cannot be guaranteed. The composition of the supervisory board differs across European countries. For instance, in Germany and the Netherlands, the supervisory board comprises employees, their representatives, trade unions, and institutional investors, mainly banks.[78]

Employees in Germany and the Netherlands are significant stakeholders and can influence executive board decision-making compared to the UK and USA, which practice the Anglo-Saxon model. Employee involvement resonates with the idea of 'codetermination,'[79] which is the German term for workers' participation. Under the codetermination act,[80] employees are empowered to play a significant role in decisions that affect workers' rights. For instance, they have the right to discuss issues relating to employment contracts, working hours, holidays, and dismissal with the executive board.[81]

4.5.3 Japanese Model

The *Keiretsu* system underpins the Japanese corporate governance model.[82] Networks of commercial relationships among companies underpin the Japanese corporate governance system, as companies usually take shares within each other business.[83] Despite these connections, the companies within the *Keiretsu* system are autonomous from each other. Notwithstanding the companies' independence under the Japanese model, there are interconnected trading activities among the companies. A significant characteristic of the system is that the companies are encouraged to trade amongst themselves and cooperate to promote the corporate governance of the different companies within the *Keiretsu* system.[84]

The *Keiretsu* system is divided into two groups: the vertical Keiretsu and the horizontal Keiretsu. The vertical *Keiretsu* comprises companies within the same supply chain, while the horizontal *Keiretsu* comprises companies that deal in similar products.[85]

The banks play a fundamental role in the rescue operation of companies under the Japanese stakeholder model. This is evident when the companies are experiencing

78 Jeroen Weimer, Joost Pape, 'A taxonomy of systems of corporate governance', *Corporate Governance: An International Review*, 7(2), April 1999
79 Codetermination Act, 1976
80 Codetermination Act, 1976
81 Codetermination Act, 1976
82 Codetermination Act, 1976, p. 160
83 Codetermination Act, 1976
84 Erik Berglöf, Enrico Perotti, 'The governance structure of the Japanese financial keiretsu', *Journal of Financial Economics*, 36(2), October 1994, pp. 259–284, 262
85 Masahiko Aoki, 'Toward an economic model of the Japanese firm', *Journal of Economic Literature*, 28(1), March 1990, pp. 1–27, 14

financial difficulties; however, the banks' role decreases when the companies become solvent. In contrast to the Anglo-Saxon model, there is no fear of a hostile takeover in the Japanese stakeholder model; there is already a friendship network among the various companies within the *Keiretsu* system. The exchange of shares in the Keiretsu system strengthens their existing relationship. Apart from the connections within the Keiretsu system, it is argued that hostile takeovers are not a prominent feature of the Japanese stakeholder model due to the undeveloped market for corporate control compared to the Anglo-Saxon model practised in the UK, where the market for corporate control serves as a disciplinary mechanism for an ineffective board.

The Japanese stakeholder model does not exhibit such characteristics of a hostile takeover because of their firm belief in familism and respect for their cultural values. For example, reaching a consensus in the decision-making process amongst companies within the *Keiretsu* system is sacrosanct because there is little or no emphasis on litigation under the Japanese stakeholder model.[86]

In some ways, the Japanese stakeholder model is similar to the Anglo-Saxon model practised in the USA and the UK. The board structure is one notable similarity between the Japanese stakeholder model and the Anglo-Saxon corporate model. Under the Japanese stakeholder model, companies operate a one-tier board system comprising the board of directors, the office of the auditors, and the office of the representative director. Like in the UK, the board of directors includes both executive and non-executive directors.[87] An example of how the non-executive directors participate in corporate governance in the Japanese *Keiretsu* system is when the top banks appoint representatives to sit on the boards as non-executive directors of the companies they do business with.

Similarities exist between the Japanese and Continental European stakeholder models, as practised in Germany. In the Japanese stakeholder model, the employees and shareholders are key stakeholders that could influence bank management decisions.[88] Consequently, Aoki argued that the Japanese stakeholder model consists of companies with a coalition of employees and shareholders facilitated by the management to strike a balance between the interests of both stakeholders.[89] Therefore, one would argue that management responsibility under the Japanese Keiretsu system is that of an impartial umpire whose role is to promote the interests of the employees and the shareholders. Finally, a significant similarity between the Continental European stakeholder model as practised in Germany and the Japanese stakeholder model is evident from the employees' involvement in the decision-making process, particularly on matters that directly affect the employees.

86 Masahiko Aoki, 'Toward an economic model of the Japanese firm', *Journal of Economic Literature*, 28(1), March 1990, pp. 1–27, 14

87 Masahiko Aoki, 'Toward an economic model of the Japanese firm', *Journal of Economic Literature*, 28(1), March 1990, pp. 1–27, 14

88 Masahiko Aoki, 'Toward an economic model of the Japanese firm', *Journal of Economic Literature*, 28(1), March 1990, pp. 1–27, 14

89 Masahiko Aoki, 'Toward an economic model of the Japanese firm', *Journal of Economic Literature*, 28(1), March 1990, pp. 1–27, 14

For example, the employees can discuss issues relating to wage determination, managerial decisions that would affect them, employment conditions, and working arrangements under the Japanese stakeholder model with the management.[90]

4.6 Stakeholders and Institutional Mechanisms in Bank Governance

The stakeholder model will employ mechanisms to protect the interests of all stakeholders in banks.[91] In contrast, the shareholder model based on the agency theory will employ mechanisms to maximise shareholder value and mitigate agency problems between shareholders and managers.[92] Corporate governance mechanisms in any jurisdiction are contingent upon various structures, such as rules, values, norms, routines, beliefs, regulatory systems, and public governance systems. This is the basis of the institutional theory, which examines how these structures become established as authoritative social behaviour guidelines.[93] This forms the basis of the institutional theory, as it examines how these structures become established as authoritative social behaviour guidelines. Corporate governance mechanisms in the banking industry can be classified into two groups: internal and external mechanisms. Internal mechanisms comprise ownership and board structures, whereas external mechanisms comprise market discipline and system regulation. While system regulation has been discussed in Chapter 3, the focus here is on ownership structure, board structure, and market discipline.

4.6.1 Ownership Structure

Banks' ownership structure and corporate governance have been a subject of debate, with divergent opinions expressed on the matter. The controversy in corporate governance and ownership research is based on the question, 'For whom and what is a business for?'[94] Wahl argued that ownership is the exclusive possession or control over any form of property.[95] While this assertion is correct regarding

90 Jeroen Weimer, Joost Pape, 'A taxonomy of systems of corporate governance', *Corporate Governance: An International Review*, 7(2), April 1999, pp. 152–166, 160

91 Ruth Aguilera, Igor Filatotchev, Howard Gospel, Gregory Jackson, 'An organizational approach to comparative corporate governance: Costs, contingencies, and complementarities', *Organization Science*, 19(3), 2008, pp. 475–492

92 Charles Oman, 'Corporate governance and national development', OECD Development Centre Working Papers, No. 180, OECD Publishing, Paris, 2001, available at: <https://doi.org/10.1787/113535588267> accessed 15 April 2024

93 OECD, 'Policy framework for investment user toolkit, chapter 6, corporate governance', 2011, p. 3, available at: <www.oecd.org/investment/toolkit/policyareas/corporategovernance/44931152.pdf>

94 Mike Franz Wahl, *Governance and Ownership: Theoretical Framework of Research School of Economics and Business Administration* (Tallinn University of Technology), p. 150, available at: <http://deepthought.ttu.ee/majandus/tekstid/TUTWPE_08_179.pdf> accessed 15 April 2024

95 Mike Franz Wahl, *Governance and Ownership: Theoretical Framework of Research School of Economics and Business Administration* (Tallinn University of Technology), p. 150, available at: <http://deepthought.ttu.ee/majandus/tekstid/TUTWPE_08_179.pdf> accessed 15 April 2024

personal property, it does not apply to banks, as shareholders cannot claim exclusive possession of the bank because of the doctrine of corporate personality.[96] Wahl's assertion is also inaccurate regarding the control of banks because it is the directors and senior management that direct and control the affairs of the banks and not the shareholders.[97]

Berle and Means' seminar work '*The Modern Corporation and Private Property*' investigates ownership structure in the corporation.[98] Their research identifies a critical problem associated with the ownership and control of firms in the United States. They argue that due to the dispersed shareholdings in most US corporations, a dilemma has arisen: ownership of wealth is without control and controllers of wealth are without ownership.[99] This view is based on firms operating in the US, controlled by specialised managers without ownership in the companies they manage. In contrast to the view expressed by Sternberg that shareholders are the owners of the companies, it is argued that shareholders of banks do not own the bank but are stakeholders by virtue of the shares they purchased in the banks.[100]

Berle and Means stated that the agency problem may arise due to the dispersed ownership structure in countries such as the UK and the US. This means that shareholders cannot exercise control over the managers who may prioritise their interests over the shareholders.' The structure of ownership differs from one jurisdiction to another. Therefore, shareholders' interests are protected against other stakeholders' interests where management and control have been merged. This fusion of management and control ensures that the typical misalignment of interest that arises in dispersed ownership structures is unlikely. Ownership structures can be classified as insider and outsider ownership.

Insider Ownership

This type of ownership structure is where the shares are owned or controlled by the bank's employees, directors, or relatives. Information asymmetry between the principal (shareholders) and the agent (managers), which is the bedrock of the agency problem, does not exist here. However, banks that adopt a concentrated ownership structure may experience certain drawbacks, such as when one family or individual acquires an excessive proportion of shares. In such instances, the management

96 *Salomon v. A Salomon & Co Ltd* [1896] UKHL 1 [1897] AC 22

97 *H L Bolton (Engineering) Co Ltd v. T J Graham & Sons Ltd* (1957) 1 QB 159

98 Adolf Berle, Gardiner Means, *The Modern Corporation and Private Property* (Macmillan Co., New York, 1932), p. 66

99 Adolf Berle, Gardiner Means, *The Modern Corporation and Private Property* (Macmillan Co., New York, 1932), p. 66

100 *Short v. Treasury Commissioners* (1948) 1 KB 116, 122, CA; *Her Majesty's Commissioners of Inland Revenue v. Laird Group Plc* [2003] UKHL 54, para 35; David Chandler, *Strategic Corporate Social Responsibility: Sustainable Value Creation* (4th ed., Sage, London, 2017), p. 119; David Chandler, *Corporate Social Responsibility: A Strategic Perspective* (Business Expert Press LLC, New York, 2015), pp. 11–13; John Kay, 'Shareholders think they own the company – they are wrong', *Financial Times*, 10 November 2015, available at: <www.ft.com/content/7bd1b20a-879b-11e5-90de-f44762bf9896> accessed 15 April 2024

may lack the autonomy to make independent decisions, as the majority shareholder wields significant influence over their actions and policies. Consequently, the traditional agency problem, which is the basis for the Anglo-Saxon model, no longer exists here, as the conflict is now between the principal (dominant shareholder) and the principal (minority shareholders). The mechanisms devised to solve the principal-agent problem may not yield the desired result if the majority shareholder acts opportunistically by taking advantage of the minority shareholders. There is also a conflict of interest between the insider owner (minority shareholders) and the creditor (debtholders).[101] This conflict is based on the relationship between the level of equity ownership by insider owners and the bank's cost of debt financing. Insider owners with a smaller share fraction are more likely to extract personal benefit by undertaking excessive risk. The bank creditors will ask for higher returns when insider owners are more likely to engage in activities that may harm them. Thus, there is a negative relationship between insider ownership (minority shareholders) and the creditor (debtholders) because of banks' debt cost.[102]

Outsider Ownership

The outsider ownership structure is a form of ownership that is characterised by a dispersed shareholder base, where no single shareholder holds a significant portion of a bank's shares. This ownership structure is prevalent in countries like the UK and the USA. Unlike insider ownership structures discussed earlier, where a small group of shareholders holds a significant amount of a bank's shares, outsider ownership structures provide a more equitable distribution of ownership. Consequently, professional managers are appointed to oversee the banks, and ownership is distinct from control, embodying the Anglo-Saxon model. Nonetheless, this outsider ownership structure presents certain challenges, such as the agency cost, which refers to the expenses incurred by bank shareholders in monitoring managers. If individual shareholders decide to monitor management independently, managers' shareholders may feel reluctant to do so because of the high cost involved. Therefore, shareholders need to work together to introduce monitoring mechanisms that will help them protect their interests. The board of directors is responsible for monitoring banks' management, which is explored in more detail in the next subsection.

4.6.2 Board of Directors as a Corporate Governance Mechanism

The board of directors is a crucial internal control mechanism that plays an instrumental role in the corporate governance of banks.[103] Under the Anglo-Saxon

101 Stefano Lugo, 'Insider ownership and the cost of debt capital: Evidence from bank loans', *International Review of Financial Analysis*, 63, 2019, pp. 357–368

102 Stefano Lugo, 'Insider ownership and the cost of debt capital: Evidence from bank loans', *International Review of Financial Analysis*, 63, 2019, pp. 357–368

103 Ooghe Hubert, Tine De Langhe, 'The Anglo-American versus the Continental European corporate governance model: Empirical evidence of board composition in Belgium', *European Business Review*, 14(6), 2002, pp. 437–449

model, the board of directors acts as a liaison between managers and shareholders, while in the stakeholder model discussed earlier, the board of directors serves as a mediator between managers and stakeholders.[104] In the Anglo-Saxon model, the shareholders appoint the board of directors to operate the banks on their behalf.[105] Hence, the board of directors functions as an internal mechanism for monitoring the management to minimise agency problems arising from the separation of ownership and control.[106] According to Armour, Hansmann, and Kraakman, managers are agents of the shareholders who have delegated their powers to the directors.[107] To ensure that managers do not abuse the authority at their disposal, the board of directors provides a formal institutional mechanism of control, which offers checks and balances. The board of directors directs the management to achieve the bank's corporate objective, which is to maximise profits for the benefit of the shareholders.[108]

There have been calls for reform in the banking industry's boardroom. These demands include separating the positions of COB and CEO, limiting directors' shareholdings, reducing the number of directors, addressing directors' pay practices, and having employee representation on the bank's board.[109] The board of directors is a crucial corporate governance mechanism in the banking industry because banking's fiduciary responsibilities extend beyond shareholders to encompass a wider stakeholder group, including employees, customers, government, creditors/depositors, and banking regulators.[110] The link between board characteristics and effective corporate governance in the banking industry has been the subject of recent debate in corporate governance discourse.[111] Some argue that board char-

104 Ooghe Hubert, Tine De Langhe, 'The Anglo-American versus the Continental European corporate governance model: Empirical evidence of board composition in Belgium', *European Business Review*, 14(6), 2002, pp. 437–449

105 Gregory Francesco Maasen, *An International Comparison of Corporate Governance Models* (3rd ed., Spencer Stuart, Amsterdam, The Netherlands, 2002), p. 48

106 Eugene Fama, Michael Jensen, 'Separation of ownership and control', *Journal of Law and Economics*, 26(2), Corporations and Private Property, 1983, pp. 301–325, available at: <https://are.berkeley.edu/~cmantinori/prclass/FamaJensen.pdf> accessed 15 April 2024

107 John Armour, Henry Hansmann, Reinier Kraakman, 'Agency problems, legal strategies and enforcement', ECGI Working Paper Series in Law, Working Paper No. 135/2009, November 2009, p. 3

108 Margaret Blair, *Ownership and Control: Rethinking Corporate Governance for the Twenty-First Century* (Brookings Institution Press, Washington, DC, 2011)

109 Corporate Governance Reform, Department for Business, Energy & Industrial Strategy, 2016, available at: <https://assets.publishing.service.gov.uk/government/uploads/system/uploads/attachment_data/file/584013/corporate-governance-reform-green-paper.pdf> accessed 15 April 2024

110 Jonathan Macey, Maureen O'Hara, 'The corporate governance of banks', *Federal Reserve Bank of New York Economic Policy Review*, 9, 2003, pp. 97–107, 94

111 Francesco Vallascas, Sabur Mollah, Kevin Keasey, 'Does the impact of board independence on large bank risks change after the global financial crisis?', *Journal of Corporate Finance*, 44, 2017, pp. 149–166; Tawei Wang, Carol Hsu, 'Board composition and operational risk events of financial institutions', *Journal of Banking & Finance*, 37(6), 2013, pp. 2042–2051; Renée Adams, Hamid Mehran, 'Bank board structure and performance: Evidence for large bank holding companies', *Journal of Financial Intermediation*, 21(2), April 2012, pp. 243–267

acteristics, such as board size, qualification of board members, board independence, CEO duality, and gender diversity, are responsible for how the board engages in its risk management and how it promotes the interests of all stakeholders in the banking industry.[112] Therefore, the characteristics of the board of directors, especially as they relate to its composition, leadership, and independence, need further consideration.

Board Size and Qualification of Board Members

The optimal size of bank boards is a topic that has sparked a debate among different stakeholders. Some scholars have argued that a larger bank board is better because it will benefit from its members' vast expertise.[113] Such a board would be equipped with an adequate workforce and resources to reduce the COB/CEO dominance.[114] Some other scholars have argued that smaller board sizes are more effective in making quick managerial decisions.[115] Although one might be inclined to agree with the latter argument at first glance, it is important to note that the size of the board does not always indicate the speed of decision-making. The urgency of a matter and the expertise of the board members are also critical factors that affect the speed of decision-making. Therefore, it is argued that a larger board with members with relevant skills, knowledge, and expertise across various fields is better equipped to make sound decisions and promote stakeholders' interests in the banking industry. For example, a large bank board with members from diverse professional backgrounds and experience will have the edge over a smaller board

112 Francesco Vallascas, Sabur Mollah, Kevin Keasey, 'Does the impact of board independence on large bank risks change after the global financial crisis?', *Journal of Corporate Finance*, 44, 2017, pp. 149–166; Tawei Wang, Carol Hsu, 'Board composition and operational risk events of financial institutions', *Journal of Banking & Finance*, 37(6), 2013, pp. 2042–2051; Renée Adams, Hamid Mehran, 'Bank board structure and performance: Evidence for large bank holding companies', *Journal of Financial Intermediation*, 21(2), April 2012, pp. 243–267

113 Francesco Vallascas, Sabur Mollah, Kevin Keasey, 'Does the impact of board independence on large bank risks change after the global financial crisis?', *Journal of Corporate Finance*, 44, 2017, pp. 149–166; Tawei Wang, Carol Hsu, 'Board composition and operational risk events of financial institutions', *Journal of Banking & Finance*, 37(6), 2013, pp. 2042–2051; Renée Adams, Hamid Mehran, 'Bank board structure and performance: Evidence for large bank holding companies', *Journal of Financial Intermediation*, 21(2), April 2012, pp. 243–267

114 Sailesh Tanna, Fotios Pasiouras, Matthias Nnadi, 'The effect of board size and composition on the efficiency of UK Banks', *International Journal of the Economics of Business*, 18(3), 2011, pp. 441–462; Renée Adams, Hamid Mehran, 'Bank board structure and performance: Evidence for large bank holding companies', *Journal of Financial Intermediation*, 21(2), April 2012, pp. 243–267

115 Michael Jensen, 'The modern industrial revolution, exit, and the failure of internal control systems', *The Journal of Finance*, 48(3), 1993, pp. 831–880; Shams Pathan, Robert Faff, 'Does board structure in banks really affect their performance?', *Journal of Banking & Finance*, 37(5), May 2013, pp. 1573–1589

regarding the robustness of debates, decision-making, and balancing of all stakeholder interests.[116]

Connected with the previous point, another important characteristic of a board is the qualifications of its members. Some commentators[117] posit that a board showcasing broad diversity will likely perform its functions effectively,[118] given the presence of members with varying degrees of experience and qualifications. A bank board consisting of directors with many years of financial experience and appropriate academic qualifications is likely to better align the interests of all stakeholders compared to a board with directors with little financial experience and a lack of relevant educational qualifications. For example, the empirical study conducted by Hau and Thum, which centred on the 29 largest banks in Germany, revealed that insufficient academic qualifications and banking-related experience of supervisory board members contributed to banking failures.[119] In light of this, the authors argued that proper educational qualifications and managerial and financial expertise are vital competencies for supervisory board members. These competencies enable them to select and effectively monitor the management board.[120] Thus, one would argue that directors must possess the requisite qualifications and experience to advise and monitor management as well as align the interests of all bank stakeholders.

Board Independence and Non-Executive Directors

Another essential characteristic of the board structure is the composition of the board of directors. A bank board of directors comprises the executive directors and the non-executive directors.[121] There is no consensus about the role of the execu-

116 Jeffrey Cohen, Ganesh Krishnamoorthy, Arnold Wright, 'Corporate governance and the audit process', 19(4), Winter 2002, pp. 573–594

117 Douglas Freeman, 'Board diversification strategy; realising a competitive advantage and shareholder value', *Organisational Science*, 15(3), 1984; Richard Allen, Gail Dawson, Kathleen Wheatley, Charles White, 'Perceived diversity and organizational performance', *Employee Relations*, 30(1), 2007, pp. 20–33, available at: <https://doi.org/10.1108/0142545081083539>; Maran Marimuthu, 'Ethnic diversity on boards of directors and its implications on firm financial performance', *Journal of International Social Research*, 1, pp. 2–15

118 Lawrence Gales, Idalene Kesner, 'An analysis of board of director size and composition in the bankrupt organizations', *Journal of Business Research*, 30(3), July 1994, pp. 271–282

119 Harald Hau, Marcel Thum, 'Subprime crisis and board (in-)competence: Private vs. public banks in Germany', ECGI Working Paper Series in Finance Working Paper No. 247/2009, p. 13, available at: <https://ecgi.global/working-paper/subprime-crisis-and-board-competence-private-vs-public-banks-germany> accessed 15 April 2024

120 Harald Hau, Marcel Thum, 'Subprime crisis and board (in-)competence: Private vs. public banks in Germany', ECGI Working Paper Series in Finance Working Paper No. 247/2009, p. 13, available at: <https://ecgi.global/working-paper/subprime-crisis-and-board-competence-private-vs-public-banks-germany> accessed 15 April 2024

121 Christopher Pass, 'Corporate governance and the role of non-executive directors in large UK companies: An empirical study', *Corporate Governance International Journal of Business in Society*, 4(2), June 2004, pp. 52–63

tive directors and that of the non-executive directors.[122] The divergence in opinions concerning their functions depends on several factors. These include the ownership structure, board composition, whether the bank is public or private, and the power between external and internal stakeholders.[123]

The UK Companies Act 2006 does not distinguish between the role of the executive directors and that of the non-executive directors.[124] Executive and non-executive directors have the same responsibilities in promoting the bank's success,[125] exercising independent judgment,[126] and avoiding conflict of interest.[127] Sir Walker outlined the responsibilities of non-executive directors as ensuring an effective executive team in place, participating in the board decision-making process, and exercising appropriate oversight over the execution of the agreed strategy by the executive team.[128] Therefore, one could argue that the two main distinctions between executive and non-executive directors are, firstly, that executive directors are typically recruited from among the bank staff, whereas non-executive directors are appointed from outside the bank. Secondly, executive directors are involved in the bank's daily operations, while non-executive directors have a crucial role in monitoring the bank's activities.[129]

The importance of having a well-composed board that promotes diversity and inclusion has received significant attention lately. In the UK, board diversity should consider various factors such as gender, ethnicity, age, disability, and culture.[130] Pande and Ford recommended that there should be a reasonable proportion of women to men on the board.[131] Empirical evidence suggests that including a fair ratio of women on a board can lead to better financial performance of banks.[132] Research has also indicated that banks with more women on their boards are less likely to be involved in scandals such as bribery, fraud, or shareholders' battles,

122 Tracy Long, Victor Dulewicz, Keith Gay, 'The role of the non-executive director: Findings of an empirical investigation into the differences between listed and unlisted UK boards', *Corporate Governance: An International Review*, 13(5), September 2005, pp. 667–679, 668

123 Tracy Long, Victor Dulewicz, Keith Gay, 'The role of the non-executive director: Findings of an empirical investigation into the differences between listed and unlisted UK boards', *Corporate Governance: An International Review*, 13(5), September 2005, pp. 667–679, 668

124 UK Companies Act 2006

125 S.172 Companies Act 2006

126 S.172 Companies Act 2006, S.173

127 S.172 Companies Act 2006, S.175

128 Sir David Walker, 'A review of corporate governance in UK banks and other financial sector entities', *The Walker Review, Secretariat*, London, 26 November 2009, p. 35

129 Michael Weisbach, 'Outside directors and CEO turnover', *Journal of Financial Economics*, 20(1–2), 1988, pp. 431–460, 433

130 José García Martín, Begoña Herrero, 'Boards of directors: Composition and effects on the performance of the firm', *Economic Research-Ekonomska Istraživanja*, 31(1), 2018, pp. 1015–1041

131 Pande, Rohini, Deanna Ford, 'Gender quotas and female leadership: A review', *World Development Report on Gender*, 2011, available at: <www.tinyurl.com/yxhp8v6z> accessed 15 April 2024

132 Carolyn Wiley, Mireia Monllor-Tormos, 'Board gender diversity in the STEM&F sectors: The critical mass required to drive firm performance', *Journal of Leadership & Organizational Studies*, 25(3), January 2018

and such boards are better at aligning the interests of all stakeholders. While the number of reported cases of corrupt women directors is low, this does not indicate that women are less likely to abuse their positions.[133] The relatively small number is due to fewer women occupying board positions compared to men, and as such, the number of women rising to become CEOs/COBs is relatively low.

Studies indicate that a notable gender imbalance exists on the board of financial services in the United Kingdom, with a lower proportion of women compared to men.[134] Presently, women constitute a mere 23% of board members in financial services companies, with only 14% of this demographic holding executive committee roles.[135] Such a disparity undoubtedly perpetuates the underrepresentation of women in leadership positions within the banking industry. Research suggests that increasing the number of women on the banks' boards can positively impact their decision-making capacity, as women tend to be more risk-averse than their male counterparts.[136] In light of this, one would argue that banks with more decisive female leadership are more likely to benefit from a better risk management framework.[137]

When considering the composition of a board, an important factor to take into account is the ratio of executive directors to non-executive directors. Lynall, Goden, and Hillman asserted that a board with many non-executive directors is superior because it will alleviate the agency's problems.[138] If the non-executive directors are not involved in the daily management of the bank, they can monitor the executive directors who oversee the bank's day-to-day running.

On the other hand, Donaldson and Davis suggest that boards composed of more executive directors function better because they are good stewards of the shareholders, working tirelessly to attain the bank's corporate objectives, which is to maximise profits for the benefit of its shareholders.[139] Proponents of a higher proportion of non-executive directors argue that it allows executive directors to concentrate

133 Scott Berinato, 'Banks with more women on their boards commit less fraud', *Harvard Business Review*, May–June 2021, available at: <https://hbr.org/2021/05/banks-with-more-women-on-their-boards-commit-less-fraud> accessed 15 April 2024

134 House of Commons Treasury Committee, 'Women in finance', Fifteenth Report of Session 2017–2019, June 2018, p. 5, available at: <https://publications.parliament.uk/pa/cm201719/cmselect/cmtreasy/477/477.pdf> accessed 15 April 2024

135 House of Commons Treasury Committee, 'Women in finance', Fifteenth Report of Session 2017–2019, June 2018, p. 5, available at: <https://publications.parliament.uk/pa/cm201719/cmselect/cmtreasy/477/477.pdf> accessed 15 April 2024

136 Linda-Eling Lee, Ric Marshall, Damion Rallis, Matt Moscardi, 'Women on boards: Global trends in gender diversity', MSCI Research, November 2015, available at: <www.msci.com/documents/10199/04b6f646-d638-4878-9c61-4eb91748a82b> accessed 15 April 2024

137 Linda-Eling Lee, Ric Marshall, Damion Rallis, Matt Moscardi, 'Women on boards: Global trends in gender diversity', MSCI Research, November 2015, available at: <www.msci.com/documents/10199/04b6f646-d638-4878-9c61-4eb91748a82b> accessed 15 April 2024

138 Matthew Lynall, Brian Golden, Amy Hillman, 'Board composition from adolescence to maturity: A multitheoretic view', *Academy oí Management Review*, 28(3), 2003, pp. 416–431, 418

139 Lex Donaldson, James Davis, 'Boards and company performance – research challenges the conventional wisdom', *Corporate Governance: An International Review*, 2(3), 1994, pp. 151–160

on the bank's day-to-day operations.[140] Moreover, a board that is duly constituted with more non-executive directors can leverage their expertise to engage in vigorous discussions during board meetings.[141] However, the validity of this argument is dependent on the true independence of the non-executive directors. If their independence has been compromised, the discussions in the boardroom would be a mere form of formality.

Separation of the Roles of Chairman of the Board (COB) and Chief Executive Officer (CEO)

The leadership structure of a bank's board depends on the corporate governance model followed in the country. The Anglo-Saxon model features a one-tier board system that combines the CEO's office with the COB's. In the Continental European model, for instance, a two-tier board system is employed in Germany, where the CEO's office is separated from the COBs. When the same person holds the positions of both COB and CEO of the bank, it is called duality. The CEO oversees the bank's day-to-day activities, while the COB ensures that the board of directors functions efficiently.[142] The issue with this arrangement is that the CEO, who also doubles as the COB, would become excessively powerful and limit the board's ability to monitor the management team effectively. Finkelstein and D'aveni have suggested separating the CEO's office from that of the COB in banking institutions.[143] They argue that when a CEO doubles as the COB, they are vested with immense power and authority, thus compromising the board's impartiality.[144]

It is argued that such fusion would hinder the effective governance of the bank because such a CEO who doubles as the COB will dominate the agenda and the content of board meetings. Critics argue that such a combination would lead to a conflict of interest, as the management may prioritise their own interests over the interests of other stakeholders.[145] Such a board would lack the independence required to observe and monitor the management team if the same person holds both offices. Some scholars who support duality argue that such a combination

140 Charlie Weir, David Laing, 'Governance structures, director independence and corporate performance in the UK', *European Business Review*, 13(2), 2001, pp. 86–95
141 Charlie Weir, David Laing, 'Governance structures, director independence and corporate performance in the UK', *European Business Review*, 13(2), 2001, pp. 86–95
142 Charlie Weir, David Laing, 'Governance structures, director independence and corporate performance in the UK', *European Business Review*, 13(2), 2001, pp. 86–95
143 Sydney Finkelstein, Richard A. D'Aveni, 'CEO duality as a double-edged sword: How boards of directors balance entrenchment avoidance and unity of command', *The Academy of Management Journal*, 37(5), October 1994, pp. 1079–1108, 1082
144 Sydney Finkelstein, Richard A. D'Aveni, 'CEO duality as a double-edged sword: How boards of directors balance entrenchment avoidance and unity of command', *The Academy of Management Journal*, 37(5), October 1994, pp. 1079–1108, 1082
145 Lex Donaldson, James Davis, 'Stewardship theory or agency theory: CEO governance and shareholder returns', *Australian Journal of Management*, 16(1), 1991, p. 51

would lead to better outcomes and performance of the bank.[146] Their argument was based on the assumption that separating both positions would cost the bank more than the benefit to be derived. However, the existing empirical evidence does not support the claim that banks with duality perform better. A study conducted using Malaysian corporations shows that about 17.9% of companies operate a duality leadership structure. The research results suggested that companies with duality are underperforming compared to companies where the role of the CEO is separated from that of the COB.[147] It is argued that duality does not guarantee the performance of banks nor does it help promote all stakeholders' interests. The board's independence is essential for the bank's performance and protection of all its stakeholders' interests among all the board's characteristics discussed earlier. The best way to achieve board independence and protect key stakeholders' interests is by separating the position of the CEO from that of the COB.

Board Committees

Board committees are another vital characteristic of the board of directors. These committees are a subset of the board of directors and may include both executive and non-executive directors. Specific committees are responsible for performing oversight functions for the board of directors. Board committees perform specific functions or ad hoc tasks the board of directors assign them as needed. For example, an audit committee of the board oversees the financial reporting process and provides recommendations to the entire board. In some countries, the corporate governance framework mandates that the board of directors have specific board committees, like in the UK Code of Corporate Governance, which requires listed companies to establish a board audit committee.[148]

Board committees are a fundamental component of corporate governance in most jurisdictions; the applicable law usually determines the number and structure of these committees.[149] The committees commonly provided for by law include the audit committee, the risk committee, the remuneration committee, and the nominations committee.[150] However, after the financial crisis of 2007–2009, CSR or sustainability committees have also become crucial, particularly in banks that have adopted the stakeholder model. The primary objective of CSR or sustainability

146 James Brickley, Jeffrey Coles, Gregg Jarrell, 'Leadership structure: Separating the CEO and chairman of the board', *Journal of Corporate Finance*, 3(3), June 1997, pp. 189–220, Elsevier

147 Rashidah Abdul Rahman, Roszaini Mohd Haniffa, 'The effect of role duality on corporate performance in Malaysia', *Corporate Ownership & Control*, 2(2), Winter 2005, p. 44

148 UK Corporate Governance Code, 'Financial reporting council', July 2018, p. 10, available at: <www.frc.org.uk/getattachment/88bd8c45-50ea-4841-95b0-d2f4f48069a2/2018-UK-Corporate-Governance-Code-FINAL.pdf> accessed 8 April 2024

149 UK Corporate Governance Code, 'Financial reporting council', July 2018, p. 10, available at: <www.frc.org.uk/getattachment/88bd8c45-50ea-4841-95b0-d2f4f48069a2/2018-UK-Corporate-Governance-Code-FINAL.pdf> accessed 8 April 2024

150 José Sánchez, María Zamanillo, Manuel Luna, 'How corporate governance mechanisms of banks have changed after the 2007–08 financial crisis', *Contemporary Issues in Banking*, 11(S1), Special Issue, January 2020, pp. 52–61

committees is to promote transparency and accountability.[151] One would argue that embedding CSR in the corporate governance of banks is one way of recognising and promoting the interests of key stakeholders.[152] In the latter part of this chapter, the role of CSR in corporate governance will be examined.

Executive Compensation

Executive compensation is an internal mechanism employed by banks to ensure that their management and directors adhere to the banks' long-term goals. Before the financial crisis of 2007–2009, concerns surfaced regarding executive remuneration, specifically, the growth and size of executive pay.[153] However, after the financial crisis, there was a greater focus on executive pay due to the link between the failure of banks and excessive risk-taking by senior management and board members in exchange for short-term bonuses[154] Lord Turner argued that directors and senior management of UK banks engaged in excessive risk-taking due to the high level of executive remuneration in UK banks, which led to significant losses during the global financial crisis.[155] In response to this finding, the UK government introduced several reforms to address banks' bonus culture and executive pay. For example, the government introduced the remuneration code for banks in September 2009, which aimed to reduce the short-termism of incentives among bank executives.[156] One of the remuneration code innovations was the delay in paying at least 50% of bank executive bonuses for three years.[157] There is a condition subsequent to the delayed payment being made based on the banks' making financial profits in the long run. Suppose the banks' future performance is adjudged as inadequate because they failed to make profits or incurred losses; any bonus amount previously paid out to directors and senior managers will be clawed back. The regulation of executive

151 José Sánchez, María Zamanillo, Manuel Luna, 'How corporate governance mechanisms of banks have changed after the 2007–08 financial crisis', *Contemporary Issues in Banking*, 11(S1), Special Issue, January 2020, pp. 52–61

152 Chris Mason, John Simmons, 'Embedding corporate social responsibility in corporate governance: A stakeholder systems approach', *Journal of Business Ethics*, 119, 2014, pp. 77–86, available at: <https://doi.org/10.1007/s10551-012-1615-9> accessed 8 April 2024

153 Lord Adair Turner, 'The Turner review: A regulatory response to the global banking crisis, FSA', March 2009, p. 79, available at: <http://news.bbc.co.uk/1/shared/bsp/hi/pdfs/18_03_09_turner_review.pdf> accessed 15 April 2024

154 Lord Adair Turner, 'The Turner review: A regulatory response to the global banking crisis, FSA', March 2009, p. 79, available at: <http://news.bbc.co.uk/1/shared/bsp/hi/pdfs/18_03_09_turner_review.pdf> accessed 15 April 2024

155 Lord Adair Turner, 'The Turner review: A regulatory response to the global banking crisis, FSA', March 2009, p. 79, available at: <http://news.bbc.co.uk/1/shared/bsp/hi/pdfs/18_03_09_turner_review.pdf> accessed 15 April 2024

156 House of Commons Treasury Committee, 'Banking crisis: Reforming corporate governance and pay in the city', Ninth Report of Session 2008–09, p. 22, available at: <https://publications.parliament.uk/pa/cm200809/cmselect/cmtreasy/519/519.pdf>

157 House of Commons Treasury Committee, 'Banking crisis: Reforming corporate governance and pay in the city', Ninth Report of Session 2008–09, p. 22, available at: <https://publications.parliament.uk/pa/cm200809/cmselect/cmtreasy/519/519.pdf>

compensation is not unique to the UK. The US enacted the Dodd-Frank Act in July 2010,[158] which contained several corporate governance provisions that dealt with directors' compensation in US banks.[159] European Union Member States also collectively attempted to tackle the bonus culture in banks in their jurisdictions by introducing reforms that targeted executive compensation.[160] This was one way to ensure that bank directors and senior management were held accountable and to mitigate the excessive risk-taking that contributed to the financial crisis.[161]

It is evident from the discussions conducted in this subsection that the board of directors constitutes a crucial corporate governance mechanism. It has become apparent that to ensure the board's performance and protect the interests of stakeholders, the composition of the board, particularly regarding qualification, diversity, and independence, is sacrosanct. One significant way of guaranteeing the board's independence is by separating the position of CEO from that of the COB. Such a separation would ensure that power is not concentrated in the hands of a domineering individual who serves as both the CEO and the COB. The concentration of power in one individual would impede the board of directors' capacity to monitor management effectively. Now that the ownership and board structures as corporate governance mechanisms have been discussed, the next subsection will examine market discipline as a form of corporate governance mechanism in the banking industry.

4.6.3 Market Discipline

External auditors play a vital role in ensuring transparent financial information, which enables stakeholders to make informed decisions while contributing to the financial soundness of banks.[162] They are expected to perform independently of the board of directors. Under the Anglo-Saxon model, external auditors are primarily responsible for safeguarding shareholders' interests by providing them with accurate and relevant information.[163] Scholars have argued that external auditors can help minimise the agency problem by ensuring that directors act in the interest of shareholders. Auditors examine bank financial statements to identify financial misstatements or fraud that could defraud shareholders.[164] Therefore, their respon-

158 Dodd-Frank Act, 2010

159 Dodd-Frank Act, 2010

160 Directive (EU) 2017/828 of the European Parliament and of the Council of 17 May 2017, Amending Directive 2007/36/EC as Regards the Encouragement of Long-Term Shareholder Engagement, available at: <http://data.europa.eu/eli/dir/2017/828/oj> accessed 15 April 2024

161 Paul Gregg, Sarah Jewell, Ian Tonks, 'Executive pay and performance: Did bankers' bonuses cause the crisis?', *International Review of Finance*, 12(1), 2012, pp. 89–122

162 The World Bank, 'Banking supervisors and external auditors: Building a constructive relationship', Centre for Financial Reporting Reform, Governance Global Practice, World Bank Group, 2015, available at: <http://hdl.handle.net/10986/25074> accessed 15 April 2024

163 Adrian Cadbury, *Report of the Committee on the Financial Aspects of Corporate Governance* (Gee and Co Ltd., London, 1992), p. 36, available at: <www.ecgi.org/codes/documents/cadbury.pdf> accessed 15 April 2024

164 Marianne Ojo, 'The role of external auditors in corporate governance: Agency problems and the management of risk', MPRA Paper, 6 July 2009, available at: <https://mpra.ub.uni-muenchen.de/28149/1/MPRA_paper_28149.pdf> accessed 28 November 2021

sibility is to express an opinion that reasonable assurance has been obtained and that the bank's financial statements are free from material misunderstanding.[165] The financial statement is prepared following the financial reporting framework of the country where the bank has its head office and in accordance with any relevant regulations established by regulators in that country.[166] External auditors must carry out their functions with due diligence and suggest suitable recommendations to improve banks' corporate governance.[167] However, some auditors compromise their professional integrity and collude with the board to falsify financial statements for personal gains while performing their statutory responsibilities.[168]

Courts have held external auditors accountable for cases of negligent misstatement and false accounting. For instance, in the recent *Assetco Plc v Grant Thornton UK LLP* case, the Court of Appeal found the auditors liable for failing to uncover fraudulent activities by Assetco's directors.[169] The auditors failed to detect substantial losses concealed in 2009 and the group's insolvency that continued into 2010 and 2011. This failure deprived Assetco of the opportunity to hold senior management accountable.[170]

The role of external auditors in the period leading up to the financial crisis of 2007–2009 has generated debates about auditing practices. Scholars have argued that the four dominant accountancy firms in the UK (Deloitte, KPMG, Pricewaterhouse-Coopers, and Ernst and Young) contributed to the global financial crisis by collecting large amounts in audit fees and providing incorrect valuations of bank assets before 2007.[171] As a result, the House of Lords Economic Affairs Committee conducted an enquiry into the UK auditing standard, which led to a referral to the Office of Fair Trading.[172] Therefore, external auditors are responsible for ensuring that they provide accurate and relevant information about the actual financial positions of banks. By

165 Basel Committee on Banking Supervision, 'The relationship between banking supervisors and banks' external auditors', January 2002, available at: <www.bis.org/publ/bcbs87.pdf> accessed 15 April 2024

166 Basel Committee on Banking Supervision, 'The relationship between banking supervisors and banks' external auditors', January 2002, available at: <www.bis.org/publ/bcbs87.pdf> accessed 15 April 2024

167 Marijana Joksimović, Alseddig Ahmed, 'The internal audit as function to the corporate governance', *Megatrend Review*, 14(2), 2017, pp. 109–126, 113

168 Julius Olatunde Otusanya, Sarah Lauwo, 'The role of Auditors in the Nigerian banking crisis', *Accountancy Business and the Public Interest*, 9, 2010, p. 179

169 [2020] EWCA Civ. 1151

170 [2020] EWCA Civ. 1151

171 Prem Sikka, 'Financial crisis and the silence of the auditors', *Accounting, Organizations and Society*, 34(6–7), 2009, pp. 868–873; Rajib Doogar, Stephen Rowe, Padmakumar Sivadasan, 'Asleep at the wheel (again)? Bank audits during the lead-up to the financial crisis', *Contemporary Accounting Research*, 32(1), Spring 2015, pp. 358–391; Adam Jones, 'Auditors criticised for role in financial crisis', *The Financial Times Newspaper*, 30 March 2011, available at: <www.ft.com/content/358b366e-59fa-11e0-ba8d-00144feab49a> accessed 15 April 2024; Nick Mathiason, 'Auditors' face being called to account for their role in the global financial crisis', *The Guardian Newspaper*, 25 October 2009, available at: <www.theguardian.com/business/2009/oct/25/auditors-role-financial-crisis> accessed 15 April 2024

172 Lords Select Committee, The Economic Affairs Committee, 'Auditors: Market concentration and their role', 2nd Report of Session, Volume I: Report, Published by the Authority of the House of Lords, London, 2010–2011

doing so, they can help protect the interests of all bank stakeholders and address the problem of information asymmetry, which causes market failure.[173]

4.7 Stakeholder Model, Corporate Governance, and Corporate Social Responsibility

There is an ongoing discussion about the relationship between corporate governance and corporate social responsibility (CSR). The debate revolves around whether banks should engage in CSR[174] and whether CSR should be a key corporate governance mechanism.[175] As corporate citizens, banks are expected to meet societal expectations, including recognising and protecting stakeholders' interests, and CSR can be instrumental in achieving these objectives.[176] The Anglo-Saxon model discussed earlier highlights the board of directors' responsibility to pursue the bank's corporate goal, profit maximisation for shareholders' benefit. However, embedding CSR in the corporate governance of banks is a medium through which the board of directors and management can promote stakeholders' interests and not just those of its shareholders.[177] Therefore, it is argued that the nexus between CSR and corporate governance focuses on the banks' responsibility to be accountable to stakeholders.[178] This responsibility may vary from one jurisdiction to another and take different approaches. For instance, CSR initiatives in the UK may not aim to provide infrastructure and social amenities because CSR policies are not globalised but context-dependent. In Nigeria, however, banks have a social responsibility to help develop infrastructure and social amenities due to the institutional environment in the country.[179] Therefore, it is argued that CSR must be embedded in the corporate governance framework in the banking industry. This will enable

173 Frederic Mishkin, 'Asymmetric information and financial crises: A historical perspective', in Glenn Hubbard (ed), *Financial Markets and Financial Crises* (University of Chicago Press, Chicago, 1991), pp. 69–108

174 Ruth Aguilera, Cynthia Williams, John Conley, Deborah Rupp, 'Corporate governance and social responsibility: A comparative analysis of the UK and the US', *Corporate Governance: An International Review*, 14(3), 2006, pp. 147–158

175 Andreas Scherer, Guido Palazzo, 'Toward a political conception of corporate responsibility: Business and society seen from a Habermasian perspective', *Academy of Management Review*, 32(4), 2007, pp. 1096–1120, 1096

176 Andreas Scherer, Guido Palazzo, 'Toward a political conception of corporate responsibility: Business and society seen from a Habermasian perspective', *Academy of Management Review*, 32(4), 2007, p. 34

177 Ruth Aguilera, Cynthia Williams, John M. Conley, Deborah Rupp, 'Corporate governance and social responsibility: A comparative analysis of the UK and the US', *Corporate Governance: An International Review*, 14(3), 2006

178 Dima Jamali, Asem Safieddine, Myriam Rabbath, 'Corporate governance and corporate social responsibility synergies and interrelationships', *Corporate Governance: An International Review*, 16(5), 14 October 2008, pp. 443–459

179 Adaeze Okoye, 'Exploring the relationship between corporate social responsibility, law and development in an African context: Should government be responsible for ensuring corporate responsibility?', *International Journal of Law and Management*, 54(5), 2012, pp. 364–378, 367

the board of directors and senior management to adhere to fundamental principles of transparency, integrity, fairness, accountability, and responsibility and help them align the interests of shareholders and other key stakeholders, regardless of the corporate governance model adopted.

4.8 Conclusion

This chapter provides an in-depth analysis of regulatory approaches governing banks' governance, specifically examining the Anglo-Saxon, Continental European, and Japanese Keiretsu models. It posits that two primary corporate governance models exist: the shareholder and stakeholder models. The chapter also identifies stakeholders in bank governance, including shareholders, employees, creditors, government, host communities, banking regulators, and supervisors. The chapter explores various corporate governance mechanisms in the banking industry, such as ownership structure, board structure, system regulation, and market discipline. Furthermore, the chapter delves into the need to incorporate CSR into the corporate governance framework in the banking industry. It argues that such an approach will promote the recognition of stakeholders and the protection of their interests, thereby leading to better bank performance.

Reference List

Abdul Rahman, Rashidah, Roszaini Mohd Haniffa, 'The effect of role duality on corporate performance in Malaysia', *Corporate Ownership & Control*, 2(2), Winter 2005, p. 44

Adams, Renée, Hamid Mehran, 'Bank board structure and performance: Evidence for large bank holding companies', *Journal of Financial Intermediation*, 21(2), April 2012, pp. 243–267

Aguilera, Ruth, Igor Filatotchev, Howard Gospel, Gregory Jackson, 'An organisational approach to comparative corporate governance: Costs, contingencies, and complementarities', *Organization Science*, 19(3), 2008, pp. 475–492

Aguilera, Ruth, Cynthia Williams, John Conley, Deborah Rupp, 'Corporate governance and social responsibility: A comparative analysis of the UK and the US', *Corporate Governance: An International Review*, 14(3), 2006, pp. 147–158

Alexander, Kern, *Principles of Banking Regulation* (Cambridge University Press, Cambridge, 2019)

Allen, Franklin, 'Corporate governance in emerging economies', *Oxford Review of Economic Policy*, 21(2), 2005, pp. 164–177, available at: <www.jstor.org/stable/23606977>

Allen, Richard, Gail Dawson, Kathleen Wheatley, Charles White, 'Perceived diversity and organizational performance', *Employee Relations*, 30(1), 2007, pp. 20–33, available at: <https://doi.org/10.1108/0142545081083539>

Aoki, Masahiko, 'Toward an economic model of the Japanese firm', *Journal of Economic Literature*, 28(1), March 1990, pp. 1–27

Armour, John, Henry Hansmann, Reinier Kraakman, 'Agency problems, legal strategies and enforcement', ECGI Working Paper Series in Law, Working Paper No. 135/2009, November 2009

Assetco Plc v. Grant Thornton UK LLP [2020] EWCA Civ. 1151

Ayadi, Rym, Sami Naceur, Barbara Casu, Barry Quinn, 'Does Basel Compliance matter for bank performance?', *Journal of Financial Stability*, 23, April 2016, pp. 15–32

Basel Committee on Banking Supervision, 'The relationship between banking supervisors and banks' external auditors', January 2002, available at: <www.bis.org/publ/bcbs87.pdf>

Basel Committee on Banking Supervision, 'The internal audit function in banks', Bank for International Settlement, June 2012 available at: <www.bis.org/publ/bcbs223.pdf>

Basel Committee on Banking Supervision, 'Corporate governance principles for banks', Bank for International Settlement, July 2015, available at: <www.bis.org/bcbs/publ/d328.pdf>

Basel Committee on Banking Supervision, 'Guidelines on the corporate governance principles for banks', pp. 1–13, available at: <https://assets.kpmg.com/content/dam/kpmg/pdf/2016/05/Corporate-Governance-Principles.pdf>

Berglöf, Erik, Enrico Perotti, 'The governance structure of the Japanese financial keiretsu', *Journal of Financial Economics*, 36(2), October 1994, pp. 259–284

Berinato, Scott, 'Banks with more women on their boards commit less fraud', *Harvard Business Review*, May–June 2021, available at: <https://hbr.org/2021/05/banks-with-more-women-on-their-boards-commit-less-fraud>

Berle, Adolf, Gardiner Means, *The Modern Corporation and Private Property* (Macmillan Co., New York, 1932)

Blair, Margaret, *Ownership and Control: Rethinking Corporate Governance for the Twenty-First Century* (Brookings Institution Press, Washington, DC, 2011)

Brickley, James, Jeffrey Coles, Gregg Jarrell, 'Leadership structure: Separating the CEO and chairman of the board', *Journal of Corporate Finance*, 3(3), June 1997, pp. 189–220, Elsevier

Cadbury, Adrian, *Report of the Committee on the Financial Aspects of Corporate Governance* (Gee and Co Ltd., London, 1992), p. 36, available at: <www.ecgi.org/codes/documents/cadbury.pdf>

Cernat, Lucian, 'The emerging European corporate governance model: Anglo-Saxon, Continental, or still the century of diversity?', *Journal of European Public Policy*, 11(1), 2004, pp. 147–166

Chandler, David, *Corporate Social Responsibility: A Strategic Perspective* (Business Expert Press LLC, New York, 2015), pp. 11–13

Chandler, David, *Strategic Corporate Social Responsibility: Sustainable Value Creation* (4th ed., Sage, London, 2017), p. 119

Chiu, Iris, Joanna Wilson, *Banking Law and Regulation* (Oxford University Press, Oxford, 2019)

Codetermination Act, 1976

Cohen, Jeffrey, Ganesh Krishnamoorthy, Arnold Wright, 'Corporate governance and the audit process', *Contemporary Accounting Research*, 19(4), Winter 2002, pp. 573–594

Commissioners of Inland Revenue v. Crossman [1937] AC 26 (HL) 66

Companies Act, 2006

Corporate Governance Reform, Department for Business, Energy & Industrial Strategy, 2016, available at: <https://assets.publishing.service.gov.uk/government/uploads/system/uploads/attachment_data/file/584013/corporate-governance-reform-green-paper.pdf>

Crow, David, 'HSBC to axe up to 10,000 jobs in cost-cutting drive', *The Financial Times*, 6 October 2019, available at: <www.ft.com/content/b43e7b3e-e6c7-11e9-b112-9624ec9edc59>

Culpepper, Pepper, Raphael Reinke, 'Structural power and bank bailouts in the UK and the US', *Politics and Society*, 42(4), December 2014, pp. 427–454, available at: <https://doi.org/10.1177/0032329214547342>

Deakin, Simon, 'Corporate governance and financial crisis in the long run', Working Papers WP417, Centre for Business Research, University of Cambridge, 2010, available at: <www.cbr.cam.ac.uk/fileadmin/user_upload/centre-for-business-research/downloads/working-papers/wp417.pdf>

Directive (EU) 2017/828 of the European Parliament and of the Council of 17 May 2017 Amending Directive 2007/36/EC as Regards the Encouragement of Long-Term Shareholder Engagement, available at: <http://data.europa.eu/eli/dir/2017/828/oj>

Dodd-Frank Act, 2010

Donaldson, Lex, James Davis, 'Stewardship theory or agency theory: CEO governance and shareholder returns', *Australian Journal of Management*, 16(1), 1991, p. 51

Donaldson, Lex, James Davis, 'Boards and company performance – research challenges the conventional wisdom', *Corporate Governance: An International Review*, 2(3), 1994, pp. 151–160

Doogar, Rajib, Stephen Rowe, Padmakumar Sivadasan, 'Asleep at the wheel (again)? Bank audits during the lead-up to the financial crisis', *Contemporary Accounting Research*, 32(1), Spring 2015, pp. 358–391

Fama, Eugene, Michael Jensen, 'Separation of ownership and control', *Journal of Law and Economics*, 26(2), Corporations and Private Property, 1983, pp. 301–325, available at: <https://are.berkeley.edu/~cmantinori/prclass/FamaJensen.pdf>

Financial Reporting Council, 'Effective corporate governance', July 2011, available at: <www.frc.org.uk/getattachment/8d5dd29f-0630-4521-86b2-f41a75d9be6b/FRC-Effective-Corporate-Governance-July-2011.pdf>

Finkelstein, Sydney, Richard A. D'Aveni, 'CEO duality as a double-edged sword: How boards of directors balance entrenchment avoidance and unity of command', *The Academy of Management Journal*, 37(5), October 1994, pp. 1079–1108, 1082

Francesco Maassen, Gregory, *An International Comparison of Corporate Governance Models* (Spencer Stuart, Amsterdam, The Netherlands, 1999)

Francesco Maasen, Gregory, *An International Comparison of Corporate Governance Models* (3rd ed., Spencer Stuart, Amsterdam, The Netherlands, 2002)

Francis, Bill, Iftekhar Hasan, Liang Song, *Corporate Governance, Creditor Protection, and Bank Loan Contracting in Emerging Markets* (Lally School of Management and Technology of Rensselaer Polytechnic Institute, New York, 2007)

Freeman, Douglas, 'Board diversification strategy; realising a competitive advantage and shareholder value', *Organisational Science*, 15(3), 1984

Fülöp, Melinda Timea, 'Why do we need effective corporate governance?', *International Advances in Economic Research*, 20, 2014, pp. 227–228, available at: <https://doi.org/10.1007/s11294-013-9430-3>

Gales, Lawrence, Idalene Kesner, 'An analysis of board of director size and composition in the bankrupt organisations', *Journal of Business Research*, 30(3), July 1994, pp. 271–282

Gilford Motor Co Ltd v. Horne [1933] Ch 935

Gregg, Paul, Sarah Jewell, Ian Tonks, 'Executive pay and performance: Did bankers' bonuses cause the crisis?', *International Review of Finance*, 12(1), 2012, pp. 89–122

Hau, Harald, Marcel Thum, 'Subprime crisis and board (in-)competence: Private vs. public banks in Germany', ECGI Working Paper Series in Finance Working Paper No. 247/2009, p. 13, available at: <https://ecgi.global/working-paper/subprime-crisis-and-board-competence-private-vs-public-banks-germany>

Her Majesty's Commissioners of Inland Revenue v. Laird Group Plc [2003] UKHL 54 para 35

H L Bolton (Engineering) Co Ltd v. TJ Graham & Sons Ltd (1957) 1 QB 159

Hopt, Klaus, 'Better governance of financial institutions, corporate governance of banks and other financial institutions after the financial crisis', in Eddy Wymeersch, Klaus Hopt, Guido Ferrarini (eds), *Financial Regulation and Supervision, a Post-Crisis Analysis* (Oxford University Press, Oxford, 2012)

House of Commons Treasury Committee, 'Banking crisis: Reforming corporate governance and pay in the city', Ninth Report of Session, 2008–2009, available at: <https://www.iasplus.com/en/binary/uk/0905treasurycommittee.pdf>

House of Commons Treasury Committee, 'Women in finance', Fifteenth Report of Session 2017–19, June 2018, p. 5, available at: <https://publications.parliament.uk/pa/cm201719/cmselect/cmtreasy/477/477.pdf>

Hubert, Ooghe, Tine De Langhe, 'The Anglo-American versus the continental European corporate governance model: Empirical evidence of board composition in Belgium', *European Business Review*, 14(6), 2002, pp. 437–449

Jamali, Dima, Asem Safieddine, Myriam Rabbath, 'Corporate governance and corporate social responsibility synergies and interrelationships', *Corporate Governance: An International Review*, 16(5), 14 October 2008, pp. 443–459

Jensen, Michael, 'The modern industrial revolution, exit, and the failure of internal control systems', *The Journal of Finance*, 48(3), 1993, pp. 831–880

Joksimović, Marijana, Alseddig Ahmed, 'The internal audit as function to the corporate governance', *Megatrend Review*, 14(2), 2017, pp. 109–126, 113

Jones, Adam, 'Auditors criticised for role in financial crisis', *The Financial Times Newspaper*, 30 March 2011, available at: <www.ft.com/content/358b366e-59fa-11e0-ba8d-00144feab49a>

Jones v. Lipman 1962 1 WLR 832, Gilford Motor Co Ltd v. Horne [1933] Ch 935

Kay, John, 'Shareholders think they own the company – they are wrong', *Financial Times*, 10 November 2015, available at: <www.ft.com/content/7bd1b20a-879b-11e5-90de-f44762bf9896>

Kenneth, Amaeshi, Bongo Adi, Chris Ogbechie, Olufemi Amao, 'Corporate social responsibility in Nigeria: Western mimicry or indigenous influences?', *The Journal of Corporate Citizenship*, 24, Winter 2006, pp. 83–99

Lee, Linda-Eling, Ric Marshall, Damion Rallis, Matt Moscardi, 'Women on boards: Global trends in gender diversity', MSCI Research, November 2015 available at: <www.msci.com/documents/10199/04b6f646-d638-4878-9c61-4eb91748a82b>

Long, Tracy, Victor Dulewicz, Keith Gay, 'The role of the non-executive director: Findings of an empirical investigation into the differences between listed and unlisted UK boards', *Corporate Governance: An International Review*, 13(5), September 2005, pp. 667–679

Lords Select Committee, The Economic Affairs Committee, 'Auditors: Market concentration and their role', 2nd Report of Session, Volume I: Report, Published by the Authority of the House of Lords, London, 2010–2011

Lugo, Stefano, 'Insider ownership and the cost of debt capital: Evidence from bank loans', *International Review of Financial Analysis*, 63, 2019, pp. 357–368

Lynall, Matthew, Brian Golden, Amy Hillman, 'Board composition from adolescence to maturity: A multitheoretic view', *Academy of Management Review*, 28(3), 2003, pp. 416–431

Macey, Jonathan, Geoffery Miller, 'Double liability of bank shareholders: History and implications', *Wake Forest Law Review*, 27, 1992, pp. 31–62

Macey, Jonathan, Maureen O'Hara, 'The corporate governance of banks', *Federal Reserve Bank of New York Economic Policy Review*, 9, 2003, pp. 97–107

Maher, Maria, Thomas Anderson, *Corporate Governance: Effects on Firm Performance and Economic Growth* (OECD Publishing, Paris, 1999)

Mahmud v. Bank of Credit and Commerce International SA [1997] UKHL 23

Malik v. Bank of Credit and Commerce International SA (1997) 3 WLR 95

Mallin, Christine, *Corporate Governance* (6th ed., Oxford University Press, Oxford, 2019)

Marimuthu, Maran, 'Ethnic diversity on boards of directors and its implications on firm financial performance', *Journal of International Social Research*, 1(4), Summer 2008, pp. 2–15

Martín, José García, Begoña Herrero, 'Boards of directors: Composition and effects on the performance of the firm', *Economic Research-Ekonomska Istraživanja*, 31(1), 2018, pp. 1015–1041

Mason, Chris, John Simmons, 'Embedding corporate social responsibility in corporate governance: A stakeholder systems approach', *Journal of Business Ethics*, 119, 2014, pp. 77–86, available at: <https://doi.org/10.1007/s10551-012-1615-9>

Mathiason, Nick, 'Auditors' face being called to account for their role in the global financial crisis', *The Guardian Newspaper*, 25 October 2009, available at: <www.theguardian.com/business/2009/oct/25/auditors-role-financial-crisis>

Michelon, Giovanna, Antonio Parbonetti, 'The effect of corporate governance on sustainability disclosure', *Journal of Management and Governance*, 16, 2012, pp. 477–509, available at: <https://doi.org/10.1007/s10997-010-9160-3>

Millstein, Ira, Michel Albert, Adrian Cadbury, Robert Denham, Dieter Fedddersen, Nobuo Tateisi, *Corporate Governance: Improving Competitiveness and Access to Capital in Global Markets: A Report to the OECD by the Business Industry Advisory Group on Corporate Governance* (OECD Publishing, Paris, 1998), available at: <https://doi.org/10.1787/9789264162709-en>

Mishkin, Frederic, 'Asymmetric information and financial crises: A historical perspective', in Glenn Hubbard (ed), *Financial Markets and Financial Crises* (University of Chicago Press, Chicago, 1991), pp. 69–108

National Audit Office, 'Maintaining the financial stability of UK banks: Update on the support schemes', available at: <www.nao.org.uk/report/maintaining-the-financial-stability-of-uk-banks-update-on-the-support-schemes/>

Nordberg, Donald, 'Edging toward "reasonably" good corporate governance', *Philosophy of Management*, 17, 2018, pp. 353–371, available at: <https://doi.org/10.1007/s40926-017-0083-9>

OECD, 'Policy framework for investment user toolkit, chapter 6, corporate governance', 2011, p. 3, available at: <www.oecd.org/investment/toolkit/policyareas/corporategovernance/44931152.pdf>

OECD, *G20/OECD, Principles of Corporate Governance* (OECD Publishing, Paris, 2015), available at: <https://doi.org/10.1787/9789264236882-en> accessed 15 April 2024

Ojo, Marianne, 'The role of external auditors in corporate governance: Agency problems and the management of risk', MPRA Paper, 6 July 2009, available at: <https://mpra.ub.uni-muenchen.de/28149/1/MPRA_paper_28149.pdf>

Okoye, Adaeze, 'Exploring the relationship between corporate social responsibility, law and development in an African context: Should government be responsible for ensuring corporate responsibility?', *International Journal of Law and Management*, 54(5), 2012, pp. 364–378, 367

Olatunde Otusanya, Julius, Sarah Lauwo, 'The role of Auditors in the Nigerian banking crisis', *Accountancy Business and the Public Interest*, 9, 2010, p. 179

Oman, Charles, 'Corporate governance and national development', OECD Development Centre Working Papers, No. 180, OECD Publishing, Paris, 2001, available at: <https://doi.org/10.1787/113535588267>

Pande, Rohini, Deanna Ford, 'Gender Quotas and Female Leadership: A Review', World Development Report on Gender, 2011, available at: <www.tinyurl.com/yxhp8v6z>

Pass, Christopher, 'Corporate governance and the role of non-executive directors in large UK companies: An empirical study' corporate governance', *International Journal of Business in Society*, 4(2), June 2004, pp. 52–63

Pathan, Shams, Robert Faff, 'Does board structure in banks really affect their performance?', *Journal of Banking & Finance*, 37(5), May 2013, pp. 1573–1589

Re A Company [1985] BCLC 333, *Conway v. Ratiu* (2006) 1 All ER 571

Re FG (Films) Ltd (1953) 1 WLR 483

Research and Market Development Department Securities and Exchange Commission, available at: <http://proshareng.com/admin/upload/reports/2625.pdf>

Salomon v. A Salomon & Co Ltd. [1896] UKHL 1 [1897] AC 22

Sánchez, José, María Zamanillo, Manuel Luna, 'How corporate governance mechanisms of banks have changed after the 2007–08 financial crisis', *Contemporary Issues in Banking*, 11(S1), Special Issue, January 2020, pp. 52–61
Scherer, Andreas, Guido Palazzo, 'Toward a political conception of corporate responsibility: Business and society seen from a Habermasian perspective', *Academy of Management Review*, 32(4), 2007, pp. 1096–1120
Short v. Treasury Commissioners (1948) 1 KB 116, 122, CA
Sikka, Prem, 'Financial crisis and the silence of the auditors', *Accounting, Organizations and Society*, 34(6–7), 2009, pp. 868–873
Tan, Zhong, 'Stewardship in the interests of systemic stakeholders: Re-conceptualising the means and ends of Anglo-American corporate governance in the wake of the global financial crisis', *Journal of Business and Technology Law*, 9(2), 2014, available at: <http://digitalcommons.law.umaryland.edu/jbtl/vol9/iss2/3>
Tanna, Sailesh, Fotios Pasiouras, Matthias Nnadi, 'The effect of board size and composition on the efficiency of UK banks', *International Journal of the Economics of Business*, 18(3), 2011, pp. 441–462
Turner, Lord Adair, 'The Turner review: A regulatory response to the global banking crisis, FSA', March 2009, p. 79 available at: <http://news.bbc.co.uk/1/shared/bsp/hi/pdfs/18_03_09_turner_review.pdf>
UK Corporate Governance Code, 'Financial reporting council', July 2018, p. 10, available at: <www.frc.org.uk/getattachment/88bd8c45-50ea-4841-95b0-d2f4f48069a2/2018-UK-Corporate-Governance-Code-FINAL.pdf>
Vallascas, Francesco, Sabur Mollah, Kevin Keasey, 'Does the impact of board independence on large bank risks change after the global financial crisis?', *Journal of Corporate Finance*, 44, 2017, pp. 149–166
Wahl, Mike Franz, *Governance and Ownership: Theoretical Framework of Research School of Economics and Business Administration* (Tallinn University of Technology), p. 150, available at: <http://deepthought.ttu.ee/majandus/tekstid/TUTWPE_08_179.pdf>
Walker, Sir David, 'A review of corporate governance in UK banks and other financial sectors entities', *The Walker Review, Secretariat*, London, 26 November 2009
Walsh, James, James Seward, 'On the efficiency of internal and external corporate control mechanisms', *The Academy of Management Review*, 15(3), July 1990, pp. 421–458
Wang, Tawei, Carol Hsu, 'Board composition and operational risk events of financial institutions', *Journal of Banking & Finance*, 37(6), 2013, pp. 2042–2051
Wang, Zhaofeng, 'Corporate governance under state control: The Chinese experience', *Theoretical Inquiries in Law*, 13(2), 2012
Wearing, Robert, *Cases in Corporate Governance* (Sage, London, 2005)
Weimer, Jeroen, Joost Pape, 'A taxonomy of systems of corporate governance', *Corporate Governance: An International Review*, 7(2), April 1999, pp. 152–166
Weir, Charlie, David Laing, 'Governance structures, director independence and corporate performance in the UK', *European Business Review*, 13(2), 86–95
Weisbach, Michael, 'Outside directors and CEO turnover', *Journal of Financial Economics*, 20(1–2), 1988, pp. 431–460
Wiley, Carolyn, Mireia Monllor-Tormos, 'Board gender diversity in the STEM&F sectors: The critical mass required to drive firm performance', *Journal of Leadership & Organizational Studies*, 25(3), January 2018
The World Bank, *Banking Supervisors and External Auditors: Building a Constructive Relationship* (Centre for Financial Reporting Reform, Governance Global Practice, World Bank Group, 2015), available at: <http://hdl.handle.net/10986/25074>
The World Bank, 'Understanding poverty: Financial inclusion', available at: <www.worldbank.org/en/topic/financialinclusion/overview>
Yeung, Karen, 'Regulatory agencies', in Peter Cane, Joanne Conaghan (eds), *The New Oxford Companion* (Oxford University Press, Oxford, 2008)

5 Corporate Governance and Banking Regulation in Nigeria

5.1 Introduction

This chapter analyses the corporate governance regulatory framework in Nigeria, with a particular focus on the protection of stakeholders' rights and interests. Drawing on institutional theory, it provides an in-depth examination of Nigeria's challenging institutional environment for corporate governance. The development of corporate governance in Nigeria is examined, thus highlighting the connection between the Anglo-Saxon corporate governance model and the corporate governance model adopted in Nigeria. It contends that the Companies and Allied Matters Act (CAMA) 2020 is Nigeria's primary legislation governing corporate law, which applies across all sectors. It is argued that CAMA is premised on Anglo-Saxon corporate governance because its primary focus is to enhance shareholders' value. Additionally, the chapter scrutinises the CBN Codes of Corporate Governance for Banks and the SEC Code of Corporate Governance for Public Listed Companies, assessing the extent to which they recognise stakeholders and protect their interests by utilising corporate governance mechanisms such as board and ownership structures and the market for corporate control. This analysis will facilitate an evaluation of the implementation of the corporate governance model in the Nigerian banking industry.

5.2 Historical Development of Corporate Governance in Nigeria

Before the British colonisation of Nigeria, the concept of corporate governance regulation was unfamiliar to the pre-colonial states, such as the Hausa Fulani Empire, Oyo Empire, Kanem Bornu Empire, the Igbo loose states, and the Benin Kingdom. The first companies that began operations in the region after the annexation of Lagos in 1862 were of British extraction and registered in England.[1] To regulate the British companies operating in Nigeria, the British government introduced the Anglo-Saxon corporate law model in Lagos, the Northern Protectorate,

1 Boniface Ahunwan, 'Corporate governance in Nigeria', *Journal of Business Ethics*, 37(3), 2002, pp. 269–287

DOI: 10.4324/9781003474418-7

and the Southern Protectorate.[2] Under the Statute of General Application, all laws in England became applicable in Nigeria on 1 January 1900.[3] The first company law in Nigeria was the Companies Ordinance 1912, which was based on the English Companies Act 1908; the Ordinance was later amended in 1922 and became the Companies Ordinance of 1922.[4] Nigeria thus inherited a corporate governance system based on the Anglo-Saxon corporate law model. The Companies Ordinance 1922 introduced several amendments in 1929, 1941, and 1954 to address the agency issue that emerged from the separation of ownership from control.[5] In England, the Anglo-Saxon corporate governance model was designed to hold the management of companies accountable to shareholders through the board of directors due to the dispersed ownership structure. Despite Nigeria's highly concentrated ownership structure, the country adopted the Anglo-Saxon corporate governance model.[6]

Since gaining independence in 1960, Nigeria's corporate governance model has remained largely unchanged. Despite amendments made to CAMA, the most recent one, re-enacted in 2020, replicates the English Companies Act 2006, which is premised on the Anglo-Saxon corporate law model. CAMA is designed to promote shareholders' interests, as shareholders' value is a fundamental part of this principal legislation. Therefore, it is important to examine the legal framework for corporate governance applicable to banks in Nigeria, including CAMA, to determine the extent to which it recognises and protects the interests of other stakeholders.

5.3 Legal Framework for Corporate Governance in Nigeria

The CAMA is Nigeria's primary legal framework for governing corporate governance practices. The law requires that all companies operating in Nigeria be registered under CAMA.[7] Therefore, banking institutions and other companies must first register as a company under CAMA before commencing any operations in Nigeria. Subsequently, they are obligated to abide by the provisions stipulated in CAMA. The corporate governance practice in Nigeria is grounded in the principle of shareholder primacy,[8] which is statutorily embedded in CAMA 2020. Several provisions in CAMA emphasise the importance of the shareholders' interests under Nigerian corporate law. For instance, CAMA, in a bid to recognise and protect

2 Emmanuel Adegbite, Chizu Nakajima, 'Corporate governance and responsibility in Nigeria', *International Journal of Disclosure and Governance*, 8(3), 2011, pp. 252–271

3 Statute of General Application, 1900

4 Boniface Ahunwan, 'Corporate governance in Nigeria', *Journal of Business Ethics*, 37(3), 2002, pp. 269–287

5 Elewechi Okike, 'Corporate governance in Nigeria: The status quo', *Corporate Governance: An International Review*, 15(2), 2007, pp. 173–193

6 Elewechi Okike, 'Corporate governance in Nigeria: The status quo', *Corporate Governance: An International Review*, 15(2), 2007, pp. 173–193

7 Section 18 CAMA, 2020

8 Joseph Olakunle Orojo, *Company Law and Practice in Nigeria* (3rd ed., Mbeyi and Associates Lagos, Nigeria, 1992), p. 1

shareholders' interests, makes it compulsory for newly incorporated companies to hold a general meeting of shareholders within six months of their registration.[9]

Directors have a legal obligation to act in the company's best interests, as prescribed by the CAMA. In discharging their fiduciary duty to the company, directors are to act in the interests of shareholders.[10] S.305 of CAMA is in *pari materia* with the provision of s.172 of the UK Companies Act 2006, which codifies the ESV theory as previously discussed.[11] In addition, CAMA has other provisions that emphasise the importance of shareholder primacy. These provisions include the following: that directors must avoid any personal conflicts of interest that could affect shareholders,[12] shareholders can bring personal and representative action against the directors, company, and third party,[13] shareholders are entitled to receive financial statements as of right,[14] shareholders' right to obtain copies of financial statements,[15] and lastly, auditors shall report to shareholders on the accounts examined by them.[16]

The separation of ownership and control underpinning the Anglo-Saxon model is incorporated in s.87(1)(3) and s.269 (1) CAMA, which provides for the directors of a company to exercise management power in the company.[17] These provisions received judicial approval in the case of *Baffa v Odili*, where the court held that company directors are persons duly appointed by the company to manage the company's business.[18] Thus, s.269 CAMA puts directors at the centre of corporate governance in a Nigerian company.[19] The shareholders delegate the management and control of the company to the board of directors; the directors are to act in the company's interest and deliver on their responsibilities. However, if the board of directors is not subject to adequate monitoring and oversight, they might pursue their interests while jeopardising the shareholders' interests to maximise profits for their benefit.[20]

The responsibilities vested in the directors, if not monitored effectively, will give rise to agency problems; s. 87 (1) CAMA vests all the powers of a company in its board of directors, except for those specifically reserved for members in the general meeting.[21] This statutory provision has been supported by numerous court cases, including *Okolo v Union Bank of Nigeria*,[22] where the Supreme

9 S.235 CAMA, 2020
10 S.305 (3)(4) CAMA, 2020
11 S.172 UK Companies Act, 2006
12 S.306 CAMA, 2020
13 S.344 CAMA, 2020
14 S.387 CAMA, 2020
15 S.392 CAMA, 2020
16 S.404 CAMA, 2020
17 S.87(1)(3) and S.269(1) CAMA, 2020
18 *Baffa v. Odili* (2001) 15 NWLR (pt 737) 709, S.269 CAMA, 2020
19 S.269 CAMA, 2020
20 S.87(1)(3) CAMA, 2020
21 S.87(1)(3) CAMA, 2020
22 3 NWLR (Pt.859) SC 87

Court declared that in the eyes of the law, a director is an agent of the company for which he acts and the general principle of the law of principal and agent applies. Therefore, if a director enters into a contract in the company's name or purports to bind the company, the company, as the principal, is liable for the contract, not the director.[23] This verdict implies that the directors are agents of the shareholders and must act in the company's best interests by promoting organisational objectives, such as profit maximisation, for the benefit of shareholders.

s.305(3)(4) CAMA requires that directors take into account the impact of the company's operations on the environment and consider the interests of employees when performing their functions.[24] However, s.305(9) CAMA restricts the power of these stakeholders to enforce this provision. Suppose the directors fail to consider the matter stated in s.305(3)(4) by failing to promote the relevant stakeholders' interests; in that case, only the company can sue the directors for breach of the provision of that section.[25] From the combined effect of these provisions, it is evident that there is limited stakeholders' recognition and protection of stakeholders' interests under Nigerian corporate law, given that CAMA is the principal legal framework for corporate law in Nigeria. Based on this example, it is important to examine further the institutional and regulatory framework that governs the corporate governance of companies in Nigeria. This examination aims to determine the role of the regulatory framework in promoting effective corporate governance in Nigeria.

5.4 Institutions for Corporate Governance of Companies in Nigeria

Corporate Affairs Commission

The Corporate Affairs Commission (CAC) was established in accordance with the Companies and Allied Matters Act to regulate the formation, incorporation, registration, management, and winding up of all companies incorporated within Nigeria.[26] The Commission regulates the formation, incorporation, registration, management, and winding up of all companies incorporated in Nigeria.[27] All companies are required to submit an audited financial statement to the Commission within 42 days after their annual general meeting. However, some have argued that the CAC has not been effective in monitoring companies' compliance with corporate governance provisions in CAMA because of the lack of rigorous enforcement mechanisms.[28] Despite the requirement for companies to file their financial statements with the Commission, most companies do not comply with the regulations.

23 As per Niki Tobi JSC (as he then was) delivering the lead judgment in the case
24 S.305(3)(4) CAMA, 2020
25 S.305(9) CAMA, 2020
26 CAC History, available at: <http://new.cac.gov.ng/home/about-us/> accessed 15 April 2024
27 S.1 (2) (b) CAMA, Cap C20 LFN, 2004
28 The World Bank, 'Reports on the observance of standards and codes', 2004 p. 30, The World Bank, available at: <www.worldbank.org/en/programs/rosc> accessed 15 April 2024; Elewechi Okike, 'Corporate audit report and the structure of the market for audit services to listed companies in

Despite its enormous power under the Act, the CAC has not applied any significant sanctions for companies' non-compliance.[29] As a result, one would argue that the Commission is ineffective in performing its functions. Customers have lodged complaints about its inability to carry out its tasks effectively,[30] with a majority of the complaints relating to staff incompetence, poor service delivery, missing documents, payment of extortion fees, data loss due to its epileptic server, and poor internet connectivity.[31]

Securities and Exchange Commission

The Securities and Exchange Commission (SEC) is the apex regulatory institution for the Nigerian capital market.[32] As such, all companies listed on the Nigerian Stock Exchange fall under its regulatory framework, which includes the listing rules and regulations[33] and the corporate governance code for publicly listed companies.[34] These various pieces of legislation issued by the SEC enable it to regulate all companies listed on the Nigerian stock exchange. The legal framework that enables the SEC to carry out these function is the Investments and Securities Act (ISA) 2007. The ISA grants the SEC the authority to regulate the capital market, including ensuring that all companies listed on the Nigerian stock exchange comply with the regulatory framework.[35] In 2003, the SEC issued the code of best practices for public companies in Nigeria.[36] The SEC code was intended to ensure accountability in all public companies in Nigeria. SEC was the first regulatory agency to have issued a corporate governance code for companies in Nigeria. The principal focus of the SEC code is to protect and enhance shareholders' value in public companies in Nigeria.[37] The extent to which the SEC code promotes stakeholders' recognition

Nigeria: A longitudinal study', A Research Report submitted to the Research Committee of the Institute of Chartered Accountants of Nigeria, 1995

29 The World Bank, 'Reports on the observance of standards and codes', 2004 p. 30, The World Bank, available at: <www.worldbank.org/en/programs/rosc> accessed 15 April 2024; Elewechi Okike, 'Corporate audit report and the structure of the market for audit services to listed companies in Nigeria: A longitudinal study', A Research Report submitted to the Research Committee of the Institute of Chartered Accountants of Nigeria, 1995

30 Bassey Udo, 'Normal business disrupted at CAC as customers protest poor services', *Premium Times Newspaper*, 15 September 2014, available at: <www.premiumtimesng.com/business/168188-normal-business-disrupted-at-cac-as-customers-protest-poor-services.html> accessed 15 April 2024; Tyavzua Saanyol, 'Customers reject courier services, protest CAC electronic delivery policy', *Nigerian Tribune*, 23 July 2020, available at: <https://tribuneonlineng.com/covid-19-customers-reject-courier-services-protest-cac-electronic-delivery-policy/> accessed 15 April 2024

31 Sonnie Ekwowusi, 'Whither corporate affairs commission?', *Thisday Newspaper*, Wednesday 14 July 2021, p. 14; Shaka Momodu, 'The CAC and ease of doing business: The commission should live up to its responsibilities', *Thisday Newspaper*, Wednesday 21 July 2021, p. 15

32 Investments and Securities Act, 2007

33 SEC Nigeria's Consolidated Rules and Regulations, 2013

34 Code of Corporate Governance for Public Companies, 4 April 2011

35 S.13 Investments and Securities Act, 2007

36 SEC, Code of Corporate Governance for Public Companies, 2003

37 Principle 2.2 Code of Corporate Governance for Public Companies in Nigeria, 2011

and the protection of stakeholders' interests is further explored in the later part of this chapter.

Central Bank of Nigeria

The Central Bank of Nigeria (CBN) was established in accordance with the Central Bank of Nigeria Act of 1958 and became operational on 1 July 1959.[38] As the apex regulatory body for banking supervision in Nigeria, the CBN is statutorily empowered to regulate the banking industry.[39] The CBN executes its legal mandate through two main pieces of legislation: the Banks and Other Financial Institutions Act (BOFIA) 2020[40] and the Central Bank of Nigeria Act 2007.[41] The Nigerian Central Bank is an autonomous body charged with the responsibility of promoting financial stability and continuity in economic management.[42] However, the mandate of CBN, to some extent, is questionable, as it is often the Minister of Finance and the President who determine the direction of the national economy, despite CBN's efforts to demonstrate its independence.[43] There are several instances where CBN independence has been eroded by the Federal Government, despite CBN pretending to be the brain behind those policies.[44] For example, suppose the CBN Governor wants to exercise his sovereignty regarding fiscal and macroeconomic policies. In that case, there are often conflicts of interest between CBN and government officials, especially the Ministry of Finance and the presidency.[45] In fact, the independence of the CBN has been eroded by the Federal Government on several occasions. For instance, when Dr. Ebele Jonathan, former Nigerian President, suspended the then Governor of CBN, Mallam Sanusi, alleging financial recklessness and misconduct after Sanusi alleged that the sum of £12 billion ($20 billion) in oil revenue had gone missing, there was a conflict of interests between CBN and government officials, especially the Ministry of Finance and the Presidency.[46] The removal of Godwin Emefiele by President Bola Ahmed Tinubu has been attributed to political revenge following Emefiele's attempts at reforming the financial

38 History of the CBN, available at: <www.cbn.gov.ng/AboutCBN/history.asp> accessed 15 April 2024
39 S.1 BOFIA, 2020
40 BOFIA, 2020
41 S.1 (3) CBN Act, 2007
42 S.2 CBN Act, 2007
43 Samuel Bandele Falegan, 'Central bank autonomy: Historical and general perspective', *Economic and Financial Review*, 33(4), 1995, pp. 416–428
44 Samuel Bandele Falegan, 'Central bank autonomy: Historical and general perspective', *Economic and Financial Review*, 33(4), 1995, pp. 416–428
45 Joseph O. Sanusi, 'Central banking authority, economic stability and the rule of law', A paper presented at the Ninth Annual Harvard International Development Conference, Boston, 4 April 2003, available at: <www.bis.org/review/r030530d.pdf> accessed 15 April 2024
46 Alexander Thurston, 'The politics of technocracy in fourth republic Nigeria', *African Studies Review*, 61, 2018, p. 215

system during the electioneering campaign.[47] These reforms made it difficult for individuals to access their money, leading to dissatisfaction and criticism. Despite Emefiele's arrest for mismanagement of public funds, he was ultimately charged with illegal possession of firearms.[48] Regrettably, these actions have raised questions about the motives of President Tinubu and his administration.

Nevertheless, the core objective of CBN under the CBN Act 2007 includes promoting a sound financial system in Nigeria, acting as the lender of last resort, and providing economic and financial advice to the Federal Government.[49] Undoubtedly, CBN faces several challenges in exercising its powers and functions under the BOFIA and CBN Act; one such challenge is regarding policy conflicts between CBN and the government. The CBN Governor cannot unilaterally carry out certain activities, for example, revoking a banking licence, without first seeking 'approval' from the President. To put it mildly, the CBN Governor must consult with the finance minister and the President most of the time before performing some of its core functions under BOFIA 2020[50] and the CBN Act 2007.[51] Such an arrangement undermines the CBN's independence to act timeously to a certain extent. As the prudential regulator and supervisor for the banking industry, the CBN has issued the corporate governance code for the banking industry to achieve a safe and healthy financial system. Like the SEC code, the CBN Code of Corporate Governance for Banks and Discount Houses in Nigeria[52] protects and enhances shareholders' value. The extent to which the CBN code promotes stakeholders' value in the Nigerian banking industry is also examined in detail in the latter part of this chapter.

National Pension Commission

The Pension Reform Act 2004 established the National Pension Commission (PENCOM) to set standards, rules, and guidelines for managing pension funds in Nigeria.[53] Subsequently, in 2008, PENCOM issued a Code of Corporate Governance for Licensed Pension Operators, an industry-specific code designed to guide pension scheme operators on the best corporate governance practices.[54] The code applies

47 Aanu Adeoye, 'Nigeria's new president suspends central bank governor; Godwin Emefiele's contentious policies raised doubts over the institution's independence', *The Financial Times*, 10 June 2023, available at: <www.ft.com/content/4d2d920f-a535-4fb9-806b-062948784063> accessed 15 April 2024

48 Roula Khalaf, 'Nigeria's economic reforms need to regain momentum', *The Financial Times*, 3 October 2023, available at: <www.ft.com/content/a8485413-215f-488f-ac25-46fba58fa2ac> accessed 15 April 2024

49 S.2 CBN Act of 2007

50 BOFIA, 2020

51 CBN Act, 2007

52 Code of Corporate Governance for Banks and Discount Houses and the Guidelines for Whistle Blowing in the Nigerian Banking Industry, 2014

53 Pension Reform Act, 2004

54 Code of Corporate Governance for Licensed Pension Operators, June 2008, p. 4, available at: <www.pencom.gov.ng/wp-content/uploads/2017/04/Code_of_Corporate_Governance_for_Licensed_Pension_Operators.pdf> accessed 15 April 2024

to banks acting as pension fund administrators or custodians. It aims to promote shareholders' value, as evident from its provision, which states that its purpose is to create the necessary conditions for shareholders to exercise an active and responsible ownership role. Consequently, the board of pension companies aligns its objectives with shareholders' interests, as the code seeks to promote their value.[55] As discussed earlier, the Anglo-Saxon corporate governance model seeks to maximise profit for the benefit of shareholders, which is the company's corporate goal. This code, along with other sectoral codes, is designed to promote shareholders' value, thus aligning the companies' corporate objectives with shareholders' interests.[56]

National Insurance Commission

The National Insurance Commission (NAICOM) was established under the National Insurance Commission Act 1997.[57] The Commission's primary responsibility is to ensure that the insurance business in Nigeria is effectively administered, supervised, regulated, and controlled.[58] Also, the Commission is tasked with protecting insurance policyholders, beneficiaries, and third parties involved in insurance contracts.[59] In 2009, NAICOM issued the Code of Good Corporate Governance for the Insurance Industry in Nigeria.[60] This code applies to banks that offer insurance services as part of their banking business. On 17 March 2021, the Commission introduced the Corporate Governance Guidelines for Insurance and Reinsurance Companies (CGGIRC) 2021, which became effective on the 1 June 2021.[61] The objective underpinning the new corporate governance code is not different from others discussed in this chapter because it is also based on the Anglo-Saxon corporate law model. The CGGIRC 2021 stipulates that directors are expected to preserve and enhance shareholders' value.[62] Despite the purported review made to the corporate governance code in the Nigerian insurance sector, it is evident that there is still a dearth of recognition of other stakeholders and protection of their interests.

Nigerian Communications Commission

The Nigerian Communications Commission (NCC) was established in accordance with the Nigerian Communications Act of 2003.[63] The Commission is responsible

55 Code of Corporate Governance for Licensed Pension Operators, June 2008, p. 4, available at: <www.pencom.gov.ng/wp-content/uploads/2017/04/Code_of_Corporate_Governance_for_Licensed_Pension_Operators.pdf> accessed 15 April 2024, Principle 3.1.1, p. 3

56 Code of Corporate Governance for Licensed Pension Operators, June 2008, p. 4, available at: <www.pencom.gov.ng/wp-content/uploads/2017/04/Code_of_Corporate_Governance_for_Licensed_Pension_Operators.pdf> accessed 15 April 2024, Principle 4.1, p. 6

57 S.1 National Insurance Act, 1997

58 S.7 National Insurance Act, 1997

59 S.7 National Insurance Act, 1997

60 Code of Good Corporate Governance for the Insurance Industry in Nigeria, 2009

61 Corporate Governance Guidelines for Insurance and Reinsurance Companies, 2021

62 Principle 2.0 Corporate Governance Guidelines for Insurance and Reinsurance Companies, 2021

63 S.3 Nigerian Communications Act, 2003

for regulating the supply of telecommunications services and facilities, promoting competition, and setting performance standards for telephone services in Nigeria.[64] In 2016, the Commission issued the Code of Corporate Governance for the Telecommunication Industry (CCGTI); like all other codes already examined, the CCGTI is designed to protect and enhance shareholders' value.[65] This is evident from several specific provisions of the CCGTI; for example, the code states that apart from the shareholders in general meetings, the board of directors shall be the highest decision-making body.[66] It also states that it is the responsibility of shareholders to appoint the board of directors.[67] Furthermore, the CCGTI requires companies to establish effective systems and structures for risk governance and a comprehensive internal controls system to safeguard shareholders' investments.[68]

Financial Reporting Council of Nigeria

The Financial Reporting Council of Nigeria (FRCN) was established by the Financial Reporting Council Act 2011.[69] The FRCN Act also established the Directorate of Corporate Governance,[70] responsible for developing sound corporate governance principles in Nigerian companies.[71] To realise these objectives and address the multiplicity of corporate governance codes and overlapping legislation, the Directorate of Corporate Governance attempted to unify the various industry-specific codes discussed earlier by issuing the National Code of Corporate Governance (NCCG) 2016, which became effective on 17 October 2016. However, this faced much resistance from various shareholders who claimed the NCCG 2016 was a disincentive to investment. On 28 October 2016, less than 12 days after the NCCG 2016 came into force, the government suspended the code.[72] This follows the decision in *Eko Hotels v FRCN*, where the court held that no law empowered the FRCN to exercise any form of regulatory power over Eko Hotels and Suites, as it was a private company.[73] It is argued that the court reached this decision because FRCN had acted *ultra vires* by requesting Eko Hotels to register with the FRCN.

64 S.1 Ibid
65 Principle 1.0 Code of Corporate Governance for the Telecommunication Industry, 2016
66 Principle 1.0 Code of Corporate Governance for the Telecommunication Industry, 2016, Principle 2.1(c)
67 Principle 1.0 Code of Corporate Governance for the Telecommunication Industry, 2016, Principle 2.1(a)
68 Principle 1.0 Code of Corporate Governance for the Telecommunication Industry, 2016, Principle 11.0
69 S.1 Financial Reporting Council of Nigeria Act, 2011
70 S.49 Financial Reporting Council of Nigeria Act, 2011
71 S.50 Financial Reporting Council of Nigeria Act, 2011
72 The Editor, '"Investors" laud suspension of FRCN corporate governance code', *The Nigerian Guardian Newspaper*, 9 November 2016, available at: <https://guardian.ng/business-services/investors-laud-suspension-of-frcn-corporate-governance-code/> accessed 15 April 2024
73 *Eko Hotels v. Financial Reporting Council of Nigeria* (Unreported: Suit No. FHC/L/CS/1430/2012 delivered, 21 March 2014 by Justice Abang

The FRCN Act only requires the registration of accountants and other professionals based on their involvement in the financial reporting process in private companies.[74]

Subsequently, the FRCN exercised its power to conduct a periodic assessment of the codes and guidelines issued by the Council and reintroduced the National Code of Corporate Governance in 2018, which applies to all companies in Nigeria.[75] The NCCG 2018 became effective on 1 January 2020.[76] The FRCN has described the NCCG 2018 as one that highlights fundamental principles that seek to institutionalise corporate governance best practices in Nigerian companies and promote public awareness of essential corporate values and ethical practices that will enhance the integrity of the business environment.[77] The NCCG 2018 attempted to recognise some stakeholders and protect stakeholders' interests, such as the principle requiring companies as responsible corporate citizens to pay adequate attention to sustainability by contributing to economic development.[78] Another of the NCCG 2018 principles dealing with stakeholders' interests is the one that requires companies to communicate and interact with stakeholders, keeping them conversant with the companies' activities and assisting them in making informed decisions.[79] Lastly, the code also recognised stakeholders' interests by requiring companies to fully and comprehensively disclose all matters material to shareholders and stakeholders and of matters set out in the code to ensure proper monitoring of its implementation.[80]

The provisions of NCCG 2018 are commendable in their attempt to recognise some stakeholders, but they are insufficient in providing the necessary protection for stakeholders' interests. This inadequacy arises from two key reasons. First, the NCCG 2018 failed to repeal sector-specific codes, such as the CBN and the SEC codes, which still dominate the banking industry and are based on the shareholder primacy model. As a result, these codes remain the governing codes for the industry, and the stakeholder innovations present in the NCCG 2018 are unlikely to offer the required protection for stakeholder interests. Second, the NCCG 2018 is subject to the primary corporate law legislation, CAMA 2020, which is also underpinned by the shareholder primacy value. Thus, the stakeholder innovations present in the NCCG 2018 are unlikely to provide the necessary protection for stakeholders in the banking industry and other companies.

74 *Eko Hotels v. Financial Reporting Council of Nigeria* (Unreported: Suit No. FHC/L/CS/1430/2012 delivered, 21 March 2014 by Justice Abang

75 Nigerian Code of Corporate Governance, 2018

76 Nelson Anumaka, 'The Nigeran code of corporate governance is principle based, flexible and scalable', Interview with the Institute of Directors of Nigeria, available at: <www.iodnigeria.org/Portals/0/Documents/The%20Nigeria%20Code%20of%20Corporate%20Governance%202018%20is%20a%20principle%20based%20flexible%20and%20scalable.pdf?ver=2020-08-02-164202-313> accessed 15 April 2024

77 Nigerian Code of Corporate Governance, 2018, p. iv

78 Principle 26 Nigerian Code of Corporate Governance, 2018

79 Principle 26 Nigerian Code of Corporate Governance, 2018, Principle 27

80 Principle 26 Nigerian Code of Corporate Governance, 2018, Principle 28

Furthermore, the NCCG 2018 did not attempt to harmonise the corporate governance provisions in CAMA 2020 with the provisions of other codes. Neither did it make its application supersede CAMA and the various other codes. Having examined the various legal and institutional frameworks for corporate governance applicable to companies generally in Nigeria, it is necessary to explore the bank-specific codes in detail, as this will help assess the extent to which these codes allow for recognising stakeholders and protecting stakeholders' interests. Before embarking on this task, it is helpful to explore the structure of the Nigerian deposit money bank.

5.5 Structure of Nigerian Deposit Money Bank

The banking industry exhibits slight variations across different countries, with their activities often extending beyond core functions such as deposit-taking and account management. These differences can be attributed to the institutional theory, which underpins establishing various structures, norms, rules, and routines as authoritative guidelines for social behaviour. Economic and legal factors primarily influence the types of banking institutions that operate in a given jurisdiction. The economic factor is based on the specific banking services that customers require, subject to the regulatory framework in that jurisdiction. For instance, regulatory bodies may issue banking licenses that specify the permitted activities of banks, such as accepting deposits and honouring customer checks, as well as prohibited activities, such as foreign exchange dealings. In such cases, banks cannot legally offer foreign exchange services, even if customers demand them, as their licenses expressly prohibit such activities.

Legal factors are another reason banking operations vary from jurisdiction to jurisdiction.[81] This depends on the prevailing banking regulatory framework in a given jurisdiction. Regulatory frameworks may prescribe universal banking models that permit banks to transform into one-stop shops and engage in a broad range of financial activities, either in the ordinary course of their conventional banking operations or indirectly through designated subsidiaries. For example, in 2000, the Central Bank of Nigeria introduced the universal banking model, which allowed banks to offer an extensive array of financial products and services, thereby facilitating their transformation into one-stop shops.[82]

Over the years, there have been significant changes in the Nigerian banking industry. These changes include alterations in the ownership structure, the number of banking institutions, and modifications to the mode of operations.[83] While there are different types of banking institutions, the focus here will be on Deposit

81 Principle 26 Nigerian Code of Corporate Governance, 2018, Principle 28

82 Ebenezer Adodo, 'Legal challenges of universal banking in Nigeria', *Modern Practice Journal of Finance & Investment Law*, 6(3–4), 2002, pp. 398–406

83 Charles Chukwuma Soludo, 'Consolidating the Nigerian banking industry to meet the development challenges of the 21st century', 6 July 2004, p. 2, available at: <www.bis.org/review/r040727g.pdf> accessed 15 April 2024

Money Banks in Nigeria (DMBs), comprising 25 commercial banks and six merchant banks.[84] The focus on these 31 banks in these categories is not because they only accept customer deposits. However, employees and customers of these banks are major victims of persistent banking failures in Nigeria; hence, they are key stakeholders that the current regulatory framework has ignored. Before delving into the corporate governance in these banks, examining the scope of DMBs in Nigeria is helpful.

Commercial banks are the oldest banking institutions in Nigeria. The first commercial bank to operate in the country was established in 1894.[85] Initially, their primary function was to accept deposits that were withdrawn by cheques.[86] Over time, commercial banking activities have expanded to include providing credit facilities for customers, acting as agents of payment through hosting internet banking, and safekeeping customer valuables. Commercial banks are crucial to the Nigerian financial system and contribute to the nation's overall economic development. Their primary functions include accepting deposits from customers, making payments upon presentation of cheques, and advancing the surplus of deposits collected as loans to borrowers in return for a profit. Moreover, commercial banks in Nigeria offer invaluable financial advice and guidance to their customers, particularly regarding financial products.

Before the 2004 consolidation/recapitalisation reform agenda by the CBN Governor, Prof. Soludo, 89 commercial banks were operating in the country. However, due to some banks' inability to raise the minimum capital within the specified time, the number was significantly reduced to 25 commercial banks. While some banks could meet the minimum capital requirement, others had to merge with other banks to achieve the same objective. The CBN revoked the operating licenses of those who could not devise a means to raise the minimum capital within the stipulated time. Nigeria has three types of commercial banks: regional, national, and international. Regional commercial banks operate in ten states or fewer and must have a minimum paid-up capital of ₦15 billion ($41.7 million). National commercial banks, on the other hand, must have a minimum capital requirement of ₦25 billion ($69.4 million) and are eligible to operate in all states in Nigeria. International commercial banks must have a minimum paid-up capital of ₦100 billion ($278 million) and are authorised to operate in Nigeria and other international destinations. Currently, 25 commercial banks are operating in Nigeria. Out of the 25, eight banks are licensed to operate globally, 12 are licensed to operate nationally, and the remaining five are licensed to operate regionally.[87]

84 CBN, 'Financial institutions', available at: <www.cbn.gov.ng/Supervision/finstitutions.asp> accessed 15 April 2024

85 First Bank of Nigeria Is the Pioneer Commercial Bank in Nigeria, Which Started a Business in 1894

86 First Bank of Nigeria Is the Pioneer Commercial Bank in Nigeria, Which Started a Business in 1894, p. 31

87 CBN, 'Supervision: List of financial institutions', available at: <www.cbn.gov.ng/supervision/Inst-DM.asp> accessed 15 April 2024. This list does not include Optimus Bank that was established in January 2023

Merchant banks are financial institutions that offer medium-term and long-term credit, equipment leasing, syndicate loans, foreign exchange services, investment advice, and portfolio management, among other services.[88] In Nigeria, the history of merchant banking dates back to 1960, when two pioneering institutions, Phillip Hill Nigeria Limited and Nigeria Acceptance Limited, began merchant banking operations. Before the 1960s, there were no merchant banks in Nigeria, as commercial banks handled investment financing; however, adopting the Universal Banking Model in 2000 led to the phasing out of merchant banking operations. Merchant banking was reintroduced on 8 August 2010 following the abolition of the Universal Banking model.[89] One of the reasons for the reintroduction of Merchant banks in Nigeria was to bridge the gap in the type of credit provided by commercial banks. Merchant banks are now required to maintain a minimum paid-up share capital of ₦15 billion ($41.7 million).[90] One could argue that the reintroduction of merchant banks became necessary to safeguard the deposits of commercial bank customers, as CBN felt that commercial banks could not carry out merchant banking activities because of their national reach and low capital base.[91]

5.6 Legal Framework for Corporate Governance in Nigerian Deposit Money Banks

As mentioned earlier, the legal framework that governs corporate governance in the Nigerian banking industry is outlined in several regulations, including CAMA 2020, BOFIA 2020, Investments and Securities Act 2007, CBN Act 2007, CBN Code of Conduct for Directors of Licensed Banks and Financial Institutions 2010, SEC Code of Corporate Governance for Public Companies 2011, Nigerian Sustainable Banking Principles 2012, CBN Code of Corporate Governance for Banks and Discount Houses, Guidelines for Whistleblowing in the Nigerian Banking industry 2014, Nigerian Code of Corporate Governance 2018, and Corporate Governance Guidelines for Banks 2023. However, compliance with these regulations may not be guaranteed, particularly with the two primary corporate governance codes for the banking industry, as the weak enforcement regime makes it unlikely that banks will be sanctioned for non-compliance.[92] Thus, it is essential to examine the two main corporate governance codes applicable to the DMBs in Nigeria in detail to

88 Ikpefan Ailemen, *Issues in Banking and Finance* (The Chartered Institute of Bankers of Nigeria 2012), p. 11

89 Alex Ehimare Omankhanlen, 'The financial sector reforms and their effect on the Nigerian economy', *Economy Transdisciplinarity Cognition*, 15(2), pp. 45–57

90 Omoh Gabriel, 'CBN re-introduces merchant banking', *The Nigerian Vanguard*, 8 August 2010, available at: <www.vanguardngr.com/2010/08/cbn-re-introduces-merchant-banking> accessed 15 April 2024

91 CBN, 'List of financial institutions: Merchant banks', available at: <www.cbn.gov.ng/Supervision/Inst-MB.asp> accessed 15 April 2024

92 Vincent Nmehielle, Enyinna Nwauche, 'External-internal standards in corporate governance in Nigeria', The George Washington University Law School Public Law and Legal Theory Working Paper, 2004, pp. 115, 1–50

ascertain to what extent they allow for the recognition of stakeholders and the protection of stakeholders' interests.

5.6.1 SEC Code of Corporate Governance for Public Companies in Nigeria

In the wake of various corporate governance scandals that occurred globally in the early 2000s, the need to revamp the corporate governance frameworks of publicly listed companies became a top priority. In Nigeria, the Securities and Exchange Commission (SEC) established a committee in 2001 to draft the Code of Best Practices for Public Companies in Nigeria. This code became operational in 2003 and applied to all listed companies, regardless of their sector. Despite its implementation, the SEC code faced criticism for its lack of enforceability. As a result, a committee was formed in September 2008 to identify the weaknesses in the SEC code that impeded effective corporate governance in public companies in Nigeria. Based on the committee's recommendations, the SEC code was revised in March 2011 to address the shortcomings of the previous code.[93]

The SEC code is a set of regulations that aims to ensure that company directors are accountable to their shareholders. However, it gives limited recognition to the interests of other stakeholders. The SEC code requires the board to protect the statutory and general rights of shareholders and to enhance their value at all times, and as a result, the interests of other stakeholders become secondary. For example, the SEC code makes it mandatory for the board to always protect shareholders' statutory and general rights.[94] It also enjoins directors to protect and enhance shareholders' value always.[95] Therefore, for the board to deliver on these provisions, other stakeholders' interest becomes secondary because the code specifies that directors must always protect shareholders' interests. According to the SEC code, one of the board's core responsibilities is to ensure effective communication with shareholders. This can be achieved by using general meetings to communicate with the shareholders and encourage their participation.[96] One would argue that directors who fail to communicate with shareholders effectively and encourage their participation may face negative consequences in the long term, as shareholders have the power to appoint directors and approve the terms and conditions of their directorships.[97] Consequently, directors who do not adhere to the provisions of the SEC code are more likely to be removed from their positions.[98]

There are several provisions in the SEC code that guarantee the protection of shareholders' interests over and above those of other stakeholders. These provisions are worth considering, as they further support the assertion that the Nigerian corporate governance model is underpinned by the Anglo-Saxon corporate law model

93 Elewechi Okike, Emmanuel Adegbite, 'The code of corporate governance in Nigeria: Efficiency gains or social legitimation?', *Corporate Ownership and Control*, 9(3), 2012, pp. 262–275

94 SEC Code, 2011 Principle 22.1

95 SEC Code, 2011 Principle 2.2

96 SEC Code, 2011 Principle 2.2, Principle 3.1(g)

97 SEC Code, 2011 Principle 2.2, Principle 13.4

98 SEC Code, 2011 Principle 2.2, Principle 19.1

designed to enhance shareholder value. The SEC code made it mandatory for the board to ensure that all shareholders are treated equally and that no shareholder should be given preferential treatment or access to information or other materials based on their shareholding.[99] In recognition of the issue between minority and majority shareholders, the SEC code made it mandatory for the board to ensure that minority shareholders are adequately protected from controlling shareholders' abusive actions.[100] The SEC code requires the board to ensure that the venue of a general meeting is accessible to shareholders and that no shareholder is disenfranchised on account of the choice of venue of the meeting.[101] Before analysing corporate governance mechanisms in Nigerian banks, the next subsection examines the CBN's code for DMBs and the Nigerian Sustainable Banking Principles to demonstrate whether it allows for recognising stakeholders and to what extent it protects other stakeholders' interests in the Nigerian banking industry.

5.6.2 CBN Corporate Governance Code and the Nigerian Sustainable Banking Principle

Following the consolidation exercise in the Nigerian banking industry, the CBN introduced the Code of Corporate Governance for Banks in Nigeria in March 2006, which became effective on 3 April 2006.[102] The code aimed to ensure good corporate governance practices in DMBs by making it mandatory for all DMBs to comply with its provisions.[103] Despite the various variations in the CBN and SEC code requirements, public listed banks must ensure compliance with both. Like the SEC code, the CBN code was criticised for its ambiguity and lack of consistency with international best practices.[104] To strengthen the corporate governance practices in the banking industry endangered by poor corporate governance practices that almost led to the failure of 10 DMBs operating in Nigeria in 2009, on the 16 May 2014, CBN issued a revised code of corporate governance applicable to DMBs, which became effective on 1 October 2014.[105]

99 SEC Code, 2011 Principle 2.2, Principle 22.2
100 SEC Code, 2011 Principle 2.2, Principle 22.3
101 SEC Code, 2011 Principle 2.2, Principle 23
102 Code of Corporate Governance for Banks in Nigeria Post Consolidation, available at: <www.cbn.gov.ng/OUT/PUBLICATIONS/BSD/2006/CORPGOV-POSTCONSO.PDF> accessed 15 April 2024
103 Code of Corporate Governance for Banks in Nigeria Post Consolidation, available at: <www.cbn.gov.ng/OUT/PUBLICATIONS/BSD/2006/CORPGOV-POSTCONSO.PDF> accessed 15 April 2024
104 Code of Corporate Governance for Banks and Discount Houses and the Guidelines for Whistle Blowing in the Nigerian Banking Industry, 2014, available at: <www.cbn.gov.ng/out/2014/fprd/circular%20on%20code%20of%20circular%20on%20corporate%20governance%20and%20whistle%20blowing-may%202014%20(3).pdf> accessed 15 April 2024
105 Code of Corporate Governance for Banks and Discount Houses and the Guidelines for Whistle Blowing in the Nigerian Banking Industry, 2014, available at: <www.cbn.gov.ng/out/2014/fprd/circular%20on%20code%20of%20circular%20on%20corporate%20governance%20and%20whistle%20blowing-may%202014%20(3).pdf> accessed 15 April 2024

Some argue that the revised CBN code, like the SEC code to a certain extent, protects other stakeholders' interests by requiring banks to establish a whistleblowing policy for reporting unethical behaviour.[106] The CBN code did not define illegal or unethical behaviours. However, it provided a list of conducts that could be construed as illegal or unethical behaviours, including financial malpractice, impropriety, fraud, failure to comply with a legal obligation or statutes, actions detrimental to health and safety or the environment, or any form of criminal activity. Improper conduct or unethical behaviour, failure to comply with regulatory directives, other forms of corporate governance breaches, connected transactions, insider abuses, non-disclosure of interest, and attempts to conceal any of these, among others, are also considered unethical.[107] Though the CBN claimed that the whistleblowing policy is intended to encourage relevant stakeholders to report perceived unethical or illegal conduct; however, stakeholders like customers and employees are reluctant to report unethical or illegal conduct due to the absence of the necessary statutory framework which protects whistleblowers if their identities were later exposed[108]

Before revising the CBN code in 2014, the CBN tried to bridge the gap between the shareholder primacy model practised in the Nigerian Banking industry and the recognition and protection of key stakeholders and their interests by introducing the Nigerian Sustainable Banking Principles.[109] The primary aim of the Nigerian Sustainable Banking Principle is to serve as a common baseline and framework for each DMB to implement its own internal corporate social responsibility policies and standards.[110] The Nigerian Sustainable Banking Principles advocate for promoting women's empowerment through gender inclusivity in the workplace,[111] promoting financial inclusion by providing financial services to individuals and communities which previously had little or no access to the formal financial sector,[112] and minimising the effects of banking operations on the environment and

106 Code of Corporate Governance for Banks and Discount Houses and the Guidelines for Whistle Blowing in the Nigerian Banking Industry, 2014, available at: <www.cbn.gov.ng/out/2014/fprd/circular%20on%20code%20of%20circular%20on%20corporate%20governance%20and%20whistle%20blowing-may%202014%20(3).pdf> accessed 15 April 2024

107 Code of Corporate Governance for Banks and Discount Houses and the Guidelines for Whistle Blowing in the Nigerian Banking Industry, 2014, available at: <www.cbn.gov.ng/out/2014/fprd/circular%20on%20code%20of%20circular%20on%20corporate%20governance%20and%20whistle%20blowing-may%202014%20(3).pdf> accessed 15 April 2024

108 Folashade Adeyemo, 'The Achilles' heel of whistleblowing: the position of Nigerian legislation', *Journal of International Banking Law and Regulation*, 31(2), 2016, pp. 105–109, 105

109 CBN, 'Nigerian sustainable banking principles', Central Bank of Nigeria, July 2012, available at: <www.cbn.gov.ng/out/2012/ccd/circular-nsbp.pdf> accessed 15 April 2024

110 CBN, 'Nigerian sustainable banking principles', Central Bank of Nigeria, July 2012, available at: <www.cbn.gov.ng/out/2012/ccd/circular-nsbp.pdf> accessed 15 April 2024

111 CBN, 'Nigerian sustainable banking principles', Central Bank of Nigeria, July 2012, available at: <www.cbn.gov.ng/out/2012/ccd/circular-nsbp.pdf> accessed 15 April 2024, Principle 4

112 CBN, 'Nigerian sustainable banking principles', Central Bank of Nigeria, July 2012, available at: <www.cbn.gov.ng/out/2012/ccd/circular-nsbp.pdf> accessed 15 April 2024, Principle 5

local communities.[113] Although these principles are admirable and expected to promote stakeholder recognition and protection of their interests, they are only recommendations and do not have the force of law like the CBN code. Consequently, DMBs have a high rate of non-compliance; this will be further explored in the next section, which focuses on corporate governance mechanisms in Nigerian DMBs.

5.7 Corporate Governance Mechanisms in DMBs in Nigeria

The ownership structure of DMBs in Nigeria is heavily concentrated among a few individuals, families, and the government to some extent.[114] The recapitalisation reform introduced by Soludo in 2004–2005 witnessed a series of mergers and acquisitions of banks, and it provided an opportunity for wealthy families, institutional investors, and affluent individuals to acquire significant equity in Nigerian DMBs. While the Central Bank of Nigeria (CBN) did not set a limit for individual or institutional shareholding, the CBN code requires individuals seeking to own more than 5% of equity to obtain CBN permission.[115] The CBN code also stipulates that the government's shareholding in any Nigerian DMB should not exceed 10% by the end of the 2007 financial year.[116] However, government shareholding in some DMBs exceeded this threshold, thus violating the CBN code. A private individual can own 100% equity in any DMB if they seek CBN's approval. The code does not specify any conditions that should be met for CBN to approve investors' equity ownership above 10%. Therefore, it is left to the discretion of CBN whether such requests are granted. It is, therefore, argued that unfettered discretionary power is likely to be abused because CBN independence, in reality, is subject to the whims and caprices of political officeholders like ministers and the President, as stated previously. Therefore, the decision to grant such requests is at the discretion of the CBN. The annual reports of some DMBs show 100% private equity ownership. For instance, in the 2007 financial year, Equitorial Trust Bank, Fidelity Bank, Standard Chartered Bank, and Union Bank had 100% private equity ownership. The concentration of ownership among a few individuals, families, and the government in Nigerian DMBs raises concerns about transparency and accountability.

Between 2007–2010 Standard Chartered Bank, a commercial bank operating in Nigeria, is wholly owned by private individuals or institutional investors of foreign origin. Consequently, it is appropriate to classify it as a foreign bank. The differentiation between foreign and domestic ownership structures is useful in demonstrating the impact of ownership structure on corporate governance. When

113 CBN, 'Nigerian sustainable banking principles', Central Bank of Nigeria, July 2012, available at: <www.cbn.gov.ng/out/2012/ccd/circular-nsbp.pdf> accessed 15 April 2024, Principle 2

114 Ikpefan Ailemen, *Issues in Banking and Finance* (The Chartered Institute of Bankers of Nigeria, 2012), p. 11

115 Ikpefan Ailemen, *Issues in Banking and Finance* (The Chartered Institute of Bankers of Nigeria, 2012), p. 11

116 Ikpefan Ailemen, *Issues in Banking and Finance* (The Chartered Institute of Bankers of Nigeria, 2012), p. 11

foreign entities own a significant amount of shares in a DMB, it is expected that the corporate governance practices employed in their country of origin will be adopted and applied in their host country.[117] The ownership structure of certain banks has undergone a shift during periods in which the government has assumed a 100% equity stake due to rescue interventions. However, the broader pattern of ownership has generally remained unchanged. Specifically, between 2011 and 2014, the government held a 100% equity stake in Mainstreet Bank, Keystone Bank, and Enterprise Bank. It is worth noting that the aforementioned equity holdings were temporary measures employed by the government to safeguard the stability of the banking industry.[118] These banks were bridge banks that CBN granted licences to take over Afribank, Bank PHB, and Spring Bank, respectively, as an interventionist approach to mitigate the possibility of a systemic financial failure.[119] Three failed banks, Afribank, Bank PHB, and Spring Bank, were acquired by AMCON, making the government own 100% equity in those banks. It is worth mentioning that during the last quarter of 2014, Skye Bank and Heritage Bank Ltd acquired Mainstreet Bank Ltd and Enterprise Bank Ltd, respectively. In 2018, CBN revoked Skye Bank's licence following a series of financial difficulties due to poor corporate governance, evidenced by its high non-performing loans and insider-related dealings.[120] AMCON established a bridge bank called Polaris Bank to take over Skye Bank's assets and liabilities. This move led to the government acquiring 100% equity in Polaris Bank.[121]

As previously discussed, the Anglo-Saxon model is predicated upon the assumption that the ownership structure is dispersed. However, this model may prove to be unsuitable in the Nigerian context, owing to the country's highly concentrated ownership structure. The Anglo-Saxon model is designed to alleviate the 'agency problem' that arises as a result of the separation of ownership and control. Therefore, it is argued that in the Nigeria's banking industry, the agency problem arising from high ownership concentration may manifest in the relationship between

117 Elewechi Okike, Emmanuel Adegbite, Franklin Nakpodia, Stephen Adegbite, 'A review of internal and external influences on corporate governance and financial accountability in Nigeria', *International Journal of Business Governance and Ethics*, 10(2), 2015, pp. 165–185

118 NDIC, 'A brief on nigeria deposit insurance corporation to the house committee on banking and currency', October 2011, p. 6, available at: <https://ndic.gov.ng/files/NDIC%20ACTIVITIES%20FOR%20THE%20HOUSE%20COMMITTEE%20ON%20BANKING%20AND%20CURRENCY.pdf> accessed 15 April 2024

119 Chijioke Ohuocha, 'Exclusive: Nigeria's banking crisis seen resolved in 2011', *Reuters*, 14 December 2011, available at: <www.reuters.com/article/businesspro-us-nigeria-amcon/exclusive-nigerias-banking-crisis-seen-resolved-in-2011-idUSTRE6BD2QK20101214> accessed 15 April 2024

120 Mohammed Kudu Ibrahim, 'Press statement on the resolution of Skye Bank Plc', Thursday, 20 September 2018, available at: <https://ndic.gov.ng/press-releases/press-statement-on-the-resolution-of-skye-bank-plc/> accessed 15 April 2024

121 Mohammed Kudu Ibrahim, 'Press statement on the resolution of Skye Bank Plc', Thursday, 20 September 2018, available at: <https://ndic.gov.ng/press-releases/press-statement-on-the-resolution-of-skye-bank-plc/> accessed 15 April 2024

majority and minority shareholders. The majority shareholders may also oversee the bank's management, thereby taking advantage of the social context and weak institutional arrangement to exploit minority shareholders. There have been many instances of banking scandals involving CEOs, one of which is the Oceanic Bank scandal. A dominant shareholder took advantage of the challenging institutional environment to perpetrate fraud. The EFCC brought charges against Mrs. Ibru, who was a CEO and a majority shareholder, for various counts of fraud and related offences that amounted to ₦160.2 billion (approximately $1.35 billion). Mrs. Ibru was ultimately found guilty of these offences and was sentenced to 18 months' imprisonment. In light of her conviction, she was required to forfeit approximately 199 assets valued at over ₦160.2 billion (approximately $1.35 billion).[122] Despite the countermeasures implemented to mitigate the agency problem, some bank CEOs and COBs circumvent the corporate governance codes and the CBN whistle-blowing policy to perpetrate various forms of fraud and other financial crimes. Therefore, it is imperative to scrutinise the board structure further as a corporate governance mechanism in Nigeria's DMBs to determine the extent to which it facilitates the recognition of stakeholders and the protection of their interests.

5.7.1 Board Appointment

The Board of Directors plays a vital role in ensuring effective corporate governance, as it sets the strategic direction of the bank.[123] The composition, leadership, integrity, and independence of the board are sacrosanct in ensuring effective corporate governance. Pursuant to s.271(1) of the CAMA 2020, all companies incorporated in Nigeria, except for small companies, must have a minimum of two directors.[124] While small companies may have one director, Nigerian banks are not included in this category due to the minimum capital requirement for their establishment.

CAMA does not specify the maximum number of directors a company can have; however, the SEC and CBN codes provide some guidelines on the size and composition of the board. The difference in the requirements of these two codes is used to determine compliance. The SEC code stipulates a minimum of five directors,[125] but it does not provide a maximum number of directors, leaving it to the banks' discretion to decide. The SEC code further recommends a board composition that is a mix of executive and non-executive directors, with a COB leading the board. In addition to non-executive directors, the SEC code suggests that most board members should be non-executive directors, with at least one independent director.

122 *Federal Republic of Nigeria v. Dr (Mrs) Cecilia Ibru*, Charge FHC/L/297C/2009

123 Section 2.3, Securities and Exchange Commission Code of Corporate Governance for Public Companies, 2011, p. 2, Section 4.2 and 4.6; Code of Corporate Governance for Banks in Nigeria Post Consolidation, 2006, p. 9, available at: <www.cbn.gov.ng/OUT/PUBLICATIONS/BSD/2006/CORPGOV-POSTCONSO.PDF> accessed 15 April 2024

124 S.271 (1) CAMA 2020

125 Section 4.1–4.4 Securities and Exchange Commission Code of Corporate Governance for Public Companies, 2011, p. 3

In relation to board size,[126] the CBN code makes no explicit reference to the minimum number of directors in the 2006 code. However, the revised CBN code stipulates that a board should consist of no fewer than five directors.[127] A divergence between the CBN code and the SEC code is the maximum number of directors. The SEC code does not specify a maximum number of directors, as it is contingent upon the size and intricacy of the company. Conversely, the CBN code establishes a limit of 20 directors. SEC and CBN codes mandated that the board should have more non-executive directors. Both the SEC and CBN codes require the board to have a greater number of non-executive directors. The CBN code is more stringent regarding board independence, mandating the appointment of at least two independent directors. In contrast, the SEC code mandates the appointment of a single independent director. As per section 275(1) of CAMA 2020, a public company is required to have no fewer than three independent directors on its board.[128] To be appointed as a director, the SEC code demands that the individual possess demonstrated integrity, core competency, and knowledge of board matters.[129] However, the CBN code also requires that such a person is of proven integrity and that the individual is knowledgeable in business and financial matters.

Based on the challenging institutional environment in Nigeria, social and political connections are key determinants when appointing directors.[130] Most directors in family-owned banks are either relative or close allies; choosing a director in most cases is unnecessary to monitor the executives, as they are also the owners of the banks.[131] Consequently, their appointment may not be based on merit and integrity but rather, on their social and political connections. The highly concentrated ownership structure of these banks further exacerbates this situation. Due to the institutional environment in Nigeria, the appointment of directors in DMBs, particularly those that are family-owned, is significantly influenced by tribalism, nepotism, and socio-political and religious connections due to the institutional environment.[132] The appointment of directors based on favouritism is believed to result in directors demonstrating loyalty to those who influenced their appointment. This is particularly true when siblings and other family members are appointed to the board, as was the case in the Oceanic Bank scandal, where the directors were

126 Section 5.3.5–5.3.6 Code for Corporate Governance for Banks in Nigeria Post Consolidation, 2006, p. 13

127 Section 2.2.1 Code of Corporate Governance for Banks and Discount Houses and the Guidelines for Whistle Blowing in the Nigerian Banking Industry, 2014

128 S 275 (1) CAMA, 2020

129 Section 4.4 Securities and Exchange Commission Code of Corporate Governance for Public Companies, 2011, p. 3

130 Muhammad Arslan, Ahmad Alqatan, 'Role of institutions in shaping corporate governance system: Evidence from emerging economy', *Heliyon*, 6(3), 2020, p. 9

131 Muhammad Arslan, Ahmad Alqatan, 'Role of institutions in shaping corporate governance system: Evidence from emerging economy', *Heliyon*, 6(3), 2020, p. 9

132 Chris Ogbechie, Dimitrios Koufopoulos, 'Corporate governance practices in publicly quoted companies in Nigeria', *International Journal of Business Governance and Ethics*, 3(4), 2007, pp. 350–381

related. In such cases, family ties supersede the interests of other stakeholders, leading to poor corporate governance in the Nigerian banking industry.[133]

5.7.2 Board Size

The SEC Code did not provide any recommendation for the maximum size of the board, while the CBN code suggested that the board should not have more than 20 members.[134] Between 2007 and 2018, none of the DMB boards exceeded the maximum size suggested by the CBN Code. Furthermore, all DMBs, during the same period, fulfilled the minimum requirement set by both codes, mandating that the board members should not be less than five persons.[135] Thus, the board size varied from six directors in Wema Bank to 20 directors in UBA, except for Spring Bank in 2007 and 2009, Stanbic IBTC in 2007, Standard Chartered Bank and Wema Bank in the years 2007 to 2009, and Equitorial Trust Bank in 2009, all DMBs had ten or more directors during the review period. In the fiscal years of 2010, 2011, and 2012, the majority of Deposit Money Banks (DMBs) exhibited a board size that was significantly above the average. However, Spring Bank, Wema Bank, and First Monument Bank had fewer than ten directors. In 2010, Spring Bank had only three directors, which was in violation of the codes that required a minimum of five board members.[136]

Between 2013 and 2015, most DMBs maintained a board size of no less than ten directors, with the exception of Standard Chartered Bank, which had a lower number. Coronation Merchant Bank and FBN Merchant Bank displayed a board size of seven directors in 2015. In the years 2016 to 2018, the average board size for all DMBs remained constant at ten directors. Furthermore, no DMB exhibited a board size below the mandated minimum of five directors as prescribed by the codes.[137]

5.7.3. Board Composition

The agency theory advocates for having more non-executive directors than executive directors on the board, which underpins both corporate governance codes.[138]

133 Chris Ogbechie, 'Corporate governance practices and leadership in Nigeria', 7 June 2019, available at: <https://ssrn.com/abstract=3400913>, Section 2.4 Code of Corporate Governance for Banks in Nigeria Post Consolidation, available at: <www.cbn.gov.ng/OUT/PUBLICATIONS/BSD/2006/CORPGOV-POSTCONSO.PDF> accessed 15 April 2024

134 Section 2.2.1 Code of Corporate Governance for Banks and Discount Houses and the Guidelines for Whistle Blowing in the Nigerian Banking Industry, 2014

135 Section 4.4 Securities and Exchange Commission Code of Corporate Governance for Public Companies, 2011 p. 3, Section 2.2.1 Code of Corporate Governance for Banks and Discount Houses and the Guidelines for Whistle Blowing in the Nigerian Banking Industry, 2014

136 Section 4.2 Securities and Exchange Commission Code of Corporate Governance for Public Companies, 2011, p. 3

137 Section 4.2 Securities and Exchange Commission Code of Corporate Governance for Public Companies, 2011, p. 3, Section 2.2.1 Code of Corporate Governance for Banks and Discount Houses and the Guidelines for Whistle Blowing in the Nigerian Banking Industry 2014

138 Section 2.2.3 Code of Corporate Governance for Banks and Discount Houses and the Guidelines for Whistle Blowing in the Nigerian Banking Industry 2014

Concerning the board composition of Deposit Money Banks (DMBs) during the fiscal periods between 2007 and 2009, all DMBs, except Oceanic Bank, Union Bank, and Zenith Bank, had more non-executive directors than executive directors on their boards in 2007. However, the following year, Afribank, Wema Bank, and Zenith Bank were found to have contravened the codes stipulating the need for more non-executive directors on their boards, violating both codes. In 2009, all DMBs, except for Afribank, Equatorial Bank Ltd, First Bank Nigeria, Spring Bank, and Wema Bank, conformed with the requirement of having a greater number of non-executive directors on the board. Nonetheless, compliance was still an issue, as evidenced by the annual reports of the CBN and the Nigerian Deposit Insurance Corporation (NDIC) during this period, which showed that a few DMBs had failed to comply.

5.7.4 Board Independence

There are several factors to consider to promote the board's independence. One of these is separating the CEO's office from the COB's. This is based on the agency theory, the basis of the Anglo-Saxon model used in the Nigerian banking industry. Combining these positions can compromise the independence of the board. The CEO oversees the bank's day-to-day operations, while the COB oversees the board of directors. Except for SEC 2003, all codes necessitate that two distinct individuals, unrelated by extended family, hold these positions. Although the SEC Code of 2003 does not mandate the segregation of both offices, it suggests that separate individuals hold the COB and CEO positions. Despite the differences between the SEC and CBN codes in this regard, all DMBs have complied with the CBN code by separating the CEO's office from the COB since the 2007 fiscal year.

One way to ensure the independence of a board is to have more non-executive directors than executive directors, with a portion of the non-executive directors being independent. While the CBN code does not define an independent director, guidelines for appointing such directors suggest that they should not represent any particular shareholder interest and should have no personal business interests in the bank.[139] For instance, the CAMA 2020 specifies that the board of a publicly listed company should have at least three independent directors.[140] The CBN code, on the other hand, mandates that two independent directors be appointed, while the SEC code requires the board to have at least one independent director. During 2007 and 2008, no DMB had an independent director on their board. By 2009, only ten DMBs had successfully complied with the requirement of having independent directors on their boards. The remaining 14 DMBs had breached the SEC and the CBN codes by not having at least one or two independent directors as mandated

139 CBN, 'Guidelines for the appointment of independent directors', Circular to All Banks, BSD/DIR/GEN/CIR/VOL.1/013, 26 OCTOBER 2007, available at: <www.cbn.gov.ng/out/circulars/bsd/2007/guidelines%20for%20the%20appointment%20of%20independent%20directors.pdf> accessed 15 April 2024

140 S. 275(1) CAMA, 2020

by the SEC or CBN codes, respectively. From 2010 to 2018, while it appeared that more DMBs had appointed one independent director on their board, many DMBs still violated the SEC code and CBN code provisions, which required them to have at least one or two independent directors, respectively.

It is argued that a board's true independence is contingent upon the presence of a greater number of independent directors. This is attributed to the fact that independent directors lack any vested interest in the bank, as opposed to non-executive directors who are appointed to represent shareholders' interests. Unfortunately, the appointment of non-executive directors is often predicated on nepotism rather than merit, compromising the board's ability to provide oversight and independence.[141] Therefore, increasing the number of independent directors appointed solely based on merit will help promote stakeholder recognition and protect stakeholders' interests.

The enforcement of the CBN code has raised significant concerns among various stakeholders. Several years following the directive to have at least two independent directors on their board, some DMBs are still in breach of the code. The primary reason for non-compliance is attributed to the CBN's ineffective supervisory and enforcement technique. Although the CBN code mandates compliance,[142] it also stipulates that failure to comply with its provisions would attract sanctions under BOFIA or any applicable legislation or regulation.[143] However, no severe actions have been taken against those who failed to comply with the code. The CBN regulatory approach is neither proactive nor reactive, as it fails to establish the necessary mechanisms to ensure that DMBs adhere to the code's requirements.

Similarly, a reactive regulator would have acted against those DMBs that do not comply with the code's requirements. The regulatory powers conferred on CBN under BOFIA empower it to impose sanctions on DMBs that failed to comply with their licence conditions; it is argued that taking such steps against the defaulters will serve as a deterrent to others.[144] Additionally, the CBN code mandates that DMBs report their compliance with the provisions of the code to the CBN quarterly. However, it remains uncertain whether these reports are being submitted to the CBN as stipulated by the code.[145]

Most of the banks' compliance statements in their annual reports indicate that they have complied with the SEC and the CBN codes. However, if there are any

141 Peter Klein, Daniel Shapiro, Jeffrey Young, 'Corporate governance, family ownership and firm value: The Canadian evidence', *Corporate Governance: An International Review*, 13(6), November 2005, pp. 769–784, Wiley Blackwell

142 Section 8.1.1 Code of Corporate Governance for Banks and Discount Houses and the Guidelines for Whistle Blowing in the Nigerian Banking Industry, 2014

143 Section 8.1.1 Code of Corporate Governance for Banks and Discount Houses and the Guidelines for Whistle Blowing in the Nigerian Banking Industry, 2014, Section 8.1.3

144 Section 8.1.1 Code of Corporate Governance for Banks and Discount Houses and the Guidelines for Whistle Blowing in the Nigerian Banking Industry, 2014

145 Section 8.1.1 Code of Corporate Governance for Banks and Discount Houses and the Guidelines for Whistle Blowing in the Nigerian Banking Industry, 2014, Section 8.1.2

discrepancies in the codes, they have only complied with the CBN code specific to the banking industry.[146] This raises concerns about the transparency of these disclosures on the part of the banks. It is important for the banks to make complete and transparent disclosures for the benefit of all stakeholders. Failure to do so would require the CBN to invoke its powers under s.33(1) BOFIA 2020 to investigate the DMBs in the public interest and impose appropriate sanctions on DMBs who default.[147] If proper investigations are carried out, CBN, as a proactive regulator, will detect non-compliance with the requirements of the code by DMBs and will be able to address the issue before it metamorphoses into a banking crisis. For example, CBN has powers under BOFIA to carry out on-site and off-site examinations of DMBs, including appointing more qualified persons other than the officers of CBN to investigate the books and affairs of the DMBs.[148]

5.7.5 Board Committees

The board of directors of DMBs in Nigeria works through subcommittees to discharge its responsibilities effectively. Both the SEC code and the CBN code require the formation of board committees. The SEC code mandates the establishment of at least three board committees, including the audit, risk management, and governance/remuneration committees.[149] The governance/remuneration committee is restricted to non-executive directors alone. However, the SEC code does not provide any guidance on the composition of the audit and risk committees. It remains unclear if these committees should be composed of executive directors, non-executive directors, or a combination of both.

According to the CBN code, DMBs are required to establish a minimum of four board committees, namely, risk management and audit functions (which can be performed by one committee, depending on the bank's size) and the board governance and nomination committees.[150] The CBN code also specifies that all board committees must have a charter that DMBs are obligated to submit to the CBN for approval.[151] The board audit committee differs from the mandatory audit committee required under s.404(3) CAMA 2020, as both committees have different functions.[152] The Board Audit Committee is a supervisory body that monitors the board's activities in general terms.

146 GTBank Annual Report, 2015, p. 15, available at: <www.gtbank.com/uploads/financial-information/2015-Year-End-Audited-Results.pdf> accessed 15 April 2024
147 S.33 (1) BOFIA, 2020
148 S.33 (2) BOFIA, 2020
149 S.9.2 Securities and Exchange Commission Code of Corporate Governance for Public Companies, 2011, p. 7
150 S.2.5.1 Code of Corporate Governance for Banks and Discount Houses and the Guidelines for Whistle Blowing in the Nigerian Banking Industry, 2014
151 S.2.5.1 Code of Corporate Governance for Banks and Discount Houses and the Guidelines for Whistle Blowing in the Nigerian Banking Industry, 2014, S.2.5.2
152 S.2.5.1 Code of Corporate Governance for Banks and Discount Houses and the Guidelines for Whistle Blowing in the Nigerian Banking Industry, 2014, S.2.5.1(i)

Conversely, the statutory Audit Committee is responsible for scrutinising the audited financial statements and accounts to ensure that external auditors maintain objectivity, integrity, and independence. Notably, it is imperative to observe that the COB is ineligible for membership in any board committee. Additionally, the COB is precluded from assuming the leadership of any board committee. The objective of this regulation is to ensure the autonomy and transparency of these committees; only non-executive directors are eligible for the leadership of board committees.[153]

Each committee's constitution depends on the board's size and the directors' availability. For instance, in the case of Wema Bank between 2007 and 2009, which had only six directors, all the directors were assigned to different committees except the COB. Consequently, all the members had to serve in all the committees except for the specific committee, which required only non-executive directors to be members, like the remuneration committee. However, the appointment of the same people to different committees, with only a change in the chairperson, is insufficient to ensure board independence, especially when the composition of these committees is not based on the qualifications, competence, and experience of its members. This approach can lead to manipulation, particularly in family-owned DMBs, where domineering CEOs/COBs can exert undue influence. For example, in the financial year ending 2009, ten DMBs, including Skye Bank, had the Risk Management Committee and the Credit Committee. These committees failed to deliver their oversight function because of the absence of an appropriate risk management framework. These committees failed to deliver their oversight function because of the absence of an appropriate risk management framework.[154] The institutional environment significantly influences the appointment of directors to the board and their allocation to board committees in Nigeria. Regrettably, the selection process often results in the appointment of individuals who do not possess the requisite skills, training, or experience necessary for the effective execution of their oversight functions. This situation arises primarily due to the absence of a merit-based selection process. Consequently, the appointment of directors with inadequate qualifications can have severe consequences for an organisation. Such individuals may lack the expertise and knowledge required to make informed decisions and provide effective oversight, which could lead to poor performance, legal issues, and reputational damage.

5.7.6 Board Gender Diversity

Board gender diversity has been a significant topic in corporate governance discourse, particularly in the banking industry. In Nigeria, it has become apparent that there is a gender imbalance in the boardrooms of DMBs. However, there are

153 S.2.5.1 Code of Corporate Governance for Banks and Discount Houses and the Guidelines for Whistle Blowing in the Nigerian Banking Industry, 2014, S.2.5.4

154 Sanusi L. Sanusi, 'Global financial meltdown and the reforms in the Nigerian banking industry', *CBN Journal of Applied Statistics*, 2(1), 2010, pp. 93–98

no specific provisions for board gender diversity in Nigerian laws, and neither the SEC nor the CBN code includes any specific provisions dealing with it. The CBN issued the 'Nigerian Sustainable Banking Principles' on 24 September 2012 to address this issue.[155] Principle Four mandates that DMBs should have at least 30% women representation on their boards, and 40% of top management positions should be occupied by women by the end of December 2014.[156] DMBs were required to disclose compliance with this directive in their annual reports by stating the statistics of female representation.[157]

It is argued that this CBN directive stimulated women's participation in national development, enabling them to contribute meaningfully to the economy and society. Prior to the issuance of this directive, women's interest in pursuing top management positions within the banking industry was minimal. One of the reasons for this was the predominance of men in the industry, which relegated women to secondary roles.[158]

On 3 March 2014, Sarah Alade, who was then the Acting Governor of the CBN, reiterated the importance of having women represented in the board and management of DMBs in accordance with the regulatory directive of the CBN.[159] According to her, CBN expects compliance from all DMBs, as there was a sense of agreement between the CBN and DMBs that they should increase the number of women on boards for economic growth sustainability.[160] She emphasised the need for the banking industry to increase the number of women participating in the decision-making process of the banks for the benefit of all stakeholders by ensuring that women should fill at least 40% of top management positions and 30% of board positions from now on.[161] One significant flaw with this regulatory directive is that it lacks a proper enforcement mechanism. It did not contain sanctions for DMBs that failed to adhere to it. One will argue that though this example is a CBN's directive, it does not mean it is less important than the code. CBN has issued this directive to promote women's participation in national development and in line with its powers to make rules and regulations for the operation and control

155 CBN, 'Nigerian sustainable banking principles', Central Bank of Nigeria, July 2012, available at: <www.cbn.gov.ng/out/2012/ccd/circular-nsbp.pdf> accessed 15 April 2024

156 CBN, 'Nigerian sustainable banking principles', Central Bank of Nigeria, July 2012, available at: <www.cbn.gov.ng/out/2012/ccd/circular-nsbp.pdf> accessed 15 April 2024, p. 19

157 CBN, 'Nigerian sustainable banking principles', Central Bank of Nigeria, July 2012, available at: <www.cbn.gov.ng/out/2012/ccd/circular-nsbp.pdf> accessed 15 April 2024, p. 21

158 Folarin Alayande, 'Where have all the women gone?', *Thisday Newspaper*, 7 March 2020, available at: <www.thisdaylive.com/index.php/2020/03/07/where-have-all-the-women-gone/> accessed 5 May 2024

159 CBN, 'Reviews 40% women board slot', *The Nation Newspaper*, 5 March 2014, available at: <https://thenationonlineng.net/cbn-reviews-40-women-board-slot/> accessed 15 April 2024

160 CBN, 'Reviews 40% women board slot', *The Nation Newspaper*, 5 March 2014, available at: <https://thenationonlineng.net/cbn-reviews-40-women-board-slot/> accessed 15 April 2024

161 CBN, 'Reviews 40% women board slot', *The Nation Newspaper*, 5 March 2014, available at: <https://thenationonlineng.net/cbn-reviews-40-women-board-slot/> accessed 15 April 2024

of all institutions under its supervision[162] and powers under s.67(1)(a) BOFIA 2020 to make regulations and issue guidelines regarding corporate governance, CBN should have imposed sanctions such as fines on DMBs for failing to comply with this directive.[163]

It could be contended that the non-compliance with the directive by DMBs can be attributed to Nigeria's institutional context. Specifically, Nigeria is a patriarchal society where the culture of male dominance and the relegation of women to secondary roles are strongly entrenched.[164] Furthermore, it is plausible that the low representation of women on the boards of DMBs is due to the banks' lack of high-quality applications from women.[165] This could be one of the possible reasons for CBN's reluctance to impose sanctions despite the insistent breaches by the DMBs to comply with the directive.[166]

The number of women who have been COBs in DMBs in Nigeria has recently been small. For example, Standard Chartered Bank and Unity Bank have had female CEOs. On 31 March 2015, GTBank appointed its first female COB, making history as the first woman to occupy that position since the bank began operating on 17 January 1990. This is a significant milestone in the banking industry, demonstrating a commitment to gender diversity and inclusivity in leadership positions. It also highlights the importance of breaking down gender barriers and promoting equal opportunities for women in the workplace.[167] On 30 July 2015, Access Bank appointed a new COB, who happened to be a woman.[168] Similarly, on 7 September 2015, First Bank Nigeria appointed a woman as the COB, making

162 S.56 (2) BOFIA, 2020

163 S.29 BOFIA, 2020, S.67(1)(a), BOFIA, 2020

164 Godiya Allanana Makama, 'Patriarchy and gender inequality in Nigeria: The way forward', *European Scientific Journal*, 9(17), June 2013, p. 115

165 Helen Ojo, 'Mojekwu, Awosika, seek adoption of 30% female representation on board of Nigerian firms', *The Guardian*, 21 September 2018, available at: <https://guardian.ng/business-services/mojekwu-awosika-seek-adoption-of-30-female-representation-on-board-of-nigerian-firms/>; Onyinye Nwachukwu, 'Emefiele: When a Central Bank governor doubles as women's cheerleader', *BusinessDay*, 4 August 2021, available at: <https://businessday.ng/features/article/emefiele-when-a-central-bank-governor-doubles-as-womens-cheerleader/> accessed 5 May 2024

166 Helen Ojo, 'Mojekwu, Awosika, seek adoption of 30% female representation on board of Nigerian firms', *The Guardian*, 21 September 2018, available at: <https://guardian.ng/business-services/mojekwu-awosika-seek-adoption-of-30-female-representation-on-board-of-nigerian-firms/>; Onyinye Nwachukwu, 'Emefiele: When a Central Bank governor doubles as women's cheerleader', *BusinessDay*, 4 August 2021, available at: <https://businessday.ng/features/article/emefiele-when-a-central-bank-governor-doubles-as-womens-cheerleader/> accessed 5 May 2024

167 Business Journal, 'GT bank appoints Osaretin Demuren as new chairman', 28 April 2015, available at: <www.businessjournalng.com/gt-bank-appoints-osaretin-demuren-as-new-chairman/> accessed 5 May 2024

168 Wale Odunsi, 'Mosun Belo-Olusoga replaces Gbenga Oyebode as access bank chairman', *Daily Post Newspaper*, 31 July 2015, available at: <https://dailypost.ng/2015/07/31/mosun-belo-olusoga-replaces-gbenga-oyebode-as-access-bank-chairman/> accessed 5 May 2024

her the first woman to hold that position since the bank was founded in 1894.[169] Although women have been appointed as CEOs or COBs in various companies in Nigeria, the number of women holding top positions in the Nigerian banking industry remains relatively small due to the domination of men in the sector. However, a few women have made it to the top, such as the woman who was appointed the CEO of Stanbic IBTC Bank from 2011 to 2012.[170] Standard Chartered Bank appointed women as CEOs from 2011 to 2018,[171] and Unity Bank, on 11 August 2015, appointed a woman as CEO, a position she still occupies to date,[172] making her the first female to occupy that position since the bank was founded in 2006. It is worth noting that Jaiz Bank had no female representation on its board in the fiscal year ending in 2015.

In 2016, there was a similar trend to the previous year in board gender diversity at banks. Only 4 out of the 25 DMBs had 30% or more female representation on their board. These four banks are Access Bank at 35.7%, Citibank Nigeria at 33.33%, Standard Chartered Bank at 42.85%, and Wema Bank at 33.33%. There was also no change in the number of women occupying the top positions of COBs/CEOs in 2016. It was found that 21 DMBs did not meet the threshold of women's participation on the board as directed by CBN. Jaiz Bank had no female participation on its board for two years in a row. This raises concerns about the enforcement mechanisms and sanctions for non-compliance, as over 80% of the DMBs still need to meet the required threshold. Since there is a reporting obligation mandating DMBs to disclose the number of women on their board in their annual reports, the CBN must be aware of such a high level of non-compliance. Otherwise, the DMBs involved failed to make complete and transparent disclosures. It is worth noting that DMBs breach the directive, which raises questions about whether the CBN intended for the directive to have no force of law and not just a mere recommendation. Even though the directive did not recommend any specific punishment for failure to comply, the CBN should have taken punitive action against defaulting DMBs. The CBN could rely on its powers under section 12 (g) of the BOFIA 2020 to sanction DMBs for breaching their licences' conditions.[173]

In the 2017 fiscal year, the number of women on the boards of DMBs has increased compared to previous years. However, 18 DMBs failed to meet the required threshold of having at least 30% female representation on their board, as directed by the Central Bank of Nigeria (CBN). Only eight DMBs met this

169 First Bank of Nigeria Board of Directors, available at: <www.firstbanknigeria.com/about-us/the-leadership/board-of-directors/ibukun-awosika-profile/> accessed 5 May 2024

170 Stanbic Bank Our Leadership, available at: <www.standardbank.com/sbg/standard-bank-group/who-we-are/our-leadership/Sola,David%E2%80%93Borha> accessed 5 May 2024

171 Standard Chartered Bank Press Release, 'We've announced key appointments in Africa', 27 December 2018 available at: <www.sc.com/en/media/press-release/weve-announced-key-appointments-in-africa/> accessed 5 May 2024

172 Unity Bank Board of Directors, available at: <www.unitybankng.com/board-of-directors> accessed 5 May 2024

173 S.12(g) BOFIA, 2020

requirement in the 2017 fiscal year, which are Access Bank (35.29%), Citibank (38.46%), Coronation Merchant Bank (30%), FSDH Merchant Bank (36.36%), FCMB (36.36%), Stanbic-IBTC (30%), Unity Bank (33.33%), and Wema Bank (33.33%). The data also revealed that Jaiz Bank and Skye Bank had no female representation on their board. Jaiz Bank had failed to comply with the regulatory directive of the CBN for three consecutive years, requiring women to fill at least 30% of board positions. Skye Bank did not comply because the CBN appointed an all-male board in 2016 when it dissolved the bank's board.[174] One would expect that the CBN should have at least complied with its directive on board gender diversity when constituting the board of Skye Bank with at least 30% of women. The report also shows no changes in the number of females who occupied the top positions of COBs/CEOs for the third year running.

In the fiscal year of 2018, only six Deposit Money Banks (DMBs) adhered to the regulation of appointing more than 30% of female representation on their board. These six DMBs are Access Bank (33.33%), Citibank (38.46%), FCMB (36.36%), GTBank (30.76%), Stanbic-IBTC (37.5%), and Wema Bank (45.45%). Jaiz Bank was the only DMB without any female representation on its board for four consecutive years.

Furthermore, the women occupying the top positions of Chairpersons of Boards/ Chief Executive Officers (COBs/CEOs) in Nigerian DMBs remained the same for the fourth year in a row. Access Bank, First Bank, and GTBank continued to have women as their COBs, while Chartered Standard Bank and Unity Bank were the only two DMBs with female CEOs.

The socio-political environment in Nigeria is a significant factor that inhibits board gender diversity, especially women's representation on the boards of DMBs. Nigeria is a patriarchal society where people tend to underestimate women's ability to contribute to economic development despite many Nigerian women excelling in various professional careers. This cultural belief extends to the banking industry, as evidenced by the level of non-compliance with the CBN regulatory requirement to promote gender diversity on the Board of DMBs. Consequently, the overall number of women on the Board of Nigerian DMBs is still below the 30% threshold the CBN set nine years after introducing the Nigerian Sustainable Banking Principles.[175] It is worth mentioning that Zenith Bank Plc has officially announced the appointment of Adaora Umeoji as the incoming CEO effective from 1 June 2024, contingent upon approval by the CBN. Umeoji will succeed the incumbent, Ebenezer Onyeagwu, whose five-year term will end on 31 May 2024.

174 CBN Press Release, 'Central Bank of Nigeria makes board and management changes at Skye Bank Plc', available at: <www.cbn.gov.ng/out/2016/ccd/cbn%20press%20statement%20on%20skye%20bankjuly%20040716.pdf> accessed 5 May 2024

175 Implementation of Sustainable Banking Principles by Banks, 'Discount Houses and Development Finance Institutions in Nigeria', CBN Circular Ref No. FPR/DIR/CIR/GEN/01/33, 24 September 2012, available at: <www.cbn.gov.ng/out/2012/ccd/circular-nsbp.pdf>

5.7.7 Executive Compensation

The issue of executive compensation in the banking industry has sparked a number of heated debates, particularly in the wake of the global financial crisis that occurred between 2007 and 2009.[176] Both the SEC and CBN codes attempted to address executive compensation in the Nigerian banking industry. The SEC code stipulates that the remuneration of executive directors should be based on their skills and experience and that only non-executive directors are eligible to determine their remuneration.[177] Similarly, the CBN code requires that all DMBs have a remuneration policy for executive directors, which must be disclosed in the bank's annual reports. The policy also makes it clear that only non-executive directors are authorised to determine the remuneration of executive directors.[178] The CBN code, like the SEC code, stipulates that only non-executive directors hold the authority to set executive directors' pay.

Nevertheless, the lack of uniformity in executive compensation within the same DMB is apparent due to several factors, such as individual experience, qualifications, and expertise. The codes themselves remain silent regarding any limit on executive director remuneration. By contrast, the UK has a separate remuneration code for banks, with the PRA and FCA Remuneration Codes designed to mitigate excessive risk-taking within the banking industry.[179] It is argued that while the SEC and the CBN codes are not expected to impose restrictions on executive remuneration, they must provide safeguards against the risks arising due to the structure of the remuneration arrangements. The CBN code requires DMBs to disclose their remuneration policy in their annual reports to shareholders. However, there is no stipulation that the policy must be subject to shareholders' approval.

In this regard, it is important to note that executive remuneration has been a subject of great debate and scrutiny in recent years. While attracting and retaining top talent is necessary, excessive executive pay can lead to a misalignment of interests between directors and shareholders. Moreover, it can lead to a negative perception of the bank in the eyes of the public. However, it is expected that during the general meeting, shareholders will vote on the remuneration of executive directors, even though it is not expressly stated in the code. However, CAMA 2020 provides that DMBs shall determine the executive directors' remuneration during the general meetings.[180] Although non-executive directors are responsible for establishing the remuneration of executive directors, it can be contended that a CEO who holds a

176 House of Commons Treasury Committee, 'Banking crisis: Reforming corporate governance and pay in the city', Ninth Report of Session 2008–2009, 12 May 2009, p. 8, available at: <https://publications.parliament.uk/pa/cm200809/cmselect/cmtreasy/519/519.pdf> accessed 5 May 2024

177 Section 14.2–14.3, Securities and Exchange Commission of Nigeria, Code of Corporate Governance for Public Companies, 2011, p. 9

178 Section 2.7.4–2.7.5, Code of Corporate Governance for Banks and Discount Houses and the Guidelines for Whistle Blowing in the Nigerian Banking Industry, 2014

179 PRA/FCA Senior Management Arrangements Systems and Controls Sourcebook, Chapter 19A, available at: <www.handbook.fca.org.uk/handbook/SYSC/19A/?view=chapter> accessed 5 May 2024

180 Section 257 CAMA, 2020

majority share can influence executive directors' pay since non-executive directors are appointed based on connections. Although CAMA 2020 aimed to establish safeguards by proposing that shareholders in general meetings should approve the remuneration of executive directors,[181] it is merely a formality because the non-executive directors are appointed based on connections; the majority shareholder will ensure that they approve the remuneration packages, especially if the DMB in question is a family-owned bank.

Directors have the right to request reimbursement of expenses incurred while attending meetings, such as travel, lodging, and dining expenses. However, there is currently no provision to regulate the maximum amount that may be claimed. This lack of control provides an avenue for corruption as directors may misuse expense claims to perpetrate fraud against the bank.[182] There are no provisions in CAMA 2020, CBN code, or SEC code prohibiting performance-related compensation to directors. The agency theory argues that if directors' compensation is not linked directly to firm value by shareholders, directors may lack incentives to maximise shareholders' interests or seek to consume the perquisites at the bank's expense.[183] It is argued that the payment of bonuses directly linked to short-term performance is one reason directors embark on excessive risk-taking, and if not checked, it can lead to bank failure.[184] Excessive risk-taking in the banking industry arises when the board incentivises directors and senior management to pursue risky ventures that yield short-term benefits.[185] Such situations often occur when strategic decisions are driven by directors' bonuses, short-term share prices, or shareholders' short-term interests rather than the bank's and its stakeholders' long-term interests, including employees and customers.[186] This phenomenon is particularly concerning, as it exposes the bank and its stakeholders to significant risk. When directors and senior management prioritise short-term gains over the long-term interests of the bank, they may engage in practices that ultimately harm the bank and its stakeholders. In addition, such practices may result in significant financial losses and reputational damage to the bank.

Therefore, boards and senior management must prioritise the bank's and its stakeholders' long-term interests when making strategic decisions. This approach

181 Section 257 CAMA, 2020

182 Olaoye Olatunji, Dada Adekola, 'Analysis of frauds in banks: Nigeria's experience', *European Journal of Business and Management*, 6(31), 2014, pp. 90–99

183 Keith Harvey, Ronald Shrieves, 'Executive compensation structure and corporate governance choices', *Journal of Financial Research*, 24(4), 2001, pp. 495–512, 497

184 Raghuram Rajan, 'The credit crisis and cycle-proof regulation', *Federal Reserve Bank of St. Louis Review*, September–October 2009, Part 1, pp. 397–402, available at: <https://doi.org/10.20955/r.91.397-402>

185 Hamid Mehran, Alan Morrison, Joel Shapiro, 'Corporate governance and banks: What have we learned from the financial crisis?', in Mathias Dewatripont, Xavier Freixas (eds), *The Crisis Aftermath: New Regulatory Paradigms* (Centre for Economic Policy Research, London, 2012), p. 11

186 Hamid Mehran, Alan Morrison, Joel Shapiro, 'Corporate governance and banks: What have we learned from the financial crisis?', in Mathias Dewatripont, Xavier Freixas (eds), *The Crisis Aftermath: New Regulatory Paradigms* (Centre for Economic Policy Research, London, 2012), p. 11

will ensure that the bank can sustainably meet the needs of its stakeholders and operate in a stable and successful manner.

The common practice in the Nigerian banking industry is that directors are paid bonuses randomly that may have no bearing on bank size, return on assets, and financial or non-financial performance.[187] Zenith Bank, for instance, offers a productivity bonus to its non-executive directors, which is disbursed at the end of every financial year.[188] However, this bonus is not based on pre-defined criteria except attendance at board and committee meetings. This has raised concerns that it depletes the bank's resources and compromises the independence of non-executive directors, which, according to the SEC code, is unacceptable.[189] The SEC code cautions against remunerating non-executive directors in ways that may compromise their independence; making such random payments violates the code. In dealing with non-executive directors' remuneration,[190] the CBN code divided it into two key components: the directors' fee and sitting allowances for attending board and committee meetings. Besides these fees, non-executive directors may claim expenses such as travel and hotel expenses incurred because of attending board or committee meetings; however, this can only be claimed where the banks have not initially covered such expenses.

According to the CBN code, non-executive directors are only entitled to directors' fees and sitting allowances for board and committee meetings and cannot receive any other benefits or salaries, such as share options or bonuses.[191] However, unlike the SEC code, the CBN code does not set a maximum threshold on the non-executive directors' fees, opening up a loophole for exploitation.[192] It is, therefore, argued that the practice of paying productivity bonuses to non-executive directors by DMBs breaches the CBN code[193] because 'productivity bonus' does not fall into any categories of compensation that non-executive directors are supposed to receive as stipulated by the codes. The categories of compensation that non-executive directors are entitled to are directors' fees, sitting allowances for board or committee meetings, and reimbursement of any expenses incurred during the attendance of meetings, such as travel and hotel expenses.

187 Appah Ebimobowei, Tebepah Sekeme Felix, Awuji Charles Evans, 'Directors' Compensation and Financial Performance of Deposit Money Banks in Nigeria', *World Journal of Finance and Investment Research*, 5(1), 2020, pp. 61–76

188 Zenith Bank Plc Annual Report, 31 December, 2018, p. 36, available at: <www.zenithbank.com/media/2755/2018-annual-report.pdf> accessed 5 May 2024

189 Section 14.6 Securities and Exchange Commission of Nigeria, Code of Corporate Governance for Public Companies, 2011, p. 10

190 Section 2.7.7, Code of Corporate Governance for Banks and Discount Houses and the Guidelines for Whistle Blowing in the Nigerian Banking Industry, 2014

191 Section 2.7.7, Code of Corporate Governance for Banks and Discount Houses and the Guidelines for Whistle Blowing in the Nigerian Banking Industry, 2014

192 Olaoye Olatunji, Dada Adekola, 'Analysis of frauds in banks: Nigeria's experience', *European Journal of Business and Management*, 6(31), 2014, pp. 90–99

193 Zenith Bank Plc Annual Report, 31 December 2018, p. 36, available at: <www.zenithbank.com/media/2755/2018-annual-report.pdf> accessed 5 May 2024

5.7.8 External Auditors

External auditors play a paramount role in ensuring the transparency and accountability of the board from an agency perspective.[194] One could argue that to some extent, CAMA 2020 has provided guidelines for the roles that external auditors should play in terms of corporate governance. Notably, section 407(1)(a)(b) mandates auditors to report accurately on the proper accounting by the banks, ensuring that the bank's balance sheet accurately reflects the accounting records and returns of the bank.[195] For the auditors to carry out their function effectively, every bank's auditor shall access the bank's books of accounts, vouchers, and information or explanations to enable them to discharge their duties.[196] The external auditors must consider the correctness of the information in the directors' annual reports for the fiscal year the accounts are being prepared; if there are any inconsistencies, the auditors shall state that fact in their reports.[197]

External auditors are an essential part of the banking industry and play a vital role in ensuring market discipline is maintained in the public interest. External auditors are responsible for scrutinising a bank's accounts carefully to protect the interests of all stakeholders. The information provided by the auditors allows stakeholders to make informed decisions. However, there may be instances when directors are not transparent in their disclosures to external auditors. These instances may involve concealing specific material facts from the auditors, which can hinder their ability to provide an accurate opinion of the bank's actual financial position. For example, directors may maintain two separate books of account and provide only one to the auditors, withholding the second book, which reflects the bank's actual financial position. External auditors must be given complete and accurate information to fulfil their responsibilities adequately. Any misleading or incomplete disclosures by directors can have significant consequences for the bank and its stakeholders. Therefore, directors must comply with their obligations and provide external auditors with all relevant information.[198]

Auditors may also conspire with the directors to misrepresent the bank's financial position.[199] A firm of auditors called Akintola Williams Deloitte was indicted for colluding with the board of directors of Afribank to overstate the bank's accounts

194 Jill Solomon, *Corporate Governance and Accountability* (4th ed., John Wiley and Sons, Inc., Chichester, 2013), p. 167

195 Section 407 (1) (a) (b) CAMA, 2020

196 Section 407 (1) (a) (b) CAMA, 2020, Section 407 (3)

197 Section 407 (1) (a) (b) CAMA, 2020, Section 407 (5)

198 Chijioke Nelson, 'Investigations uncover serial alleged frauds by Skye Bank Plc's managers', *The Guardian Newspaper*, 14 November 2018, available at: <https://guardian.ng/business-services/investigations-uncover-serial-alleged-frauds-by-skye-bank-plcs-managers/> accessed 5 May 2024

199 Owolabi Bakare, 'The unethical practices of accountants and auditors and the compromising stance of professional bodies in the corporate world: Evidence from corporate Nigeria', *Accounting Forum*, 31(3), pp. 277–303, 279, available at: <www.tandfonline.com/doi/pdf/10.1016/j.accfor.2007.06.001> accessed 21 May 2024

intentionally.[200] Other accounting firms like KPMG, PricewaterhouseCoopers, and Ernest and Young have been implicated in allegations of financial misappropriation, false accounting, deliberate financial engineering, and financial misstatements of audited accounts of DMBs in Nigeria.[201] These auditing firms were responsible for auditing the financial reports of Nigerian DMBs that collapsed in 2009. Therefore, no punishment for auditors who engage in malpractices is mentioned beyond the provision of auditory functions in the CBN and SEC codes.

Nevertheless, external auditors are now obligated to owe duties to the company, shareholders, and other stakeholders who may suffer loss or damage due to the auditor's negligence.[202] Despite this right, the threshold required for success in suing auditors is incredibly high. Plaintiffs must demonstrate that the auditors were aware that the financial statements would be provided to them and that they would rely on them, even if it were to their detriment. In light of the critical role external auditors played in the 2009 banking crisis, it is surprising that no cases concerning auditors' liability have been reported so far in the Nigerian banking industry.

5.8 Corporate Social Responsibility in the Nigerian Banking industry

As mentioned earlier, CSR is pivotal in ensuring that stakeholders are recognised and their interests are protected. In this regard, it is necessary to investigate the extent to which the CSR regulatory framework in Nigeria has contributed to the promotion of stakeholders' recognition and protection of interests in the banking industry.

5.8.1 Regulatory Framework for CSR in Nigerian Banks

In 2008, Senator Chukwumerije, a member of the Nigerian Senate, sponsored the CSR Senate Bill No.27.[203] The bill aimed to establish a Corporate Social Responsibility Commission and create a uniform CSR framework that would require companies to allocate at least 3.5% of their gross profits to CSR initiatives.[204] Although some countries have introduced a specific form of legislated CSR, the bill faced

200 Owolabi Bakare, 'The unethical practices of accountants and auditors and the compromising stance of professional bodies in the corporate world: Evidence from corporate Nigeria', *Accounting Forum*, 31(3), pp. 277–303, 279, available at: <www.tandfonline.com/doi/pdf/10.1016/j.accfor.2007.06.001> accessed 21 May 2024

201 Julius Otusanya, Sarah Lauwo, 'The role of auditors in the Nigerian banking crisis', *Accountancy Business and the Public Interest*, 9, 2010, pp. 159–204, 179

202 *Hedley Byrne & Co Ltd v. Heller & Partners Ltd* [1964] A.C. 465

203 Adaeze Okoye, 'Exploring the relationship between corporate social responsibility, law and development in an African context: Should government be responsible for ensuring corporate responsibility?' *International Journal of Law and Management*, 54(5), 2012, pp. 364–378, 371

204 Adaeze Okoye, 'Exploring the relationship between corporate social responsibility, law and development in an African context: Should government be responsible for ensuring corporate responsibility?' *International Journal of Law and Management*, 54(5), 2012, pp. 364–378, 371

criticism from corporations questioning the rationale for regulating CSR. For instance, under the Indian Companies Act 2013, listed companies are required to spend a minimum of 2% of their average net profits of the preceding three years on annual CSR activities in India.[205] Similarly, in 2007, Indonesia amended its Companies and Investment Law to enable it to regulate its CSR activities.[206] While CSR in developed economies often emphasises consumer protection, fair trade, green marketing, climate change, and socially responsible investments, CSR in Nigeria may need to address a distinct set of concerns. These concerns may include poverty eradication, healthcare provision, infrastructural development, financial inclusion, gender equality, and access to education. Nigeria's existing socio-economic developmental challenges have arisen from the government's inability to provide basic amenities to its citizens. As such, as good corporate citizens, DMBs are required to contribute to Nigerian society on many fronts by helping to alleviate the plight of the citizens by providing social and infrastructural facilities, amongst others. Therefore, CSR initiatives in Nigeria must approach these challenges to align with the country's socio-economic realities.

Apart from the attempt to introduce a CSR Bill in Nigeria, several other attempts have been made to regulate CSR activities in the country. One such initiative is the Corporate Social Responsibility Bill 2015, House of Representatives Bill No.117.[207] The bill made it mandatory for companies with a net profit of N500 million during any financial year[208] to spend at least 1% of their average net profits of the preceding three years on yearly CSR activities in Nigeria.[209] This requirement is in *pari materia* with the provision introduced by the Indian Companies Act 2013, with the only difference being that the Indian CSR law mandates the payment of 2% of their average net profits of the preceding three years on yearly CSR activities, while the Nigerian CSR Bill 2015 requires companies to spend at least 1% of their average net profits of the preceding three years on yearly CSR activities. The CSR Bill of 2015 was initially introduced to the House of Representatives on 8 December 2015. It underwent a second reading on 15 December of the same year. Subsequently, it was referred to the House Committees on Commerce and Justice for further deliberation. However, similar to the 2008 version, the 2015 bill could not progress to its third reading.

Another effort worthy of mention is the Financial Reporting Council of Nigeria Act (Amendment) Bill 2018, House of Representatives Bill No.1314.[210] The bill seeks to compel companies to adopt CSR in their corporate policies. The bill proposed that a mandatory percentage of the companies earning an average of

205 S135 Indian Company Act, 2013

206 Armand Maris, 'Compulsory CSR: Indonesia takes a tough stance but clarity on definitions is lacking', available at: <www.ipra.org/news/itle/compulsory-csr-indonesia-takes-a-tough-stance-but-clarity-on-definitions-is-lacking/> accessed 21 May 2024

207 CSR (Special Provisions, etc.) Bill, 2015

208 S.1 CSR (Special Provisions, etc.) Bill, 2015

209 S.3 CSR (Special Provisions, etc.) Bill, 2015

210 Financial Reporting Council of Nigeria Act (Amendment) Bill, 2018

N50 million and above in profits in three succeeding years be spent on CSR.[211] The 2018 bill was presented before the House of Representatives for the first reading on 7 February 2018 and the second on 5 July 2018. After the second reading, the bill was referred to the Committee on Commerce for further deliberation; however, like the previous ones, it did not make it past the committee stage. As it presently stands, Nigeria's statutory framework for CSR is derived from the provision of s.43 CAMA 2020. This section gives the companies the status of a natural person with the power to donate to further their business or objects in as much as the companies' memorandum or any other existing laws do not prohibit it.[212] The effect of this provision is that CSR is seen as a form of corporate philanthropy. In other words, the provision suggests that engaging in CSR in the Nigerian banking industry is nothing more than banks doing some voluntary good to society as good corporate citizens. In light of the previous section, the next section examines the CSR initiative in the Nigerian banking industry.

5.8.2 Stakeholders and CSR Practice of DMBs in Nigeria

All the DMBs are part of the Nigerian society, and as successful businesses, they are expected to engage in CSR for the benefit of stakeholders.[213] Nigerian DMBs view CSR as an elective philanthropic endeavour that affords employees, depositors, host communities, and investors a supportive environment. All the Nigerian banks claim to engage in their CSR initiative based on Carroll's CSR pyramid. Carroll explains CSR from four angles of responsibility by corporations. At the bedrock of the pyramid is economic responsibility, which means that the banks must be profitable; however, one would argue that economic responsibility transcends beyond profit maximisation for the benefit of shareholders. Stakeholder engagement by empowering women to participate in financial and commercial activities falls within the banks' economic responsibility parameters. Next on the pyramid is legal responsibility, which means banks should obey the law. Therefore, one would argue that obeying the laws means compliance with all regulations, including full compliance with the corporate governance codes and regulatory directives. The third responsibility on the pyramid is the ethical responsibility, which means that banks must be fair, just, and transparent in all circumstances; being ethical in how the DMBs operate means that the banks must always consider the impact of their operation on the environment. Occupying the least on the pyramid is philanthropic responsibility; as good corporate citizens, banks are expected to give back

211 Section 49 (h) Financial Reporting Council of Nigeria Act (Amendment) Bill, 2018
212 Section 43 (1)(2) CAMA, 2020
213 Zenith Bank Website, available at: <www.zenithbank.com/csr/>; GT Bank Website, available at: <www.gtbank.com/about/corporate-social-responsibility>; Fidelity Bank Website, available at: <https://csr.fidelitybank.ng/about/>; UBA Website, available at: <www.ubagroup.com/uba-foundation/>; Access Bank Website, available at: <www.accessbankplc.com/pages/sustainable-banking/our-community-investments/Community-Support.aspx>; WEMA Bank Website, available at: <www.wemabank.com/csr/>

to society. There are many benefits for the banks to engage in CSR; besides the fact that such CSR activities enhance their reputation and legitimacy, they also gain the trust of other stakeholders.

CSR will help in the recognition of stakeholders and the protection of stakeholders' interests. The CSR initiatives of DMBs in Nigeria regarding their overall spending on CSR activities compared to the profit after tax needed to be compared. This comparison was necessary, especially since various legislative attempts have failed to ensure that banks spend a certain percentage of their annual net profit on CSR. This comparison will undoubtedly help decide the likelihood of DMBs engaging in any mandatory form of CSR, particularly as it relates to having a minimum percentage of their profit before tax is spent on CSR initiatives. Some might argue that imposing such a percentage on DMBs to spend on CSR negates CSR objectives; however, CSR is context-dependent.[214] The subject of legislated CSR has been a topic of ongoing debate;[215] several countries have embraced some form of legislated CSR by recommending that a certain percentage of companies' profits be spent on CSR. For example, India, Indonesia, the Philippines, and the UAE all have mandated CSR forms.[216]

DMBs in Nigeria allocated less than 1% of their profit after tax to CSR initiatives on average between 2007 and 2018. While this may seem commendable, it is argued that the amount is relatively low considering the profits generated by these DMBs during that period. Furthermore, the allocation of funds for CSR initiatives by DMBs is concerning. The trend among DMBs is to disburse funds across various CSR initiatives, such as healthcare, sports, education, intervention projects, and conferences.[217] The amount that some DMBs allocate to CSR initiatives in Nigeria is deemed to be insignificant when considering the role that CSR is expected to play in addressing the country's socio-economic developmental challenges. It is important to note that CSR in the African context differs from how it is perceived in developed economies. Therefore, if DMBs' CSR initiatives aim to achieve the desired outcome of alleviating extreme poverty by 2030, more needs to be done regarding the percentage of their net profit allocated to CSR initiatives and

214 Adaeze Okoye, 'Exploring the relationship between corporate social responsibility, law and development in an African context: Should government be responsible for ensuring corporate responsibility?', *International Journal of Law and Management*, 54(5), 2012, pp. 364–378, 367

215 Doreen McBarnet, 'Corporate social responsibility beyond law, through law, for law', University of Edinburgh School of Law Working Paper No. 2009/03, 27 March 2009, available at: <https://ssrn.com/abstract=1369305 or http://dx.doi.org/10.2139/ssrn.1369305>

216 Panwar Rajat, Shweta Nawani, Vivek Pandey, 'Legislated CSR: A brief introduction', in *Corporate Social Responsibility Business and Society 360* (Vol. 2, Emerald Publishing Limited, Bingley, 2018), pp. 133–146, available at: <https://doi.org/10.1108/S2514-175920180000002004>

217 Zenith Bank Website, available at: <www.zenithbank.com/csr/>; GT Bank Website, available at: <www.gtbank.com/about/corporate-social-responsibility>; Fidelity Bank Website, available at: <https://csr.fidelitybank.ng/about/>; UBA Website, available at: <www.ubagroup.com/uba-foundation/>; Access Bank Website, available at: <www.accessbankplc.com/pages/sustainable-banking/our-community-investments/Community-Support.aspx>; WEMA Bank Website, available at: <www.wemabank.com/csr/>

the nature of the projects being embarked upon. This would require careful consideration of the projects that would be most impactful in meeting the needs of the local communities while also aligning with the strategic goals of the DMBs. Only through such initiatives can DMBs significantly contribute to the nation's development while fulfilling their social responsibility.[218] CSR initiatives in Nigeria should not only be meaningful but should also be impactful. Therefore, for banks to contribute towards attaining sustainable development goals, particularly eradicating extreme poverty, CSR must address the shortage of infrastructural development, human capacity building, financial inclusion, and women's empowerment.[219] CSR must be understood differently from its interpretation under the Anglo-Saxon model.[220] A more stakeholder-oriented CSR with government participation to provide a regulatory framework for implementing and enforcing DMB CSR obligations is extremely important.[221]

5.9 Conclusion

This chapter provides an examination of the current state of corporate governance regulations in Nigeria. The central argument presented is that the Nigerian corporate governance model is built upon the Anglo-Saxon model, which was transplanted from Britain to Nigeria due to the country's colonial past. From the analysis, the corporate governance framework in Nigeria presents significant institutional challenges that have resulted in limited recognition and protection of stakeholders' interests. Specifically, the corporate governance framework, generally applicable to companies, has demonstrated limited recognition and protection of stakeholders' interests. Moreover, the corporate governance framework for Nigerian Deposit Money Banks has further exemplified the challenging institutional context in Nigeria. This has manifested in the limited recognition and protection of stakeholders' interests in the Nigerian banking industry.

218 United Nation Sustainable Development Goals, available at: <www.un.org/sustainabledevelopment/poverty/> accessed 21 May 2024

219 Victor Ediagbonya, 'Incorporating CSR in corporate governance of banking institutions in a challenging institutional context: A case study of Nigeria', in David Crowther, Shahla Seifi (eds), *Governance and Sustainability: Approaches to Global Sustainability, Markets, and Governance* (Springer, Singapore, 2020), pp. 21–41

220 Victor Ediagbonya, 'Incorporating CSR in corporate governance of banking institutions in a challenging institutional context: A case study of Nigeria', in David Crowther, Shahla Seifi (eds), *Governance and Sustainability: Approaches to Global Sustainability, Markets, and Governance* (Springer, Singapore, 2020), pp. 21–41

221 Victor Ediagbonya, 'Incorporating CSR in corporate governance of banking institutions in a challenging institutional context: A case study of Nigeria', in David Crowther, Shahla Seifi (eds), *Governance and Sustainability: Approaches to Global Sustainability, Markets, and Governance* (Springer, Singapore, 2020), pp. 21–41

Reference List

Access Bank Website, available at: <www.accessbankplc.com/pages/sustainable-banking/our-community-investments/Community-Support.aspx>

Adegbite, Emmanuel, Chizu Nakajima, 'Corporate governance and responsibility in Nigeria', *International Journal of Disclosure and Governance*, 8(3), 2011, pp. 252–271

Adeoye, Aanu, 'Nigeria's new president suspends central bank governor; Godwin Emefiele's contentious policies raised doubts over the institution's independence', *The Financial Times*, 10 June 2023, available at: <www.ft.com/content/4d2d920f-a535-4fb9-806b-062948784063>

Adeyemo, Folashade, 'The Achilles' heel of whistleblowing: The position of Nigerian legislation', *Journal of International Banking Law and Regulation*, 31(2), 2016, pp. 105–109

Adodo, Ebenezer, 'Legal challenges of universal banking in Nigeria', *Modern Practice Journal of Finance & Investment Law*, 6(3–4), 2002, pp. 398–406

Ahunwan, Boniface, 'Corporate Governance in Nigeria', *Journal of Business Ethics*, 37(3), 2002, pp. 269–287

Ailemen, Ikpefan, *Issues in Banking and Finance* (The Chartered Institute of Bankers of Nigeria 2012), p. 11

Alayande, Folarin, 'Where have all the women gone?', *Thisday Newspaper*, 7 March 2020, available at: <www.thisdaylive.com/index.php/2020/03/07/where-have-all-the-women-gone/>

Anumaka, Nelson, 'The Nigeran code of corporate governance is principle based, flexible and scalable', interview with the Institute of Directors of Nigeria, available at: <www.iodnigeria.org/Portals/0/Documents/The%20Nigeria%20Code%20of%20Corporate%20Governance%202018%20is%20a%20principle%20based%20flexible%20and%20scalable.pdf?ver=2020-08-02-164202-313>

Arslan, Muhammad, Ahmad Alqatan, 'Role of institutions in shaping corporate governance system: Evidence from emerging economy', *Heliyon*, 6(3), 2020

Baffa v. Odili (2001) 15 NWLR (pt 737) 709, S.269 CAMA, 2020

Bakare, Owolabi, 'The unethical practices of accountants and auditors and the compromising stance of professional bodies in the corporate world: Evidence from corporate Nigeria', *Accounting Forum*, 31(3), pp. 277–303, 279, available at: <www.tandfonline.com/doi/pdf/10.1016/j.accfor.2007.06.001>

Banks and Other Financial Institutions Act, 2020

Business Journal, 'GT bank appoints Osaretin Demuren as new chairman', 28 April 2015, available at: <www.businessjournalng.com/gt-bank-appoints-osaretin-demuren-as-new-chairman/>

CAC History, available at: <http://new.cac.gov.ng/home/about-us/>

CBN, 'Guidelines for the appointment of independent directors', Circular to All Banks, BSD/DIR/GEN/CIR/VOL.1/013, 26 October 2007, available at: <www.cbn.gov.ng/out/circulars/bsd/2007/guidelines%20for%20the%20appointment%20of%20independent%20directors.pdf>

CBN, 'Nigerian sustainable banking principles', Central Bank of Nigeria, July 2012, available at: <www.cbn.gov.ng/out/2012/ccd/circular-nsbp.pdf>

CBN, 'Reviews 40% women board slot', *The Nation Newspaper*, 5 March 2014, available at: <https://thenationonlineng.net/cbn-reviews-40-women-board-slot/>

CBN, 'Financial institutions', available at: <www.cbn.gov.ng/Supervision/finstitutions.asp>

CBN, 'List of financial institutions: Merchant banks', available at: <www.cbn.gov.ng/Supervision/Inst-MB.asp>

CBN, 'Supervision: List of financial institutions', available at: <www.cbn.gov.ng/supervision/Inst-DM.asp> accessed 15 April 2024, This list does not include Optimus Bank that was established in January 2023

CBN Press Release, 'Central Bank of Nigeria makes board and management changes at Skye Bank Plc', available at: <www.cbn.gov.ng/out/2016/ccd/cbn%20press%20statement%20on%20skye%20bankjuly%20040716.pdf>
Central Bank of Nigeria Act, 2007
Code for Corporate Governance for Banks in Nigeria Post Consolidation, 2006
Code of Corporate Governance for Banks and Discount Houses and the Guidelines for Whistle Blowing in the Nigerian Banking Industry, 2014
Code of Corporate Governance for Banks in Nigeria Post Consolidation, available at: <www.cbn.gov.ng/OUT/PUBLICATIONS/BSD/2006/CORPGOV-POSTCONSO.PDF>
Code of Corporate Governance for Licensed Pension Operators, June 2008
Code of Corporate Governance for Public Companies, 2003
Code of Corporate Governance for Public Companies in Nigeria, 2011
Code of Corporate Governance for the Telecommunication Industry, 2016
Code of Good Corporate Governance for the Insurance Industry in Nigeria, 2009
Companies Act, 2006
Companies and Allied Matters Act, 2020
Corporate Governance Guidelines for Insurance and Reinsurance Companies, 2021
CSR (Special Provisions, etc.) Bill, 2015
Ebimobowei, Appah, Tebepah Sekeme Felix, Awuji Charles Evans, 'Directors' compensation and financial performance of deposit money banks in Nigeria', *World Journal of Finance and Investment Research*, 5(1), 2020, pp. 61–76
Ediagbonya, Victor, 'Incorporating CSR in corporate governance of banking institutions in a challenging institutional context: A case study of Nigeria', in David Crowther, Shahla Seifi (eds), *Governance and Sustainability: Approaches to Global Sustainability, Markets, and Governance* (Springer, Singapore, 2020), pp. 21–41
The Editor, 'Investors' laud suspension of FRCN corporate governance code', *The Nigerian Guardian Newspaper*, 9 November 2016, available at: <https://guardian.ng/business-services/investors-laud-suspension-of-frcn-corporate-governance-code/>
Eko Hotels v. Financial Reporting Council of Nigeria, Unreported: Suit No. FHC/L/CS/1430/2012
Ekwowusi, Sonnie, 'Whither corporate affairs commission?', *Thisday Newspaper*, Wednesday 14 July 2021
Falegan, Samuel Bandele, 'Central bank autonomy: Historical and general perspective', *Economic and Financial Review*, 33(4), 1995, pp. 416–428
Federal Republic of Nigeria v. Dr (Mrs) Cecilia Ibru, Charge FHC/L/297C/2009
Fidelity Bank Website, available at: <https://csr.fidelitybank.ng/about/>; UBA Website, available at: <www.ubagroup.com/uba-foundation/>
Financial Reporting Council of Nigeria Act, 2011
Financial Reporting Council of Nigeria Act (Amendment) Bill, 2018
First Bank of Nigeria Board of Directors, available at: <www.firstbanknigeria.com/about-us/the-leadership/board-of-directors/ibukun-awosika-profile/>
First Bank of Nigeria Is the Pioneer Commercial Bank in Nigeria, Which Started a Business in 1894
Gabriel, Omoh, 'CBN re-introduces merchant banking', *The Nigerian Vanguard*, 8 August 2010, available at: <www.vanguardngr.com/2010/08/cbn-re-introduces-merchant-banking> accessed 15 April 2024
GT Bank Annual Report, 2015, p. 15, available at: <www.gtbank.com/uploads/financial-information/2015-Year-End-Audited-Results.pdf>
GT Bank Website, available at: <www.gtbank.com/about/corporate-social-responsibility>
Harvey, Keith, Ronald Shrieves, 'Executive compensation structure and corporate governance choices', *Journal of Financial Research*, 24(4), 2001, pp. 495–512
Hedley Byrne & Co Ltd v. Heller & Partners Ltd. [1964] A.C. 465
History of the CBN, available at: <www.cbn.gov.ng/AboutCBN/history.asp>
House of Commons Treasury Committee, 'Banking crisis: Reforming corporate governance and pay in the city', Ninth Report of Session 2008–09, 12 May 2009, p. 8, available at: <https://publications.parliament.uk/pa/cm200809/cmselect/cmtreasy/519/519.pdf>

Ibrahim, Mohammed Kudu, 'Press statement on the resolution of Skye Bank Plc', Thursday, 20 September 2018, available at: <https://ndic.gov.ng/press-releases/press-statement-on-the-resolution-of-skye-bank-plc/> accessed 15 April 2024

Implementation of Sustainable Banking Principles by Banks, 'Discount houses and development finance institutions in Nigeria', CBN Circular Ref No. FPR/DIR/CIR/GEN/01/33, 24 September 2012, available at: <www.cbn.gov.ng/out/2012/ccd/circular-nsbp.pdf>

Indian Company Act, 2013

Investments and Securities Act, 2007

Khalaf, Roula, 'Nigeria's economic reforms need to regain momentum', *The Financial Times*, 3 October 2023, available at: <www.ft.com/content/a8485413-215f-488f-ac25-46fba58fa2ae>

Klein, Peter, Daniel Shapiro, Jeffrey Young, 'Corporate governance, family ownership and firm value: The Canadian evidence', *Corporate Governance: An International Review*, 13(6), November 2005, pp. 769–784. Wiley Blackwell

Makama, Godiya Allanana, 'Patriarchy and gender inequality in Nigeria: The way forward', *European Scientific Journal*, 9(17), June 2013, p. 115

Maris, Armand, 'Compulsory CSR: Indonesia takes a tough stance but clarity on definitions is lacking', available at: <www.ipra.org/news/itle/compulsory-csr-indonesia-takes-a-tough-stance-but-clarity-on-definitions-is-lacking/>

McBarnet, Doreen, 'Corporate social responsibility beyond law, through law, for law', 27 March 2009, University of Edinburgh School of Law Working Paper No. 2009/03, available at: <https://ssrn.com/abstract=1369305 or http://dx.doi.org/10.2139/ssrn.1369305>

Mehran, Hamid, Alan Morrison, Joel Shapiro, 'Corporate governance and banks: What have we learned from the financial crisis?', in Mathias Dewatripont, Xavier Freixas (eds), *The Crisis Aftermath: New Regulatory Paradigms* (Centre for Economic Policy Research, London, 2012)

Momodu, Shaka, 'The CAC and ease of doing business: The commission should live up to its responsibilities', *Thisday Newspaper*, Wednesday 21 July 2021

National Insurance Act, 1997

NDIC, 'A brief on Nigeria deposit insurance corporation to the house committee on banking and currency', October 2011, p. 6, available at: <https://ndic.gov.ng/files/NDIC%20ACTIVITIES%20FOR%20THE%20HOUSE%20COMMITTEE%20ON%20BANKING%20AND%20CURRENCY.pdf>

Nelson, Chijioke, 'Investigations uncover serial alleged frauds by Skye Bank Plc's managers', *The Guardian Newspaper*, 14 November 2018, available at: <https://guardian.ng/business-services/investigations-uncover-serial-alleged-frauds-by-skye-bank-plcs-managers/>

Nigerian Code of Corporate Governance, 2018

Nigerian Communications Act, 2003

Nmehielle, Vincent, Enyinna Nwauche, 'External-internal standards in corporate governance in Nigeria', The George Washington University Law School Public Law and Legal Theory Working Paper, 2004

Nwachukwu, Onyinye, 'Emefiele: When a Central Bank governor doubles as women's cheerleader', *BusinessDay*, 4 August 2021, available at: <https://businessday.ng/features/article/emefiele-when-a-central-bank-governor-doubles-as-womens-cheerleader/>

Odunsi, Wale, 'Mosun Belo-Olusoga replaces Gbenga Oyebode as Access Bank Chairman', *Daily Post Newspaper*, 31 July 2015, available at: <https://dailypost.ng/2015/07/31/mosun-belo-olusoga-replaces-gbenga-oyebode-as-access-bank-chairman/>

Ogbechie, Chris, 'Corporate governance practices and leadership in Nigeria', 7 June 2019, available at: <https://ssrn.com/abstract=3400913>

Ogbechie, Chris, Dimitrios Koufopoulos, 'Corporate governance practices in publicly quoted companies in Nigeria', *International Journal of Business Governance and Ethics*, 3(4), 2007, pp. 350–381

Ohuocha, Chijioke, 'Exclusive: Nigeria's banking crisis seen resolved in 2011', *Reuters*, 14 December 2011, available at: <www.reuters.com/article/businesspro-us-nigeria-amcon/exclusive-nigerias-banking-crisis-seen-resolved-in-2011-idUSTRE6BD2QK20101214>

Ojo, Helen, 'Mojekwu, Awosika, seek adoption of 30% female representation on board of Nigerian firms', *The Guardian*, 21 September 2018, available at: <https://guardian.ng/business-services/mojekwu-awosika-seek-adoption-of-30-female-representation-on-board-of-nigerian-firms/>

Okike, Elewechi, 'Corporate audit report and the structure of the market for audit services to listed companies in Nigeria: A longitudinal study', A Research Report submitted to the Research Committee of the Institute of Chartered Accountants of Nigeria, 1995

Okike, Elewechi, 'Corporate governance in Nigeria: The status quo', *Corporate Governance: An International Review*, 15(2), 2007, pp. 173–193

Okike, Elewechi, Emmanuel Adegbite, 'The code of corporate governance in Nigeria: Efficiency gains or social legitimation?', *Corporate Ownership and Control*, 9(3), 2012, pp. 262–275

Okike, Elewechi, Emmanuel Adegbite, Franklin Nakpodia, Stephen Adegbite, 'A review of internal and external influences on corporate governance and financial accountability in Nigeria', *International Journal of Business Governance and Ethics*, 10(2), 2015, pp. 165–185

Okolo v. Union Bank of Nigeria (2004) 3 NWLR (Pt.859) SC 87

Okoye, Adaeze, 'Exploring the relationship between corporate social responsibility, law and development in an African context: Should government be responsible for ensuring corporate responsibility?', *International Journal of Law and Management*, 54(5), 2012, pp. 364–378

Olatunji, Olaoye, Dada Adekola, 'Analysis of frauds in banks: Nigeria's experience', *European Journal of Business and Management*, 6(31), 2014, pp. 90–99

Omankhanlen, Alex Ehimare, 'The financial sector reforms and their effect on the Nigerian economy', *Economy Transdisciplinarity Cognition*, 15(2), 2012, pp. 45–57

Orojo, Joseph Olakunle, *Company Law and Practice in Nigeria* (3rd ed., Mbeyi and Associates, Lagos, Nigeria, 1992)

Otusanya, Julius, Sarah Lauwo, 'The role of auditors in the Nigerian banking crisis', *Accountancy Business and the Public Interest*, 9, 2010, pp. 159–204, 179

Pension Reform Act, 2004

PRA/FCA Senior Management Arrangements Systems and Controls Sourcebook, Chapter 19A, available at: <www.handbook.fca.org.uk/handbook/SYSC/19A/?view=chapter>

Rajan, Raghuram, 'The credit crisis and cycle-proof regulation', *Federal Reserve Bank of St. Louis Review*, September–October 2009, Part 1, pp. 397–402, available at: <https://doi.org/10.20955/r.91.397-402>

Rajat, Panwar, Shweta Nawani, Vivek Pandey, 'Legislated CSR: A brief introduction', in *Corporate Social Responsibility Business and Society 360* (Vol. 2, Emerald Publishing Limited, Bingley, 2018), pp. 133–146, available at: <https://doi.org/10.1108/S2514-175920180000002004>

Saanyol, Tyavzua, 'Customers reject courier services, protest CAC electronic delivery policy', *Nigerian Tribune*, 23 July 2020, available at: <https://tribuneonlineng.com/covid-19-customers-reject-courier-services-protest-cac-electronic-delivery-policy/>

Sanusi, Joseph O., 'Central banking authority, economic stability and the rule of law', A paper presented at the Ninth Annual Harvard International Development Conference, Boston, 4 April 2003, available at: <www.bis.org/review/r030530d.pdf>

Sanusi, Sanusi L., 'Global financial meltdown and the reforms in the Nigerian banking industry', *CBN Journal of Applied Statistics*, 2(1), 2010, pp. 93–98

SEC Nigeria's Consolidated Rules and Regulations, 2013

Section Securities and Exchange Commission Code of Corporate Governance for Public Companies, 2011

Solomon, Jill, *Corporate Governance and Accountability* (4th ed., John Wiley and Sons, Inc., Chichester, 2013)

Soludo, Charles Chukwuma, 'Consolidating the Nigerian banking industry to meet the development challenges of the 21st century', 6 July 2004, p. 2, available at: <www.bis.org/review/r040727g.pdf>

Stanbic Bank Our Leadership, available at: <www.standardbank.com/sbg/standard-bank-group/who-we-are/our-leadership/Sola,David%E2%80%93Borha>

Standard Chartered Bank Press Release, 'We've announced key appointments in Africa', 27 December 2018, available at: <www.sc.com/en/media/press-release/weve-announced-key-appointments-in-africa/>

Statute of General Application, 1900

Thurston, Alexander, 'The politics of technocracy in fourth Republic Nigeria', *African Studies Review*, 61, 2018, p. 215

Udo, Bassey, 'Normal business disrupted at CAC as customers protest poor services', *Premium Times Newspaper*, 15 September 2014, available at: <www.premiumtimesng.com/business/168188-normal-business-disrupted-at-cac-as-customers-protest-poor-services.html>

United Nation Sustainable Development Goals, available at: <www.un.org/sustainable development/poverty/>

Unity Bank Board of Directors, available at: <www.unitybankng.com/board-of-directors>

WEMA Bank Website, available at: <www.wemabank.com/csr/>

The World Bank, 'Reports on the observance of standards and codes', The World Bank, 2004, p. 30, available at: <www.worldbank.org/en/programs/rosc>

Zenith Bank Plc Annual Report, 31 December 2018, p. 36, available at: <www.zenithbank.com/media/2755/2018-annual-report.pdf>

Zenith Bank Website, available at: <www.zenithbank.com/csr/>

6 Corporate Governance and Banking Regulation in South Africa

6.1 Introduction

This chapter focuses on the corporate governance framework applicable to DMBs in South Africa. It begins by discussing the historical development of corporate governance in the country. It argues that the South African corporate governance model is based on the Anglo-Saxon model, which originated from the UK due to its colonial past. Furthermore, this chapter delves into the corporate governance framework in the South African banking sector to determine if it recognises stakeholders and safeguards their interests. It also scrutinises the political and socio-economic factors that impact corporate governance in the South African banking sector. Some key legislation, notably the Companies Act 71 of 2008 and the King IV Corporate Governance Code, will be examined to identify and evaluate the major challenges to effective corporate governance in the South African banking sector. Additionally, this chapter highlights the nature and scope of CSR in the South African banking sector.

6.2 Historical Development of Corporate Governance in South Africa

South Africa is known for its unique history of corporate governance practices, which have been influenced by the concentration of ownership structure in the hands of a minority white population.[1] The country's corporate structure is similar to the Anglo-Saxon shareholder model, which emphasises maximising profit for the benefit of shareholders.[2] South Africa operates a single-tier board structure, similar to the board structure of Nigerian DMBs, as examined in the previous chapter. However, South Africa has witnessed various corporate scandals due to

1 T. Nag, 'Corporate governance in South Africa', in A. Banik, A. Das Gupta, P.K. Bhaumik (eds), *Corporate Governance, Responsibility and Sustainability* (Palgrave Macmillan, London, 2015), available at: <https://doi.org/10.1057/9781137361851_5>

2 T. Nag, 'Corporate governance in South Africa', in A. Banik, A. Das Gupta, P.K. Bhaumik (eds), *Corporate Governance, Responsibility and Sustainability* (Palgrave Macmillan, London, 2015), available at: <https://doi.org/10.1057/9781137361851_5>

DOI: 10.4324/9781003474418-8

governance failures and corporate practices. Examples of corporate failures include Fidentia, MacMed, Randgold, Regal Bank, and Saambou.[3] Furthermore, besides the various corporate scandals, the global financial crisis from 2007 to 2009 has re-emphasised the importance of effective corporate governance by implementing adequate organisational risk management.[4]

The corporate governance landscape in South Africa reflects the country's history of colonialism and apartheid. Apart from South Africa being a formal British colony, thus inheriting the corporate law and corporate governance practice, another significant factor that has shaped the corporate governance framework in South Africa is the apartheid period that promoted white dominance of the economy, thereby limiting the access of black people to leadership and managerial positions. Despite the end of apartheid, the white population still largely dominates the economy of South Africa.[5] Various measures have been implemented to address this imbalance, including the enactment of legislation to empower and integrate the black population after the demise of apartheid. These measures have significant implications for corporate governance practices in South Africa. Corporate governance codes in South Africa have undergone refinements and updates over the years, leading to improvements in corporate practices.

The South African Government has made several attempts to promote effective corporate governance since 1994, when it introduced the King I Report, followed by King II in 2002, King III in 2009, and most recently, King IV in 2016. The King IV Report, enacted on 1 November 2016, became effective on 1 April 2017. It places significant emphasis on the importance of risk management and recommends that the risk committee comprise a majority of non-executive members of the governing body.

South Africa's corporate governance model has been primarily based on the Anglo-Saxon model, where corporations are expected to be able to consider the interests of other shareholders apart from those of shareholders.[6] However, post-apartheid corporate governance reforms, especially the 2002 King Report, require South African corporations to explicitly comply with several affirmative action and stakeholder corporate governance provisions to address historical socio-economic inequalities between minority white and majority black South

3 T. Nag, 'Corporate governance in South Africa', in A. Banik, A. Das Gupta, P.K. Bhaumik (eds), *Corporate Governance, Responsibility and Sustainability* (Palgrave Macmillan, London, 2015), available at: <https://doi.org/10.1057/9781137361851_5>

4 Collins G. Ntim, Sarah Lindop, Dennis A. Thomas, 'Corporate governance and risk reporting in South Africa: A study of corporate risk disclosures in the pre- and post-2007/2008 global financial crisis periods', *International Review of Financial Analysis*, 30(C), 2013, pp. 363–383, Elsevier

5 C.G. Ntim, 'Corporate governance, affirmative action and firm value in post-apartheid South Africa: A simultaneous equation approach', *African Development Review*, 25, 2013, pp. 148–172, available at: <https://doi.org/10.1111/j.1467-8268.2013.12021.x>

6 C.G. Ntim, 'Corporate governance, affirmative action and firm value in post-apartheid South Africa: A simultaneous equation approach', *African Development Review*, 25, 2013, pp. 148–172, available at: <https://doi.org/10.1111/j.1467-8268.2013.12021.x>

Africans.[7] This has resulted in South African corporations exhibiting some of the key features of the Anglo-Saxon and Continental European models of corporate governance in their annual reports, thus making the South African corporate governance model a hybrid form of corporate governance.[8]

6.3 Legal Framework for Corporate Governance in South African Banks

South Africa has attempted to strengthen its corporate governance framework by enacting several rigorous laws, including the Companies Act 71 of 2008, the Banking Act 94 of 1990, the Johannesburg Stock Exchange Listing Rules 2007, and the Financial Sector Regulation Act 9 of 2017. Additionally, South Africa has also introduced a myriad of corporate governance codes in recent times. The South African King Commission has introduced several reports that set out the philosophy, practices, principles, and outcomes that primarily set the standard for corporate governance in South Africa. The various reports from the King Commission include the King I Report, introduced in 1994; the King II Report, introduced in 2002; the King III Report, introduced in 2009; and the King IV Report, introduced in 2016. According to the South African Institute of Director, several corporate governance changes taking place both locally and internationally have necessitated the changes from King III to King IV which is founded on the African philosophy of Ubuntu instigating an unprecedented global interest in corporate governance in Africa. The King IV Report emphasises enhancing accountability by disclosing executive remunerations in three sections of the financial report: the overview of the remuneration policy, background statement, and implementation report. The King IV applies to all organisations irrespective of their incorporation or form status. One would argue that despite several attempts to enhance the corporate governance framework in South Africa, the country has been affected by major corporate governance failures in recent years due to weak implementation and enforcement of these legislations. This results from the country's context-specific issues ranging from lack of director independence to poor director disclosure occasioned by interference from control blocs and family owners, negatively impacting the banking sector. The following key legislation needs further explanation in order to understand the legal framework of corporate governance in the South African banking industry.

6.3.1 Companies Act 71 of 2008

The Companies Act No. 71 of 2008 serves as the principal legal framework governing companies, including banks, in South Africa. This legislation falls under

7 C.G. Ntim, 'Corporate governance, affirmative action and firm value in post-apartheid South Africa: A simultaneous equation approach', *African Development Review*, 25, 2013, pp. 148–172, available at: <https://doi.org/10.1111/j.1467-8268.2013.12021.x>

8 C.G. Ntim, 'Corporate governance, affirmative action and firm value in post-apartheid South Africa: A simultaneous equation approach', *African Development Review*, 25, 2013, pp. 148–172, available at: <https://doi.org/10.1111/j.1467-8268.2013.12021.x>

the oversight of the Department of Trade and Industry (DTI) through the Registrar of Companies. It delineates numerous regulatory requirements for interactions between a bank and its directors, shareholders, and other stakeholders. In South Africa, companies can establish themselves as private or public entities, each subject to distinct requirements. According to the Companies Act No. 71 of 2008, the board of directors is responsible for supervising the bank in accordance with the Articles of Association and the Memorandum of Incorporation, which define the bank's capacity, legal powers, and governance.

One would argue that Companies Act No. 71 of 2008 is more inclined to promote shareholders' value; this is because s.112 tend to guarantee the protection of shareholders against directors and management by requiring that any disposal of the whole undertaking or assets may be disposed of only after authorisation by members in the form of a special resolution.[9] The board of directors is responsible for managing a bank and has the authority to exercise all powers and functions unless the Companies Act or Memorandum of Incorporation specifies otherwise.

In accordance with the Companies Act No. 71 of 2008, publicly listed banks are required to have an audit committee. Additionally, public and private banks that meet specific criteria, such as workforce size, turnover, and the nature and extent of their activities, must appoint a social and ethics committee highlighting the importance of ethics in governance. Furthermore, publicly listed banks must appoint a COB to lead the board and a CEO to oversee management. In order to ensure the independence of the board, separate individuals must hold these positions as per listing requirements; however, there are instances where a temporary dispensation may be granted.

6.3.2 Johannesburg Stock Exchange Listing Requirements

The JSE, standing as Africa's largest stock market and ranked as the 17th largest globally, boasts a market capitalisation of $1.356 trillion as of 2023. In addition to providing listings for local and foreign companies, the JSE grants access to over 800 listed securities encompassing approximately 400 listed companies. Its listing requirements encompass diverse continuing disclosure obligations and overarching principles pertaining to disclosures by listed companies within their annual reports and financial statements. The exchange ensures comprehensive disclosure of corporate activities. In June 2022, the JSE released the Sustainability and Climate Disclosure Guidance, aimed at fostering transparency, upholding robust governance practices, and directing listed entities towards optimal environmental, social, and governance (ESG) disclosure practices. A bank listed on the JSE must include specific information in its annual report and financial statements regarding its adherence to the King Code. This includes a statement addressing the bank's implementation of the King Code. In particular, the bank is required to have a policy that ensures a clear balance of power and authority at the board level, preventing any single director from having unrestricted decision-making powers.

9 S.112 Companies Act No. 71, 2008

Additionally, the bank must have a separate COB and a CEO, with the same individual prohibited from simultaneously holding both positions. The COB must be an independent non-executive director, or the bank must provide a satisfactory explanation for any deviation from this requirement.

The JSE listing regulations necessitate the appointment of an audit committee, a remuneration committee, and a social and ethics committee by the bank to facilitate effective oversight. The composition of these board committees must adhere to the Companies Act and comply with the recommended practices in the King Code. The bank's annual reports are required to disclose a concise description of the mandates of the board committees and the number of meetings conducted. Additionally, the audit committee must ensure that the auditor's appointment is presented as a resolution at the bank's annual general meeting and confirm to the shareholders that these responsibilities have been fulfilled.

Furthermore, the JSE listing rules mandate that the board of directors or the nomination committee have a policy on promoting broader diversity at the board level, particularly regarding gender, race, culture, age, knowledge, skills, and experience. The board must disclose to shareholders in its annual report on how the board or the nomination committee has considered and applied the policy in the nomination and appointment of directors.

6.3.3 King Report on Corporate Governance

In 1994, the King Committee, chaired by Mervyn King, published the King I Report on Corporate Governance. Notably, this report represented a pioneering effort in South Africa by advocating for the implementation of the highest standards of corporate governance.[10] The King I Report incorporated numerous corporate governance standards and principles similar to those in other jurisdictions like the United Kingdom.[11] However, some have argued that the King I Report differs from the UK Cadbury 1992 code due to its introduction of an integrated approach to corporate governance. This approach encompasses ethical, social, and environmental practices, aiming to cater to a broader range of stakeholders.[12] The corporate governance codes in South Africa have undergone significant evolution, with periodic refinements and updates leading to enhancements in corporate practices. The current operational code in South Africa reflects these progressive changes.

As stated earlier, the King IV Report came into effect on 1 April 2017 and applies to all companies. The King IV Report defines corporate governance as the exercise of ethical and effective leadership by the governing body towards the achievement of these four governance outcomes: ethical culture, strong performance, effective

10 Institute of Directors, King I Code, 1994

11 P. Armstrong, N. Segal, B. Davis, *Corporate Governance, South Africa, a Pioneer in Africa* (South African Institute of International Affairs, 2005)

12 P. Armstrong, N. Segal, B. Davis, *Corporate Governance, South Africa, a Pioneer in Africa* (South African Institute of International Affairs, 2005)

control, and legitimacy.[13] The objectives of King IV encompass the promotion of corporate governance as integral to the operation of an organisation and the achievement of governance outcomes, including an ethical culture, strong performance, effective control, and legitimacy. Additionally, King IV Report aims to broaden the acceptance of its principles by ensuring accessibility and suitability for implementation across diverse sectors and organisational types. It further seeks to emphasise corporate governance as a comprehensive and interconnected set of arrangements to be comprehended and executed in an integrated manner and to advocate for transparent and meaningful reporting to stakeholders. Lastly, the King IV Report presents corporate governance as concerned with not only structure and process but also with ethical consciousness and conduct.[14]

The King IV Report is designed to be universally applicable, regardless of an organisation's incorporation status. Its principal objective is to enhance the scope of corporate governance, ensuring its suitability for implementation across diverse sectors and organisational structures.[15] In order to achieve this objective, the King IV Report contains additional guidance for specific sectors, thereby facilitating their application by those organisations.[16] The King IV Report moved away from 'apply or explain of the King III Report to 'apply and explain', driving boards to focus on compliance and outcomes. It is argued that stakeholders receive wider discretion to examine whether the four governance outcomes are achieved through the 'apply-and-explain' approach. By adopting the apply-and-explain approach, the King IV Report framework is implemented proportionally, providing adaptability in the execution of diverse practices tailored to the organisation's available resources, the extent and complexity of activities, and the size of turnover and workforce.[17] It is argued that the King III Report made it easier to report non-compliance, as the King IV Report requires the bank to comply and explain, so by reading the integrated report, one would be overwhelmed by the amount of explanation relating to compliance rather than whether the banks complied with the code or have provided an explanation for their non-compliance.

6.3.4 Banks Act 94 of 1990

The Banks Act, previously known as the Deposit-Taking Institutions Act 94 of 1990, is an important piece of legislation governing DMBs in South Africa. The Act aims to regulate and supervise the business activities of public companies that accept deposits from the public. The Act has undergone several amendments, with the most recent one being made by the Financial Sector Laws Amendment Act 23 of 2021, which became effective on 1 June 2023.

13 King IV Report, Institute of Directors of South Africa, 2016, p. 20
14 King IV Report, Institute of Directors of South Africa, 2016, p. 22
15 King IV Report, Institute of Directors of South Africa, 2016, p. 35
16 King IV Report, Institute of Directors of South Africa, 2016, p. 35
17 King IV Report, Institute of Directors of South Africa, 2016, p. 37

The Banks Act focuses on corporate governance within the banking industry, particularly in Chapter V, section 60B of the Act. According to the Act, a bank's board of directors and executive officers must establish and maintain an adequate and effective process of corporate governance that aligns with the nature, complexity, and inherent risks in the activities and business of the bank concerned.[18] The Banks Act also requires that the process of corporate governance should be established to achieve the bank's strategic and business objectives efficiently, effectively, ethically, and equitably within acceptable risk parameters. This is to ensure, *inter alia*, compliance with the strategic framework and guidelines established for the bank or controlling company,[19] including that the board and officers shall ensure compliance with all applicable laws and corporate behaviour that is universally recognised as correct and proper.[20] It should also promote a balance of interests of the shareholders and other interested persons who may be affected by the conduct of directors or executive officers of the bank or controlling company within a framework of effective accountability.[21] Additionally, mechanisms and procedures are established and maintained to minimise or avoid potential conflicts of interests between the business interests of the bank or controlling company and the personal interests of directors or executive officers of the bank or controlling company.[22] Lastly, the timely, accurate, and meaningful disclosure of matters that are material to the business of the bank or controlling company or to the interests of the shareholders of or other persons having an interest in the bank or controlling company.[23]

Based on this example, one could argue that the corporate governance regulation in the Banks Act is premised on the Anglo-Saxon corporate governance model, which prioritises the interests of shareholders over and above those of other stakeholders in the banks.

6.4 Institutional Framework for Corporate Governance of Banks in South Africa

The South African Reserve Bank (SARB) is the central bank of the Republic of South Africa and is established under s.223 of the Constitution of the Republic of South Africa.[24] The SARB is charged with upholding financial stability and plays a supervisory role over the National Payment System. Additionally, the bank's Financial Surveillance Division is entrusted with the administration of exchange controls within South Africa.[25] By virtue of s.224 of the South African Constitution

18 Banks Act 94 of 1990, s.60B (1)
19 Banks Act 94 of 1990, s.60B (2) (a)
20 Banks Act 94 of 1990, s.60B (2) (b)
21 Banks Act 94 of 1990, s.60B (2) (c)
22 Banks Act 94 of 1990, s.60B (2) (d)
23 Banks Act 94 of 1990, s.60B (2) (g)
24 s. 223 of the Constitution of the Republic of South Africa, 1996
25 South African Reserve Bank, 'Financial stability', available at: <www.resbank.co.za/en/home/what-we-do/financial-stability> accessed 27 June 2024

1996, the SARB's primary object is to protect the currency's value in the interest of balanced and sustainable economic growth in the Republic.[26] The Constitution further states that the SARB, in support of its primary objective, must perform its functions independently and without fear, favour, or prejudice.[27]

South Africa adopts a twin peaks approach for overseeing the financial sector. This framework was initiated by enacting the Financial Sector Regulation Act 9 of 2017, leading to the establishment of the Prudential Authority and the Financial Sector Conduct Authority (FSCA) in April 2018.[28] The FSCA is a statutory body that oversees market conduct related to offering financial products and services in South Africa. This includes monitoring the conduct of licensed financial institutions, such as banks, insurers, retirement funds, administrators, and market infrastructures, in accordance with various financial sector laws.[29]

The Prudential Authority is established as an independent regulatory body in accordance with s.32 FSRA. The Prudential Authority, operating within the administration of the SARB, is primarily responsible for overseeing banks, insurers, co-operative financial institutions, and financial conglomerates. Its primary objective is to uphold the safety and soundness of market infrastructures and financial institutions that offer financial products and services.[30] In addition, it protects customers against systemic financial risks from financial institutions that fail to meet their statutory and operational obligations.[31]

6.5 The South African Banking Industry

The South African banking industry is the largest in sub-Saharan Africa, with the aggregate tier 1 capital of the leading South African banks reaching approximately $42 billion in 2023.[32] There are 17 commercial banks, 5 mutual banks, 11 branches, 5 co-operative banks, and 30 representative offices.[33] The South African banking industry had total assets worth R7.5 billion. However, despite the number

26 s. 224 (1) of the Constitution of the Republic of South Africa, 1996

27 s. 224 (2) of the Constitution of the Republic of South Africa, 1996

28 South African Reserve Bank, 'Financial prudential regulation', available at: <www.resbank.co.za/en/home/what-we-do/Prudentialregulation> accessed 27 June 2024

29 South African Reserve Bank, 'Financial prudential regulation', available at: <www.resbank.co.za/en/home/what-we-do/Prudentialregulation> accessed 27 June 2024

30 South African Reserve Bank, 'Financial prudential regulation: Function of prudential authority', available at: <www.resbank.co.za/en/home/what-we-do/Prudentialregulation/functions-of-the-prudential-authority> accessed 27 June 2024

31 South African Reserve Bank, 'Financial prudential regulation: Function of prudential authority', available at: <www.resbank.co.za/en/home/what-we-do/Prudentialregulation/functions-of-the-prudential-authority> accessed 27 June 2024

32 South African Reserve Bank, 'Selected South African banking sector trends', 2024, available at: <www.resbank.co.za/content/dam/sarb/publications/prudential-authority/pa-statistics-selected-trends-monthly/2024/April%202024.pdf> accessed 29 June 2024

33 South African Reserve Bank, 'Selected South African banking sector trends', 2024, available at: <www.resbank.co.za/content/dam/sarb/publications/prudential-authority/pa-statistics-selected-trends-monthly/2024/April%202024.pdf> accessed 29 June 2024

of banks, the banking industry remains predominately dominated by the six largest banks: Standard Bank, FirstRand, Absa Bank, Nedbank, Investec Bank, and Capitec Bank, accounting for over 90% of the banking industry's total assets.[34] The South African banking system has experienced several failures caused by corporate governance issues. For instance, between 2013 and 2018, major banking crises occurred involving African Bank Investment Limited and VBS Mutual Bank. The collapse of African Bank can be attributed, in part, to its sole reliance on unsecured loans as its primary source of income and its acquisition of Ellerines in 2007. Commissioner Myburgh pointed to inadequate fiduciary oversight by the Board of African Bank Investment Ltd as a contributing factor. To rescue the bank, the South African government initiated a bail-out by investing R3 billion rand (approximately £127 million), resulting in the government obtaining a 50% ownership stake in African Bank Investment Limited. The African Bank Investment Limited and VBS Mutual Bank collapsed for similar reasons, including corporate governance failures, poor or corrupt corporate practices, reckless lending in one case, and reckless conducting of banking business in both crises.[35] Consequently, given these example, it is argued that the South African banking industry is not immune to failures and faces various challenges despite the banking regulation and corporate governance reforms.

6.6 Corporate Governance Mechanisms in Commercial Banks in South Africa

The principal corporate governance mechanism in Commercial Banks in South Africa is the board of directors. The Companies Act states that the board of directors of a bank is responsible for managing its affairs.[36] Therefore, effective corporate governance in the banking industry relies on the directors effectively fulfilling their duties and roles. The South African financial sector is primarily dominated by six major banks: Standard Bank, FirstRand, Absa Bank, Nedbank, Investec Bank, and Capitec Bank. When examining the corporate governance mechanisms in the South African banking industry, it is pertinent to direct attention to these six major banks not only due to their industry dominance but also to emphasise that the regulations outlined in the Banks Act do not apply to mutual or co-operative banks as distinct statutes govern these particular institutions. The discussion regarding corporate governance mechanisms within the board of directors will primarily focus on the following: board structure, board composition, and board committees.

34 The Banker Database, *Financial Times*, available at: <www.thebankerdatabase.com/index.cfm/search/ranking?CFID=adbff447-b60c-4e10-b1d8-34a83db41850&CFTOKEN=0> accessed 29 June 2024

35 Stephanie Giamporcaro, Matthew Marrian, 'African Bank Investment Ltd (ABIL): A South African corporate governance failure', *Emerald Emerging Markets Case Studies*, 8(2), 2018, available at: <https://doi.org/10.1108/EEMCS-05-2017-0094>

36 S.66(1) Companies Act No. 71, 2008

Board Structure

South African DMBs operate a unitary board system where the board of directors performs both managerial and supervisory functions, mirroring the Anglo-Saxon model prevalent in the United Kingdom. The appointment of the board of directors is the prerogative of the shareholders, serving to advance their interests. The delineation of the board of directors' management obligations is articulated in section 66 (1) of the Companies Act No. 71 of 2008. This section stipulates that the bank's business and affairs are to be administered by, or under the guidance of, its board. The board is vested with the authority to wield all the powers and execute any of the bank's functions, save for instances where this Act or the bank's Memorandum of Incorporation dictates otherwise.[37]

Board Composition

There is no limit to the maximum number of directors a bank can have in South Africa. The Companies Act No. 71 of 2008 provided for a publicly listed company to have at least a minimum of three directors.[38] Bank directors are required to have a basic understanding of the banking business, related laws, codes of conduct, and customs that govern the activities of such institutions.[39] The competence of bank directors should match the nature and scale of the bank's business. They are expected to carry out their duties diligently, with care, and with a reasonable level of competence.[40]

To ensure the board's independence, the Banks Act 94 of 1990 provides that not more than 49%, rounded off to the next lower integral number, of the directors of a *bank* shall be employees of that *bank* or of any of its subsidiaries, or of such *bank*'s *controlling company*, or of any of such *controlling bank's* subsidiaries.[41] A controlling company shall be employees of that company or of any bank in respect of which that company is registered as a controlling company, and at least two directors must be employees of the bank.[42] Furthermore, the Banking Regulation stipulates that the chairperson of the board of directors of a bank shall not be an employee of the bank, any of the subsidiaries of the bank, the controlling company of the bank, or any subsidiary of the controlling company.[43] Looking at the six largest South African banks – Standard Bank, FirstRand, Absa Bank, Nedbank, Investec Bank, and Capitec Bank – none of the board of directors were below the minimum number stipulated by the Companies Act No. 71 of 2008.[44] However, the

37 S.66(1) Companies Act No. 71, 2008
38 S.66(2) Companies Act No. 71 of 2008
39 Regulation 40(1) of the Banking Regulations
40 Regulation 40(2) of the Banking Regulations
41 S. 60 (3)(a) Banks Act 94 of 1990
42 S. 60 (3)(b) Banks Act 94 of 1990
43 Regulation 41(1) of the Banking Regulations
44 S.66(2) Companies Act No. 71 of 2008

board size varied considerably, with Nedbank having the highest number of directors, 14,[45] and Absa Bank having the lowest number of directors, seven.[46]

Another important factor to consider when discussing board composition is gender diversity. In South Africa, no specific legislation mandates the percentage of females to be included in the board of directors, resulting in varying percentages across different boards. For instance, a few DMBs' boards of directors have an average of 40% women,[47] while others have less than 30% representation of women on their boards.[48] The representation of women on the boards of directors in South African DMBs remains significantly low despite a substantial presence of female employees within these banking institutions. Based on this example, one would argue that advancing to managerial positions and directorships within these banks presents formidable challenges for women.

Board Committees

The board of directors' committees is an important way for the board to deliver most of its responsibilities. According to the King IV corporate governance code, it is mandated that the board of directors of DMBs should have the following at least five board committees: the audit committee, nomination committee, risk committee, remuneration committee, and social and ethics committee.[49] This, to an extent, differs from the provision of s.72 (1)(a) and (b) Companies Act No. 71 of 2008, which stipulates that except to the extent that the memorandum of incorporation of a company provides otherwise, the board of a company may appoint any number of committees of directors and delegate to any committee any of the authority of the board.[50] Therefore, the board of directors is responsible for ensuring that each committee has the necessary knowledge, skills, experience, and capacity to perform its duties effectively.[51] According to the extant law, each committee should comprise at least three members.[52] All DMBs have, at minimum, all five recommended committees and fulfil the minimum membership requirement. However, it is worth mentioning that there are fewer female members within the committees relative to the overall number of female representatives on the board of directors.

45 Nedbank Group Board of Director, available at: <www.nedbank.co.za/content/nedbank/desktop/gt/en/aboutus/about-nedbank-group/board-of-directors.html> accessed 28 July 2024
46 Absa Board of Directors, available at: <www.absa.co.za/about-us/absa-bank/absa-bank-board/> accessed 28 July 2024
47 Board Composition, 'An experienced and diverse team', Investec Group Integrated Annual Report, 2024, available at: <www.investec.com/content/dam/international/corporate-governance/2024/Board-Composition.pdf> accessed 28 July 2024
48 Nedbank Board of Directors, available at: <www.nedbank.co.za/content/nedbank/desktop/gt/en/aboutus/about-nedbank-group/board-of-directors.html> accessed 24 July 2024
49 King IV Report, Institute of Directors of South Africa, 2016, pp. 55–57
50 S.72 (1)(a) and (b) Companies Act No. 71 of 2008
51 King IV Report, Institute of Directors of South Africa, 2016, p. 55
52 King IV Report, Institute of Directors of South Africa, 2016, p. 55

6.7 Corporate Social Responsibility in the South African Banking Industry

CSR constitutes an integral component of the South African corporate governance framework, as this is enshrined in the principal legislation. Section 72 (4) of the Companies Act No. 71 of 2008 empowers the Minister, through regulation, to mandate that a company or a category of companies establish a social and ethics committee if it is deemed to be in the public interest, taking into consideration its annual turnover, the scale of its workforce, and the nature and scope of its operations.[53] Regulation 43(1) of the Companies Regulations 2011 aligns with Section 72(4) of the Companies Act No. 71 of 2008. Regulation 43 (1) applies to all state-owned companies,[54] listed public companies such as DMBs,[55] and any other company that has scored above 500 points in at least two of the previous five years.[56] The social and ethics committee must consist of no fewer than three directors or prescribed officers, at least one of whom must be a director not involved in the day-to-day management of the bank's business and must not have been so involved within the previous three financial years.[57] The responsibilities and functions of the social and ethics committee are specifically delineated under Regulation 43 (5) to encompass the oversight of the bank's operations in accordance with pertinent legislation, legal requirements, and prevailing best practice codes.[58] This encompasses social and economic development matters, including the bank's adherence to the principles delineated in the United Nations Global Compact Principles and the OECD recommendations on corruption.[59]

The social and ethics committee is tasked with addressing issues related to good corporate citizenship,[60] encompassing the bank's promotion of equality, prevention of unfair discrimination, and mitigation of corrupt practices.[61] Additionally, the social and ethics committee is mandated to review the impact of the bank's activities on the environment, health, public safety, consumer relationships, and labour and employment.[62] The social and ethics committee is authorised to bring pertinent matters to the board's attention as deemed necessary and to present a report, through one of its members, to the shareholders during the bank's annual general meeting on matters within its purview.[63]

The central argument presented in this book emphasises that there is limited stakeholder recognition and protection of stakeholders' interests. Hence, this point

53 Section 72 (4) of the Companies Act No. 71 of 2008
54 Regulation 43(1) (a) of the Companies Regulations, 2011
55 Regulation 43(1) (b) of the Companies Regulations, 2011
56 Regulation 43(1) (c) of the Companies Regulations, 2011
57 Regulation 43(4) of the Companies Regulations, 2011
58 Regulation 43(5) (a) of the Companies Regulations, 2011
59 Regulation 43(5)(a) (i) of the Companies Regulations, 2011
60 Regulation 43(5)(a) (ii) of the Companies Regulations, 2011
61 Regulation 43(5)(a) (ii) (aa) of the Companies Regulations, 2011
62 Regulation 43(5)(a) (iv) of the Companies Regulations, 2011
63 Regulation 43(5)(b) and (c) of the Companies Regulations, 2011

aligns with the CSR framework designed to promote the interests of shareholders. This justification necessitates the mandatory annual reporting obligation of the social and ethics committee to shareholders. A thorough examination of the CSR framework articulated in Regulation 43 of the Companies Regulations 2011 reveals several deficiencies in the CSR provision; it is necessary to highlight some of the deficiencies inherent in the regulation. Firstly, the mandate given to the social and ethics committee is too broad. Providing specific terms of reference would have given the committee the necessary direction. Secondly, there are ambiguities regarding the nature and extent of the matters encompassed by the mandate of the social and ethics committee. This lack of clarity inhibits the committee's ability to address these matters comprehensively. Thirdly, the vagueness and absence of explicit definitions within Regulation 43 pose further challenges. For instance, the term 'social and economic development,' to which the committee is legally required to monitor and report on, lacks definitional clarity within Regulation 43 or other law. Fourthly, the reference to the Employment Equity Act as it concerns 'social and economic development' lacks definitive guidance on whether the social and ethics committee should assume responsibility for employment equity matters and the employment equity plan, as stipulated by the Employment Equity Act. Finally, the absence of a clear CSR developmental plan, despite the monitoring and reporting obligations of the social and ethics committee to shareholders at the annual general meeting, is a notable deficiency. A well-defined CSR development plan has the potential to help DMBs carry out their CSR initiatives in a more meaningful and impactful way. Currently, CSR activities undertaken by DMBs lack coordination, with individual banks conducting their initiatives without proper engagement with key stakeholders.

6.8 Conclusion

The chapter explored the corporate governance framework in South African DMBs in order to understand the extent to which it allows for the recognition of stakeholders and the protection of stakeholder interests. The chapter explores the historical development of corporate governance in South Africa; it reveals that the corporate governance framework in South African DMBs is in *pari materia* with the corporate governance framework practised in Nigeria, both of which can be traced back to the United Kingdom due to both countries being formal British colonies. The United Kingdom's corporate governance framework is designed to promote shareholders' value at the expense of other key stakeholders. Its relative success in the United Kingdom is premised on the present functional institutions; therefore, transplanting the corporate governance model from developed countries like the United Kingdom has exacerbated challenges confronting DMBs due to the differences in the institutional environment in both countries. Therefore, in light of the argument made throughout this book that corporate governance should be context-dependent, the current corporate governance framework in Africa needs to be reformulated in line with the challenging institutional context in Africa.

Reference List

Absa Board of Directors, available at: <www.absa.co.za/about-us/absa-bank/absa-bank-board/>

Armstrong, P., N. Segal, B. Davis, *Corporate Governance, South Africa, a Pioneer in Africa* (South African Institute of International Affairs, 2005)

The Banker Database, *Financial Times*, available at: <www.thebankerdatabase.com/index.cfm/search/ranking?CFID=adbff447-b60c-4e10-b1d8-34a83db41850&CFTOKEN=0>

Banks Act 94, 1990

Board Composition, 'An experienced and diverse team', Investec Group Integrated Annual Report, 2024, available at: <www.investec.com/content/dam/international/corporate-governance/2024/Board-Composition.pdf>

Companies Act No. 71, 2008

Constitution of the Republic of South Africa, 1996

Giamporcaro, Stephanie, Matthew Marrian, 'African Bank Investment Ltd (ABIL): A South African corporate governance failure', *Emerald Emerging Markets Case Studies*, 8(2), 2018, available at: <https://doi.org/10.1108/EEMCS-05-2017-0094>

Institute of Directors, King I Code, 1994

King IV Report, Institute of Directors of South Africa, 2016

Nag, T., 'Corporate governance in South Africa', in A. Banik, A. Das Gupta, P.K. Bhaumik (eds), *Corporate Governance, Responsibility and Sustainability* (Palgrave Macmillan, London, 2015), available at: <https://doi.org/10.1057/9781137361851_5>

Nedbank Board of Directors, available at: <www.nedbank.co.za/content/nedbank/desktop/gt/en/aboutus/about-nedbank-group/board-of-directors.html>

Nedbank Group Board of Director, available at: <www.nedbank.co.za/content/nedbank/desktop/gt/en/aboutus/about-nedbank-group/board-of-directors.html>

Ntim, Collins G. 'Corporate governance, affirmative action and firm value in post-apartheid South Africa: A simultaneous equation approach', *African Development Review*, 25, 2013, pp. 148–172, available at: <https://doi.org/10.1111/j.1467-8268.2013.12021.x>

Ntim, Collins G., Sarah Lindop, Dennis A. Thomas, 'Corporate governance and risk reporting in South Africa: A study of corporate risk disclosures in the pre- and post-2007/2008 global financial crisis periods', *International Review of Financial Analysis*, 30(C), 2013, pp. 363–383, Elsevier

Regulation 40 of the Banking Regulations, 1949

Regulation 41 of the Banking Regulations, 1949

Regulation 43 of the Companies Regulations, 2011

South African Reserve Bank, 'Financial prudential regulation', available at: <www.resbank.co.za/en/home/what-we-do/Prudentialregulation>

South African Reserve Bank, 'Financial prudential regulation: Functions of prudential authority', available at: <www.resbank.co.za/en/home/what-we-do/Prudentialregulation/functions-of-the-prudential-authority>

South African Reserve Bank, 'Financial stability', available at: <www.resbank.co.za/en/home/what-we-do/financial-stability>

South African Reserve Bank, 'Selected South African banking sector trends', 2024, available at: <www.resbank.co.za/content/dam/sarb/publications/prudential-authority/pa-statistics-selected-trends-monthly/2024/April%202024.pdf>

Part C

Redefining Corporate Governance Model for Africa

7 A Case for a More Efficient Corporate Governance for Banks in Africa

7.1 Introduction

Based on the findings from the preceding chapters, it is clear that Nigerian and South African banks follow a corporate governance system based on the Anglo-Saxon model, which tends to prioritise shareholders' interests over other stakeholders. Although examining corporate governance in South Africa was important for understanding the institutional context there, it is important to note that the South African corporate governance model is also rooted in the Anglo-Saxon model despite the King IV Report on Corporate Governance advocating a stakeholder-inclusive approach in which the governing body takes into account the legitimate and reasonable needs, interests, and expectations of all material stakeholders in the execution of its duties, in the best interests of the company. This provision is in *pari materia* with s.305(3)(4) CAMA. Directors are to consider the impact of the company's operations on the environment in the community, and directors are also required to consider employees' interests when performing their functions.[1] However, s.305(9) CAMA 2020 took away the power of enforcement from these stakeholders by stating that only the shareholders can enforce against the directors for breach of duty.[2] Consequently, both countries encounter similar challenges, such as limited protection for stakeholders and recognition of their interests, as well as instances of banking failure due to corruption and non-compliance with regulations. Furthermore, the proliferation of corporate governance regulations presents challenges in terms of enforcement. Because both countries face similar challenges and have a similar institutional context, the remaining discussion in this chapter and the next will focus on Nigeria, as the proposed recommendations can be relevant to banks in Africa with a similar institutional context.

1 S.305 (3)(4) CAMA, 2020
2 S.305 (9) CAMA, 2020

DOI: 10.4324/9781003474418-10

7.2 A Case for Change of Corporate Governance Direction for African Banks

As evident from the discussions in Chapters 5 and 6, the Nigeria and South African corporate governance model is premised on the shareholder primacy model. However, the shareholder primacy model has been criticised for relying on flawed assumptions, rendering it normatively indefensible. The shareholder primacy model has been rebranded as the ESV model because of its many criticisms. The ESV model purports to recognise some stakeholders and their interests by requiring directors to consider the interests of stakeholders like employees and customers when promoting the company's success for the benefit of its shareholders.[3] However, it is argued that although, theoretically, the ESV model mandates directors to have regard to constituents listed in the relevant section of the Act,[4] such as employees and customers, this is the mere codification of the common law objective of the corporate which is profits maximisation for shareholders' benefit and nothing more.

Furthermore, the ESV model has been criticised for imposing a subjective standard by requiring directors to act in good faith, which appears to be counterproductive to the stakeholders listed in the section.[5] It does not appear to set any standard for directors to follow.[6] All that matters is for the directors to show that they acted in good faith regardless of their decision. Besides these shortcomings and others already discussed in Chapter 3,[7] it is argued that the shareholder primacy model is not intended to flourish in countries with challenging institutional settings such as Nigeria. To thrive, shareholder primacy model requires functioning and enabling institutional arrangements. For example, the corporate governance framework in the UK is based on the shareholder primacy model. Its relative success is premised on a strong legal system, robust capital markets, and active participation by civil societies, amongst others.

On the other hand, literature on corporate governance has presented the stakeholder model as a normatively attractive alternative to the shareholder-oriented model. However, in a bid to remedy the criticisms of the shareholder-oriented model, the stakeholder theorists have developed a theoretical framework that is not only confusing but also impracticable.[8] It is argued that the confusion arises from the dif-

3 S.172, UK Companies Act, 2006

4 S.172, UK Companies Act, 2006

5 Victor Ediagbonya, 'The scope of directors duties under the provision of section 172 of companies act of UK, corporate law', *Corporate Governance Journal*, 6 June 2017, available at: <http://dx.doi.org/10.2139/ssrn.2982033>

6 Victor Ediagbonya, 'The scope of directors duties under the provision of section 172 of companies act of UK, corporate law', *Corporate Governance Journal*, 6 June 2017, available at: <http://dx.doi.org/10.2139/ssrn.2982033>

7 See the section on ESV under theories of Corporate Governance

8 Henry Hansmann, Reinier Kraakman, 'The end of history for corporate law', Discussion Paper No. 280, The Centre for Law, Economics, and Business, Harvard Law School Cambridge, MA, March 2000, p. 7, available at: <www.law.harvard.edu/programs/olin_center/papers/pdf/280.pdf> accessed 21 June 2024

ficulty in identifying stakeholders and balancing their interests adequately.[9] Thomas Clarke argues that the stakeholder theory is intellectually appealing in its practical application; however, it gives the management excessive liberty to manoeuvre the process due to its multiple stakeholders' responsibilities.[10] Furthermore, the broad stakeholder model is also inadequate for promoting effective corporate governance in the Nigerian banking sector because of its many criticisms and Nigeria's challenging and non-enabling institutional environment. Virginia Ho argued that the theoretical framework which underpins the corporate governance model should transcend beyond the shareholders-stakeholders divide.[11] This is particularly true of countries like Nigeria and South Africa, faced with several challenges, including faulty legal transplantation, the multiplicity of regulations, systemic corruption, nepotism, tribalism, gender imbalances, and inadequate enforcement mechanisms revealed in the preceding chapters.

Keay also argued that the stakeholder theory is naïve, superficial, and unrealistic. He further states that the theory is dangerous and wholly unjustified because it undermines private property rights, denies agents' duties to principals, and destroys wealth.[12] Similarly, the shareholder theory also undermines other social actors in the corporation apart from the shareholders. Consequently, both theories are inadequate for promoting effective corporate governance in today's business world in general and Nigeria in particular.[13] Therefore, there is a need to develop an alternative corporate governance model that recognises stakeholders and protects stakeholders' interests in the Nigerian banking sector,[14] as the interest of the shareholders alone should not be the overriding purpose for which the banks exist. As discussed in Chapter 2, the banks have a key role in realising an inclusive, equitable, and sustainable economy in the countries where they operate.

Furthermore, the interests of the depositors should take precedence over those of the shareholders, as the depositors are the ones who ensure the continued existence of these banks because, without their patronage, the banks would go out of business. It is argued that apart from shareholders, there are other stakeholders the banks must recognise and protect their interests, such as depositors, employees,

9 Henry Hansmann, Reinier Kraakman, 'The end of history for corporate law', Discussion Paper No. 280, The Centre for Law, Economics, and Business, Harvard Law School Cambridge, MA, March 2000, p. 7, available at: <www.law.harvard.edu/programs/olin_center/papers/pdf/280.pdf> accessed 21 June 2024, p. 8

10 Thomas Clarke, *International Corporate Governance: A Comparative Approach* (Routledge, Abingdon, Oxon, 2007), p. 29

11 Virginia Harper Ho, 'Enlightened shareholder value: Corporate governance beyond the shareholder-stakeholder divide', *Journal of Corporation Law*, 36, 2010, p. 59

12 Andrew Keay, 'Stakeholder theory in corporate law: Has it got what it takes?', *Richmond Journal of Global Law and Business*, 9, 2010, p. 249, available at: <http://scholarship.richmond.edu/global/vol.9/iss3/2>

13 Andrew Keay, *The Corporate Objective Corporations, Globalisation, and the Law* (Edward Elgar Publishing Ltd., Cheltenham, 2011), p. 16

14 Andrew Keay, *The Corporate Objective Corporations, Globalisation, and the Law* (Edward Elgar Publishing Ltd., Cheltenham, 2011), p. 18

creditors, government, customers, and local communities. These are the key stakeholders in the Nigerian banking sector on which the FSM framework is built on. Therefore, it is imperative to consider the justification of the FSM here before proceeding to explore the FSM in detail in the next chapter.

The theoretical justifications for banking regulation, as well as the positive and normative theories of banking regulation, were examined in Chapter 3. The aim was to demonstrate that these theories, particularly the market failure theory, which is a form of positive theory and the interest group theories, particularly those that concern stakeholders' interests in regulation, which is a form of the normative theory, provided the rationale for banking regulation. The analysis highlighted the fundamental assumptions of the positivist theory of banking regulation that government intervention through regulation is necessary because of market failures. The positivist theorists contended that there is no perfect market due to information asymmetries, negative externalities, risk culture, and moral hazards. These market failures were discussed earlier in Chapter 3, thus forming the primary justification for banking regulation.

The findings from the two preceding chapters show that government interventions have not entirely resolved poor corporate governance in the Nigerian and South African banking sectors. The problems continue despite the interventionist approach to ensure a sound and safe banking system. This book acknowledges that government intervention through regulation is justified when the right corporate governance model has the required legal backing. The FSM draws on the assumption of the positive and the normative theories of banking regulation to justify applying the model in the Nigerian banking sector as it addresses the core issues that border on market failure. For example, information asymmetry is a fundamental problem for external stakeholders, such as customers dealing with the banks. These stakeholders are not employees, or board members will have difficulty dealing with the banks because of the limited information at their disposal, as banking operations are entrenched in secrecy. The findings revealed that most Nigerian banks do not provide full and honest disclosure as the law requires. Therefore, the FSM incorporates an enforcement mechanism to ensure banks regularly disclose financial and non-financial information to stakeholders. This ensures that stakeholders' interests are protected because access to relevant information will enable stakeholders to make informed decisions. Providing such information to all stakeholders enhances the board's accountability and transparency.

The OECD guidelines for corporate governance influenced the drafting of CBN and SEC codes. Despite the CBN and SEC corporate governance codes purporting to adopt the OECD guidelines, the codes have not yielded the desired result. It is argued that the OECD guidelines also have limitations because the guidelines suggest applying soft law by implementing voluntary codes.[15] The voluntariness originates through the use of the comply-or-explain approach.[16] Many European countries have adopted the comply-or-explain mechanism; for example, the UK,

15 Andrew Keay, *The Corporate Objective Corporations, Globalisation, and the Law* (Edward Elgar Publishing Ltd., Cheltenham, 2011), p. 18

16 Andrew Keay, *The Corporate Objective Corporations, Globalisation, and the Law* (Edward Elgar Publishing Ltd., Cheltenham, 2011), p. 18

Belgium, and Germany use the comply-or-explain approach.[17] Some countries in Asia have also adopted the comply-or-explain approach; for example, in Singapore, the corporate governance code is based on the comply-or-explain approach.[18]

Despite the flexibility of the comply-or-explain regulatory approach, such as allowing different banks to adopt the code based on the size and nature of their business, one would argue that such an approach will give banks the freedom to choose and implement the most advantageous provisions of the codes. A simple way to avoid discharging their obligation under the codes would be to explain why they have not complied with those provisions. However, scholars have raised serious concerns about the quality of the explanations given by many corporations to avoid compliance with relevant provisions of the codes.[19] Andrew Keay argued that despite the incontrovertible benefits of the comply-or-explain approach, it had been criticised heavily, and there is a need for reform in this area of law.[20] Therefore, the FSM is not based on the OECD recommendation, which suggests applying soft law by adopting the comply-or-explain approach. From the findings, it was established that most Nigerian banks do not comply with the codes. If the comply-or-explain regulatory framework is adopted, most banks will prefer to explain the reason for not complying, as that may seem like the easy way out.

Because there is no convergence of institutional environments, adopting an international framework without any modifications is problematic, especially if the success of such a framework depends on the availability of functional institutions. Banks in Nigeria operate in a challenging institutional environment. The Basel guidelines are international standards that banks are expected to adopt; however, adopting the guidelines without any amendments and without considering the institutional voids in these countries would also be problematic. To a certain extent, the Basel guidelines differ from the OECD guidelines, as the former is a sector-specific guideline aimed at the banking sector, unlike the latter, which applies to banks and non-banking corporations. Both guidelines acknowledge the need for an effective board to promote sound corporate governance. However, the requirement for an effective board for banking and non-banking institutions would not necessarily be the same; for example, in terms of board composition, qualification, responsibilities, and practices, the requirement in the banking sector will be higher than that of non-bank corporations. Banks are subjected to higher requirements because of the risky nature of the banking business. Based on this argument, the Basel guidelines

17 Paul Sanderson, David Seidl, John Roberts, Bernhard. Krieger, 'Flexible or not? The comply-or-explain principle in UK and German corporate governance', Working Papers, Centre for Business Research, University of Cambridge, 2010

18 Singapore Code of Corporate Governance, 2018, available at: <www.mas.gov.sg/-/media/MAS/Regulations-and-Financial-Stability/Regulatory-and-Supervisory-Framework/Corporate-Governance-of-Listed-Companies/Code-of-Corporate-Governance-6-Aug-2018.pdf> accessed 21 June 2024

19 Sergakis Konstantinos, 'EU corporate governance: A new supervisory mechanism for the comply or explain principle?', *European Company and Financial Law Review*, 10(3), 2013, pp. 394–431

20 Andrew Keay, 'Comply or explain in corporate governance codes: In need of greater regulatory oversight?', *Legal Studies*, 34(2), 2014, pp. 279–304

are more relevant to the banking sector; however, both can still be useful as a guide in designing the FSM.

7.3 Conclusion

Based on the analysis in the preceding chapters, this chapter argues for a new shift in the corporate governance framework for banks in Africa. The main argument is that corporate governance in Nigerian banks is primarily focused on promoting the interests of shareholders, often at the expense of other stakeholders in the corporation. Both debtholders and employees are essential to the ongoing operations and success of the bank, and therefore, their interests should be protected. The current legislation allows directors to consider other stakeholders when promoting the success of the company for the benefit of its members. However, there is no regulatory framework in place to hold directors accountable if they fail to do so. Consequently, FSM, the proposed model, seeks to rectify this imbalance by ensuring that all relevant stakeholders are recognised and their interests protected.

Reference List

Clarke, Thomas, *International Corporate Governance: A Comparative Approach* (Routledge, Abingdon, Oxon, 2007), p. 29

Companies Act, 2006

Companies and Allied Matters Act, 2020

Ediagbonya, Victor, 'The scope of directors duties under the provision of section 172 of companies act of UK, corporate law', *Corporate Governance Journal*, 6 June 2017, available at: <http://dx.doi.org/10.2139/ssrn.2982033>

Hansmann, Henry, Reinier Kraakman, 'The end of history for corporate law', Discussion Paper No. 280, The Centre for Law, Economics, and Business, Harvard Law School Cambridge, MA, March 2000, p. 7, available at: <www.law.harvard.edu/programs/olin_center/papers/pdf/280.pdf>

Ho, Virginia Harper, 'Enlightened shareholder value: Corporate governance beyond the shareholder-stakeholder divide', *Journal of Corporation Law*, 36, 2010, p. 59

Keay, Andrew, 'Stakeholder theory in corporate law: Has it got what it takes?', *Richmond Journal of Global Law and Business*, 9, 2010, p. 249, available at: <http://scholarship.richmond.edu/global/vol9/iss3/2>

Keay, Andrew, *The Corporate Objective Corporations, Globalisation, and the Law* (Edward Elgar Publishing Ltd., Cheltenham, 2011), p. 16

Keay, Andrew, 'Comply or explain in corporate governance codes: In need of greater regulatory oversight?', *Legal Studies*, 34(2), 2014, pp. 279–304

Konstantinos, Sergakis, 'EU corporate governance: A new supervisory mechanism for the comply or explain principle?', *European Company and Financial Law Review*, 10(3), 2013, 394–431

Sanderson, Paul, David Seidl, John Roberts, Bernhard Krieger, 'Flexible or not? The comply-or-explain principle in UK and German corporate governance', Working Papers, Centre for Business Research, University of Cambridge, 2010

Singapore Code of Corporate Governance, 2018, available at: <www.mas.gov.sg/-/media/MAS/Regulations-and-Financial-Stability/Regulatory-and-Supervisory-Framework/Corporate-Governance-of-Listed-Companies/Code-of-Corporate-Governance-6-Aug-2018.pdf>

8 A Functional Stakeholder Model of Corporate Governance for Africa

8.1 Introduction

In light of the preceding discussion on the imperative to reform the corporate governance framework for banks in Nigeria, this chapter proposes an alternative corporate governance framework specifically tailored to the Nigerian banking sector. It proposes the functional stakeholder model, designed to accommodate the unique characteristics of the challenging institutional environment in Nigeria. It argues that adopting and implementing the functional stakeholder model in the Nigerian banking sector would address the imbalance, thus allowing for the recognition of relevant stakeholders and protecting their interests. The remainder of this chapter is structured as follows: The next section explores the potential of the functional stakeholder model and summarises its key components. The second section addresses the meaning and components of the functional stakeholder model. The third section discusses the role of the board of directors as a mechanism under the functional stakeholder model. The fourth section analyses the role of CSR in the functional stakeholder model, arguing that improving CSR practices and embedding mandatory CSR obligations in the corporate governance of banks will further enhance stakeholders' recognition and protection of interests. The fifth section of this chapter explores the enforcement mechanism for the functional stakeholder model. It argues that poor enforcement mechanisms have weakened corporate governance in the Nigerian banking sector. The chapter suggests an alternative enforcement regime through the functional stakeholder model by engaging key stakeholders who will supervise the enforcement framework of the proposed model. The final section summarises the key discussions in this chapter.

8.2 Potentials of the Functional Stakeholder Model

Before embarking on the discussion on the functions and components of the FSM framework, it is necessary to summarise the key elements of the FSM to provide an insight into the potential of the model. The functional stakeholder model acknowledges the importance of international standards for promoting effective corporate governance in the banking sector. These international standards, such as the OECD guidelines and Basel principles, highlighted the need for

DOI: 10.4324/9781003474418-11

transparency, responsibility, accountability, stakeholders' engagement, and financial and non-financial disclosures in the banking sector. These principles/guidelines are undoubtedly fundamental in promoting effective corporate governance in the banking sector; however, the country's institutional environment must also be considered where these principles and guidelines are to be implemented. Therefore, where the institutional environment is challenging, as in the case of Nigeria, the international principles/guidelines need to be modified due to the institutional voids in the country, as its application should be context-dependent.

Given the challenging institutional environment, the FSM argues that several factors are necessary to ensure board effectiveness in the Nigerian banking sector. One of those factors is to have an inclusive board, as a more inclusive board composed of shareholders' and other stakeholders' representatives is a more effective board. Such a board will effectively ensure that it balances the interests of all stakeholders. Additionally, engaging non-shareholder stakeholders, like customers, employees, auditors, and bankers' associations, should promote good corporate governance in the Nigerian banking sector. Therefore, FSM is an important framework in ensuring that the board of directors and management of banks are accountable to all other stakeholders; it is a framework designed to balance the interests of all stakeholders in the Nigerian banking sector, including those of the shareholders. Apart from having an effective board, an adequate enforcement mechanism is also a core component of effective corporate governance. As such, FSM provides appropriate accountability mechanisms[1] that consider the institutional voids in Nigeria. Furthermore, having such an enforcement mechanism will ensure that all stakeholders' interests are adequately protected.

As stated earlier, the FSM draws on the non-enabling institutional environment in Nigeria to design a model that will help promote effective corporate governance in the Nigerian banking sector. It identifies key stakeholders in the banking sector that will help promote effective corporate governance. It argues that although Nigerian banks' stakeholders' group is too broad, engaging all the potential stakeholders in the corporate governance framework will be problematic and an exercise in futility. It will be challenging to incorporate the entire stakeholders' group into the corporate governance framework in the banking sector because of the number of stakeholders involved. Therefore, FSM had to devise a means of identifying those relevant stakeholders who will best serve the interest of all stakeholders either by their inclusion on the board of directors or by giving them some powers of enforcement of the corporate governance code in the Nigerian banking sector. As a result, FSM identified relevant stakeholders, including debtholders, employees, bankers' associations, Attorney-Generals, legal practitioners, judges, and customers in host communities, as the stakeholders that will help achieve effective corporate in the Nigerian banking sector.

1 Andrew Keay, Joan Loughrey, 'The framework for board accountability in corporate governance', *Legal Studies*, 35(2), 2015, pp. 252–279, ISSN 0261-3875, available at: <https://doi.org/10.1111/lest.12058>, accessed 25 July 2024

One of the innovations of FSM is its recognition of the importance of CSR within the model. The model emphasises CSR as a key element in addressing the issue of limited recognition and protection of stakeholders' interests. It suggests that CSR should be integrated into the corporate governance framework of banks in Nigeria. The FSM provides various recommendations for incorporating CSR in the corporate governance of banks, such as mandatory CSR training, inclusion of CSR in the bankers' curriculum, and monthly CSR training as part of the banks' continuous professional development requirement. Additionally, FSM proposes a mandated form of CSR, requiring banks to allocate a certain amount of their post-tax profits to CSR initiatives. FSM also advocates for DMBs to involve their customers in host communities in their CSR projects. To ensure the effective discharge of banks' CSR obligations, FSM suggests the establishment of a mandatory CSR committee within the board with the primary responsibility of ensuring banks' compliance with their CSR commitments.

8.3 Meaning and Components of the Functional Stakeholder Model

The book proposes a corporate governance model for the Nigerian banking sector, known as the functional stakeholder model (FSM). This model is not a hybrid combining two theoretical corporate governance models. The combination of the shareholder primacy and stakeholder models would be futile, as both models have been heavily criticised. In light of the findings, the existing corporate governance models are inappropriate for the Nigerian banking sector. As an alternative, FSM is a more practical corporate governance model that aims to improve the recognition and protection of stakeholders' interests in the Nigerian banking sector. FSM is envisioned to address the challenges of implementing effective corporate governance in the Nigerian banking sector, including the multiplicity of codes, multiple regulatory agencies, lack of effective sanctions, lack of accountability, ineffective board, poor judicial administration system, inadequate enforcement regime, and corruption.

Before discussing the specifics of FSM, it is necessary to explore the meaning of functional stakeholders. The word 'functional' originates from the functionalist theoretical perspective, also called functionalism, which posits that society is a social system primarily composed of different stakeholders working together to promote and protect the interests of all the stakeholders.[2] Functionalism is a general idea that can be implemented in different ways; the essence of functional analysis is the part-whole relationship, with the part being understood in terms of its contribution to the whole.[3] The functionalist theorists argue that society is

2 Jonathan Turner, 'Functionalism', in B.S. Turner (ed), *The Wiley-Blackwell Encyclopedia of Social Theory* (Wiley-Blackwell, 2017), available at: <https://doi.org/10.1002/9781118430873.est0135>

3 Wes Sharrock, John Hughes, Peter Martin, *Understanding Modern Sociology* (Sage, London, 2003), p. 15

primarily composed of social institutions, each designed to fill different needs by working together to maintain a state of balance and social equilibrium for all stakeholders.[4]

The functional theoretical perspective emphasises the interconnectedness of society by focusing on how each part can affect and is affected by other parts.[5] Emile Durkheim, one of the pioneer proponents of the functionalist theory, argued that the division of labour is key to regulating modern societies; with the division of labour, stakeholders contribute to the functioning of the social body by performing their individual assigned tasks.[6] According to Durkheim, collective consciousness, values, and rules are critical to a functioning society. Therefore, the stakeholders in performing their tasks help create a value consensus of shared common goals that help society function properly.[7] For Durkheim, societies needed to create a sense of social solidarity, making stakeholders feel a sense of belonging. Such a belief helps create social order through a commitment to shared value consensus.[8] Another renowned functionalist theorist, Talcott Parsons, who built on the work of Durkheim, sought to answer the question: How is social order possible?[9] Parsons argued that social order is possible through a central value system that provides the framework for socially acceptable behaviours. Social order is only possible if all stakeholders accept the norms and values as the fundamental guiding principle that binds the society together.[10]

Like every other theory, functionalist theorists have been criticised for portraying societies as basically harmonious.[11] It is argued that the tendency to ask what conditions incline a system towards integration and equilibrium does not necessarily exclude all possible breakdowns and the disturbance of equilibrium.[12] Therefore, this book discounts the earlier criticism because the critics had erroneously mistaken the functionalist theorists' abstract theoretical system for an empirical description of actual societies.[13]

4 Jonathan Turner, Alexandra Maryanski, *Functionalism* (The Benjamin, Cummings Publishing Company Philippines, 1979), p. 13
5 Jonathan Turner, Alexandra Maryanski, *Functionalism* (The Benjamin, Cummings Publishing Company Philippines, 1979), p. 13
6 Jonathan Turner, Alexandra Maryanski, *Functionalism* (The Benjamin, Cummings Publishing Company Philippines, 1979), p. 13
7 Jonathan Turner, Alexandra Maryanski, *Functionalism* (The Benjamin, Cummings Publishing Company Philippines, 1979), p. 13
8 Jonathan Turner, Alexandra Maryanski, *Functionalism* (The Benjamin, Cummings Publishing Company Philippines, 1979), p. 13
9 Wes Sharrock, John Hughes, Peter Martin, *Understanding Modern Sociology* (Sage, London, 2003), p. 54
10 Wes Sharrock, John Hughes, Peter Martin, *Understanding Modern Sociology* (Sage, London, 2003), p. 54
11 Wes Sharrock, John Hughes, Peter Martin, *Understanding Modern Sociology* (Sage, London, 2003), p. 53
12 Wes Sharrock, John Hughes, Peter Martin, *Understanding Modern Sociology* (Sage, London, 2003), p. 53
13 Wes Sharrock, John Hughes, Peter Martin, *Understanding Modern Sociology* (Sage, London, 2003), p. 53

In the beginning chapters of this book, the concept of stakeholders was extensively discussed, and the definition by Edward Freeman was adopted. He defined stakeholders as any group or individual who can affect or is affected by the organisation's objectives.[14] However, some scholars have also attempted to classify the stakeholders' group into instrumental versus critical or narrow versus broad distinctions.[15] Stakeholders are instrumental if they are intended to support the realisation of the overall corporate objective of the bank; here, stakeholders' engagement is viewed as a means to an end.[16] A critical view of the stakeholder groups is premised on the assumption that values must be given explicit consideration.[17] This deals with values that matter to the organisations, and such values may not be effectively balanced; the organisation may take some values more seriously than others. Identifying what values matter more to all stakeholders is critical, and balancing the choices can help achieve the desired outcome. The narrow stakeholders' view generally concerns individuals in an organisation who make its operation possible by interacting with the organisation.[18] The broad stakeholders' view is premised on the notion that all stakeholders are actually or potentially affected by the organisation's operations, not just those directly interacting with the organisation.[19]

Adopting the broad stakeholders' view might be problematic, as those who can affect or are affected by the achievement of the organisation's objectives are not easily identifiable in certain organisations because their business networks keep expanding due to the interconnectedness between businesses. For example, Business A relies on Business B for its supplies, Business B also relies on Business C for its supplies, and Business C relies on Business D for its supplies. All the businesses in the supply chain have various stakeholders, so the list keeps expanding because of the size of the business network. Therefore, one would argue that in most corporations, stakeholders generally include shareholders, investors, creditors, customers, suppliers, government, corporate regulators and supervisors, business partners, competitors, media, host communities, employees, financial institutions, and public interest groups.

14 Edward Freeman, *Strategic Management: A Stakeholder Approach* (Pitman, Boston, 1984), p. 34
15 Amanda Gregory, Jonathan Atkins, Gerald Midgley, Anthony Hodgson, 'Stakeholder identification and engagement in problem structuring interventions', *European Journal of Operational Research*, 283(1), 2019, pp. 321–340, available at: <https://doi.org/10.1016/j.ejor.2019.10.044>
16 Amanda Gregory, Jonathan Atkins, Gerald Midgley, Anthony Hodgson, 'Stakeholder identification and engagement in problem structuring interventions', *European Journal of Operational Research*, 283(1), 2019, pp. 321–340, available at: <https://doi.org/10.1016/j.ejor.2019.10.044>
17 Amanda Gregory, Jonathan Atkins, Gerald Midgley, Anthony Hodgson, 'Stakeholder identification and engagement in problem structuring interventions', *European Journal of Operational Research*, 283(1), 2019, pp. 321–340, available at: <https://doi.org/10.1016/j.ejor.2019.10.044>
18 Amanda Gregory, Jonathan Atkins, Gerald Midgley, Anthony Hodgson, 'Stakeholder identification and engagement in problem structuring interventions', *European Journal of Operational Research*, 283(1), 2019, pp. 321–340, available at: <https://doi.org/10.1016/j.ejor.2019.10.044>
19 Amanda Gregory, Jonathan Atkins, Gerald Midgley, Anthony Hodgson, 'Stakeholder identification and engagement in problem structuring interventions', *European Journal of Operational Research*, 283(1), 2019, pp. 321–340, available at: <https://doi.org/10.1016/j.ejor.2019.10.044>

In discussions regarding corporate governance within the banking sector, some scholars maintain that only stakeholders assuming risk through capital investment will qualify as relevant stakeholders.[20] However, FSM adopts the classification of stakeholders by Rodriguez, Ricart, and Sanchez, who divide stakeholders into consubstantial, contractual, and contextual.[21] Consubstantial stakeholders are essential for the company to exist; they include shareholders, creditors, investors, employees, and business partners.[22] Contractual stakeholders are those with whom the company has some form of a contractual relationship, like the banks, subcontractors, suppliers, and customers.[23] Finally, contextual stakeholders represent the social and natural system in which the company operates, and these stakeholders are host communities, society, the environment, government, and regulators.[24]

Based on this example, the FSM has identified the following stakeholders covering the three categories of stakeholders identified earlier as relevant stakeholders that will help achieve effective corporate governance in the Nigerian banking sector: employees, debtholders, customers, bankers' associations, the Attorney-General, lawyers, judges, host community, banking regulators, and public interest groups. The FSM is developed to address poor corporate governance in the Nigerian banking sector, considering Nigeria's socio-cultural, economic, and political environment. The FSM is based on the argument that the bank should be governed for stakeholders' benefit and not just to maximise shareholder profits. The FSM model did not include shareholders as part of those who will promote effective corporate governance, not because they are not relevant stakeholders but because the existing laws already offer them enough recognition and protection. For example, they have the power to appoint and remove directors. FSM advocates improving stakeholders' recognition and protecting their interests in the Nigerian banking sector. It is worth considering the roles and the nature of the stakeholders' involvement in the FSM in detail to establish how they can contribute to effective corporate governance in the Nigerian banking sector.

20 Andrew Keay, 'Stakeholder theory in corporate law: Has it got what it takes?', *Richmond Journal of Global Law and Business*, 9, 2010, p. 249, available at: <http://scholarship.richmond.edu/global/vol.9/iss3/2>

21 Miguel Rodriguez, Joan Ricart, Pablo Sanchez, 'Sustainable development and the sustainability of competitive advantage: A dynamic and sustainable view of the firm', *Creativity and Innovation Management*, 11(3), 2002, pp. 135–146, 140

22 Miguel Rodriguez, Joan Ricart, Pablo Sanchez, 'Sustainable development and the sustainability of competitive advantage: A dynamic and sustainable view of the firm', *Creativity and Innovation Management*, 11(3), 2002, pp. 135–146, 140

23 Miguel Rodriguez, Joan Ricart, Pablo Sanchez, 'Sustainable development and the sustainability of competitive advantage: A dynamic and sustainable view of the firm', *Creativity and Innovation Management*, 11(3), 2002, pp. 135–146, 140

24 Miguel Rodriguez, Joan Ricart, Pablo Sanchez, 'Sustainable development and the sustainability of competitive advantage: A dynamic and sustainable view of the firm', *Creativity and Innovation Management*, 11(3), 2002, pp. 135–146, 140

8.4 Board Composition under the Functional Stakeholder Model

The OECD guidelines and the Basel principles emphasise the importance of a strong board to promote good corporate governance in banking. It is essential for the board to be independent from the influence of a dominant CEO/COB to be effective. Given the unique nature of banks, it's crucial to reconsider how the board is composed. The first key factor for an effective board is its independence, reflected in the number of independent directors. However, there are conflicting requirements for independent directors in the CAMA, CBN, and SEC codes, while FSM advocates for a board with more independent directors. Research shows that a sufficient number of independent directors is needed to bring about meaningful change.[25] Including more independent directors on the board can bring a range of skills, qualifications, experiences, and expertise necessary to effectively monitor the management team for the benefit of all stakeholders.[26] It is argued that a board with more independent directors will be better at promoting and protecting stakeholders' interests because the independent directors come from diverse backgrounds and are not influenced by the management's incentives. Independent directors are likely to understand the evolving demands and needs of stakeholders in the banking sector and will work to balance their interests. Additionally, it is argued that independent directors will not be afraid to advocate any costly or unpopular decisions, especially regarding compliance issues, because they are not dependent on the CEO/COB or management for their incentives.[27]

Another unique characteristic of FSM is its emphasis on promoting gender diversity on boards. It is evident from the findings on the Nigerian corporate governance in DMBs demonstrate that despite the CBN's directives requiring DMBs to have at least 30% female representation on their boards and 40% of top management positions by December 2014,[28] almost all DMBs consistently failed to meet this directive. Though agitations for more gender balance boards in banks are primarily premised on the normative grounds of equity and fairness, a balanced gender composition on the board will likely result in better monitoring of the management team, as having more women on the board increases its independence.[29]

25 Bin Srinidhi, Ye Sun, Hao Zhang, Shiqiang Chen, 'How do female directors improve board governance? A mechanism based on norm changes', *Journal of Contemporary Accounting and Economic*, 16(1), April 2020, available at: <https://doi.org/10.1016/j.jcae.2019.100181>

26 Silvia Ayuso, Antonio Argandoña, 'Responsible corporate governance: Towards a stakeholder board of directors?', IESE Business School Working Paper No. 701, July 2007, available at: <https://core.ac.uk/download/pdf/6536252.pdf> accessed 25 July 2024

27 Silvia Ayuso, Antonio Argandoña, 'Responsible corporate governance: Towards a stakeholder board of directors?', IESE Business School Working Paper No. 701, July 2007, available at: <https://core.ac.uk/download/pdf/6536252.pdf> accessed 25 July 2024

28 CBN, 'Nigerian sustainable banking principles', Central Bank of Nigeria, July 2012, p. 19, available at: <www.cbn.gov.ng/out/2012/ccd/circular-nsbp.pdf> accessed 25 July 2024

29 David Carter, Frank D'Souza, Betty Simkins, Gary Simpson, 'The gender and ethnic diversity of US boards and board committees and firm financial performance', *Corporate Governance: An International Review*, 18(5), 2010, pp. 396–414

Additionally, it is argued that having more female directors on the board is more likely to enhance the board implementation of CSR strategies, as this is one way of recognising stakeholders and protecting stakeholders' interests.[30] Carter, D' Souza, Simkins, and Simpson argued that a board with more gender balance is unlikely to collude with CEOs and management to subvert all stakeholders' interests compared to a homogenous board.[31] Consequently, FSM advocates for a legislated female directorship quota on banks' boards. The Nigerian DMB boards should comprise at least 40% of women to ensure the board's independence. Such a board, with a prescribed quota of female directorship, is more inclined to prioritise CSR strategies aimed at promoting and protecting all stakeholders' interests and not only the interest of shareholders.[32]

The next aspect to consider in board composition under FSM is stakeholders' directorship. As it became evident from the findings in this book, under the shareholder primacy value model or the enlightened shareholders' value, non-shareholder stakeholders are not allowed on the board, apart from shareholders. Agency theory does not support the addition of stakeholders' directors to the board because the board's primary purpose is to align the interests of shareholders with those of directors. Additionally, according to agency theorists, having non-shareholder stakeholders on the board may lead to conflicts, such as prioritising stakeholders' interests over those of shareholders.[33] In the context of the Continental European model, it is notable that the supervisory board includes employee representatives and creditors, such as banks or their appointed representatives. However, it is imperative to mention that FSM does not endorse implementing a dual board system akin to the Continental European model. Instead, the FSM proposes appointing stakeholders' directors, specifically, creditors and employees or their representatives, to sit as directors on the boards of Nigerian DMBs.

Employee representation on the board of directors has been a prominent contemporary issue,[34] particularly in light of recent UK reforms aimed at enhancing

30 Nabil Ibrahim, John Angelidis, 'Effect of board members gender on corporate social responsiveness orientation', *Journal of Applied Business Research*, 10(1), 1 January 1994, pp. 35–40

31 David Carter, Frank D'Souza, Betty Simkins, Gary Simpson, 'The gender and ethnic diversity of US boards and board committees and firm financial performance', *Corporate Governance: An International Review*, 18(5), 2010, pp. 396–414

32 Richard Bernardi, Veronica Threadgill, 'Women directors and corporate social responsibility', *Electronic Journal of Business Ethics and Organization Studies*, 2010, 15(2), pp. 15–21; Eunjung Hyun, Daegyu Yang, Hojin Jung, Kihoon Hong, 'Women on boards and corporate social responsibility', *Sustainability Journal*, 8(4), pp. 1–26; Alison Cook, Christy Glass, 'Women on corporate boards: Do they advance corporate social responsibility?', *Human Relations*, 71(7), pp. 897–924

33 Richard Bernardi, Veronica Threadgill, 'Women directors and corporate social responsibility', *Electronic Journal of Business Ethics and Organization Studies*, 2010, 15(2), pp. 15–21; Eunjung Hyun, Daegyu Yang, Hojin Jung, Kihoon Hong, 'Women on boards and corporate social responsibility', *Sustainability Journal*, 8(4), pp. 1–26; Alison Cook, Christy Glass, 'Women on corporate boards: Do they advance corporate social responsibility?', *Human Relations*, 71(7), pp. 897–924

34 Charlotte Villiers, 'Corporate governance, employee voice and the interests of employees: The broken promise of a "world leading package of corporate reforms" ', *Industrial Law Journal*, dwaa017, available at: <https://doi.org/10.1093/indlaw/dwaa017>

employee engagement in corporate governance. As integral stakeholders, employees play a pivotal role in the operational continuity of banks; amongst other things, they invest their human resources to ensure that the banks remain a going concern. Having employees or their representatives on the board of directors will ensure that their voices are heard at the highest level, fostering mutual trust and instilling a sense of belonging.[35] Employee participation on the board is a common feature in Continental European countries, irrespective of the board structure. For example, Germany operates a dual board system comprising the management board and the supervisory board; one-third to half of the supervisory board comprises employees.[36] In contrast, Denmark operates a single-tier board system and has its boards comprising one-third of employee representatives.[37]

Employees have been identified as consubstantial stakeholders in the Nigerian DMBs under the proposed FSM. They use their skills and experience to ensure that the banks remain a going concern. As a workforce, they invest their human resources to ensure that the banks succeed, making them one of the residual risk bearers in the bank. The FSM suggests that involving employees as board directors is a fundamental step in ensuring effective corporate governance in the banking sector. This is one way to ensure adequate recognition of stakeholders and protection of stakeholders' interests.

In order to enhance employee engagement in the corporate governance framework of Nigerian DMBs, it is proposed that employees have the opportunity to elect a minimum of two and a maximum of three representatives from among themselves to serve as executive directors on the board. This excludes top management staff who may already serve on the board in an executive director capacity due to their positions. This measure aims to prevent management from influencing the election of employee directors, thus safeguarding the board's independence. Non-managerial employees would be eligible to stand for election as employee representatives on the board for a maximum of two terms, each spanning four years. This provision ensures that employees are not precluded from aspiring to managerial positions and allows for regular turnover of employee directors to bring in fresh perspectives. Additionally, employees who are elected as directors can resign at any time to pursue other career opportunities.

35 Charlotte Villiers, 'Corporate governance, employee voice and the interests of employees: The broken promise of a "world leading package of corporate reforms" ', *Industrial Law Journal*, dwaa017, available at: <https://doi.org/10.1093/indlaw/dwaa017>

36 Thomas Steger, 'Context, enactment and contribution of employee voice in the boardroom: Evidence from large German companies', *International Journal of Business Governance and Ethics*, 6, 2011, pp. 111–134, available at: <https://doi.org/10.1504/IJBGE.2011.039965> accessed 25 July 2024

37 Thomas Steger, 'Context, enactment and contribution of employee voice in the boardroom: Evidence from large German companies', *International Journal of Business Governance and Ethics*, 6, 2011, pp. 111–134, available at: <https://doi.org/10.1504/IJBGE.2011.039965> accessed 25 July 2024

It is argued that incorporating employees' representatives as directors on DMBs board will not only provide a unique opportunity for employees' voices to be heard in the boardroom but such inclusion will also help protect all stakeholder interests. Additionally, besides the skills and expertise that the employee directors can bring to the board, as insiders, employee directors can provide exclusive bank information when undertaking various board responsibilities, thereby eradicating information asymmetry and improving board efficiency.[38]

Another stakeholder's director who can help protect stakeholders' interests is the creditor. It is argued that creditors are less risk-prone than shareholders; having them directly on the board or indirectly through representatives will help mitigate excessive risk-taking by the executive directors and senior management of DMBs.[39] Consequently, FSM identifies creditors as consubstantial stakeholders in the Nigerian banking sectors because they provide finance for the continuous existence of the banks. Although there are two broad categories of creditors, the secured and unsecured, having both on the board might lead to duplication and conflict of interest. For example, a secured creditor, like banks and other financial institutions, may not have the same level of concern as a fixed deposit account operator with a considerable sum. Theoretically, secured creditors' investments are protected if the bank becomes insolvent, as the current legal framework prioritises secured creditors over unsecured creditors and shareholders.[40]

Based on this example, FSM proposes appointing a specific category of unsecured creditors, the debtholders, as directors to serve on the boards of Nigerian DMBs over other unsecured creditors. It is, therefore, imperative to differentiate between debtholders and ordinary depositors. Depositors refer to bank customers who possess current or savings accounts and retain the ability to withdraw their funds at any time.[41] In the event of concerns regarding the bank's solvency, depositors may collectively withdraw their funds, particularly if the deposits exceed the compensation they will receive through the deposit insurance scheme.[42] Such withdrawals can potentially deplete the bank's liquidity, and in most instances, the banks will not be able to meet the withdrawal demands of their customers.

Conversely, debtholders are bank customers who maintain fixed-term deposit accounts. These accounts prohibit premature withdrawal of funds but allow for withdrawal or renewal at the conclusion of the fixed term. So the longer the term, the better the interest on the money.

38 Inger Hagen, Morten Huse, 'Do employee representatives make a difference on corporate boards? Examples from Norway', in Gunnar Folke Schuappert (ed), *Perspective of Corporate Governance* (Nomos Verlagsgesellschaft, Baden-Baden, Germany, 2007), pp. 156–181

39 Klaus Hopt, 'Corporate governance of banks and financial institutions: Economic theory, supervisory practice, evidence and policy', ECGI Working Paper Series in Law, Working Paper No. 507/2020, 2020, p. 10, available at: <http://ssrn.com/abstract_id=3553780> accessed 25 July 2024

40 Section 657(6)(a) CAMA, 2020

41 Rajkama Iyerl, Manju Puri, 'Understanding bank runs: The importance of depositor-bank relationships and networks', *The American Economic Review*, 102(4), 2012, pp. 1414–1445

42 Rajkama Iyerl, Manju Puri, 'Understanding bank runs: The importance of depositor-bank relationships and networks', *The American Economic Review*, 102(4), 2012, pp. 1414–1445

The FSM advocates for debtholders to be appointed as stakeholder's directors so long as their deposits are within a minimum of two years of maturity from the time of appointment to the board. Their participation on the board is intended to enhance risk management, ultimately benefiting all stakeholders. Because they are aware that they cannot access their deposits until the maturity date, they are inclined to mitigate the risk taken by executive directors and management. Their focus would be directed towards ensuring responsible actions by executive directors rather than solely prioritising short-term profits as a result of the bonus they would derive from making those profits in the short term. Engaging in excessive risk-taking for immediate gains could undermine the banks' long-term viability. Some could argue that debtholders may exhibit reluctance in regulating the excessive risk appetite of directors, considering the safeguard of their deposits through deposit insurance in the event of a bank failure.[43] This can be particularly true of banks in developed economies; for example, in the UK, the maximum claim for deposit insurance compensation is £85,000 per customer in a bank regardless of the number of accounts held by the customer, and in the case of a joint account, the maximum amount that can be claimed is £170,000.[44] However, deposit insurance compensation paid to a bank customer in Nigeria is limited to ₦500,000 (approximately £1000).[45] This compensation amount is not enough incentive for debtholders to be reluctant to ensure effective risk management for the benefit of all stakeholders. Debtholders will not be indifferent to ensuring effective risk management; getting the deposit insurance compensation usually takes much time due to bureaucracies and bottlenecks compared to the time it takes for their fixed-term deposits to mature.

Because of the maximum amount of compensation depositors are eligible to claim in the event of bank failure in Nigeria, debtholders are like depositors without any deposit insurance cover. In most cases, the compensation they receive is relatively insignificant compared to the amount they have in the bank. FSM is based on the belief that debtholders, represented by creditors on the boards of DMBs, will actively protect the interests of all stakeholders by effectively monitoring and supervising executive directors. Eisenbeis and Kaufman argued that in the absence of a deposit insurance scheme, having depositors like creditors monitor and supervise the banks' performance would put management in check, as the threat of charging higher interest rates on credits or withdrawing funding would induce managers to act responsibly.[46] However, some might argue that such a threat by the creditors could lead to a boardroom squabble. Therefore, FSM will limit debtholder directors from unnecessarily increasing the interest they charge on their

43 Robert Eisenbeis, George Kaufman, 'Deposit insurance issue in the post-2008 crisis world', in Allen Berger, Philip Molyneux, John Wilson (eds), *The Oxford Handbook of Banking* (2nd ed., Oxford University Press, Oxford, 2015), p. 537

44 Financial Service Compensation Scheme, 'Compensation limit', available at: <www.fscs.org.uk/what-we-cover/banks-building-societies/>accessed 25 July 2024

45 Section 20(1)(b) NDIC Act, 2006

46 Robert Eisenbeis, George Kaufman, 'Deposit insurance issue in the post-2008 crisis world', in Allen Berger, Philip Molyneux, John Wilson (eds), *The Oxford Handbook of Banking* (2nd ed., Oxford University Press, Oxford, 2015), p. 538

deposits. Additionally, debtholders cannot withdraw their money until the maturity date, so it is unlikely to cause a bank run because the banks will be prepared to pay them when their money becomes due.

8.5 Role of CSR in the Functional Stakeholder Model

CSR is an integral element of FSM. Given its pivotal role in achieving effective corporate governance, it is imperative that CSR becomes ingrained within the corporate governance framework to enhance to enhance stakeholder recognition and protect their interests. The FSM advocates for a form of legislated CSR that must consider Nigeria's socio-cultural, economic, and political environment. Besides all stakeholders identified as relevant stakeholders earlier that would help protect stakeholders' interests in the Nigerian banking sector, the bankers' association, customers in the host communities, and the government are contextual stakeholders because they are in one way or another affected by the banks' operation. These contextual stakeholders will assist in implementing the CSR element of the FSM, which is geared towards stakeholders' recognition and protection of stakeholders' interests.

The Chartered Institute of Bankers in Nigeria (CIBN) serves as a professional institution for bankers in Nigeria. Presently, CIBN lacks a specific mandate for advancing an effective corporate governance framework in the Nigerian banking sector. Nevertheless, it carries out essential responsibilities, such as maintaining the register of bankers in Nigeria, formulating the bankers' training curriculum, administering professional examinations, and advocating for ethical standards and professionalism within the banking profession in Nigeria.[47] FSM aims to enhance the current responsibilities of CIBN, ensuring the organisation assumes a more active role in promoting effective corporate governance in the Nigerian banking sector. Given CIBN's responsibility for defining the knowledge and competencies necessary for prospective bankers, it becomes imperative to include CSR as an integral component of the bankers' curriculum. This approach will ensure that aspiring bankers are introduced early on to the significance of CSR as a foundational element of the corporate governance framework within the banking sector.

Additionally, FSM proposes that the responsibility of conducting CSR training should be assigned to CIBN. It recommends that all banking practitioners registered with CIBN participate in annual mandatory 12-hour continuous professional development (CPD) training focusing on CSR. This training should include at least one hour every month to keep bankers informed of their responsibility to ensure all stakeholders are fully engaged and their interests protected.

The level of stakeholder engagement with banks' CSR remains constrained, and Nigerian banks have pursued CSR initiatives from a philanthropic standpoint,

47 CIBN, 'Our principal responsibilities', available at: <www.cibng.org/institute-brief#corporate-info> accessed 25 July 2024

purporting to give back to society as corporate citizens.[48] However, these initiatives by Nigerian DMBs have been implemented without due consideration of the interconnection between purpose-driven CSR and the realisation of Sustainable Development Goals, particularly within an environment characterised by deficient basic human needs and infrastructural provisions. The CSR undertakings of Nigerian DMBs diverge from societal expectations, as the prevailing anticipation is for these initiatives to directly address the socio-economic developmental challenges in the country, including but not limited to poverty alleviation, healthcare access, infrastructure development, and educational support. Nevertheless, the DMBs' average expenditure on CSR stands at less than 1% of their post-tax profits, posing challenges in meeting the societal expectations of the Nigerian populace, particularly within the communities where these banks conduct their operations.

Therefore, FSM recommends establishing the CSR committee as a mandatory board committee tasked with engaging with customers in host communities by implementing regular consultations such as holding town hall meetings. The input of stakeholders should drive the selection of CSR projects, and following due consultation, the CSR committee will determine feasible CSR projects based on the bank's resources. In addition, the CSR committee will be responsible for drafting a contractual agreement between customers and the bank. This agreement will serve as evidence of the bank's intention to be legally bound by its commitments rather than merely offering a gratuitous promise to undertake CSR projects as a philanthropic gesture. Consequently, failure to fulfil the responsibilities outlined in the contract would constitute a breach on the part of the banks. One would argue that because legal remedies for breaches of contracts are outlined in the law, customers can have legitimate expectations of receiving remedial action for any breaches by the banks regarding the agreed projects.

Despite several attempts being made to have a legislated CSR, all failed because of a lack of consensus among the legislators. Drawing on the Indian experience, FSM proposes that there should be a CSR provision mandating banks to spend at least 3% of their average profits after tax in the preceding three years on CSR projects.[49] In addition, the CSR committee must provide regular updates regarding the CSR consultations and projects they have embarked upon in that fiscal year. The CSR committee must produce a detailed CSR report as part of the banks' annual report. The CSR report will include the composition of the CSR committee, CSR consultations for the year, selected CSR activities for the year, the funding earmarked for the CSR projects, whether the minimum threshold has been met, and the due date for completion of the projects if not already completed.

Consequently, the FSM will broaden the scope of corporate governance in the Nigerian banking sector by making CSR reporting an integral part of strategic

48 Kenneth Amaeshi, Bongo Adi, Chris Ogbechie, Olufemi Amao, 'Corporate social responsibility in Nigeria: Western mimicry or indigenous influences?', *The Journal of Corporate Citizenship, Corporate Social Responsibility in Emerging Economies*, Winter 2006, pp. 83–99

49 S135 Indian Company Act, 2013

management disclosure in the Nigerian banking sector. As a result, banks will not only be required to report on their CSR projects in annual reports but also become a binding contract between customers and the banks. Failure to execute the agreed CSR projects or any related matter in breach of the CSR contracts can be enforceable through the courts by the Attorney-General on behalf of the customers. For example, in the *People v Grasso*,[50] the Attorney-General of the State of New York brought an action on behalf of customers against Richard Grasso, the former Chairman of the New York Stock Exchange, for receiving excessive compensation. The case concerned a fundamental breakdown of corporate governance predicated upon numerous breaches of fiduciary duty when Mr. Grasso handpicked compensation committee members who determined his compensation by ignoring the benchmark set for calculating executive compensation when calculating Grasso's compensation.[51] Although this case was decided in Mr. Grasso's favour due to a legal loophole, the court found the compensation paid to Mr. Grasso was unjustifiable.[52] Therefore, in Nigeria, due to the challenging institutional context, the Attorney-General is appropriately positioned to take action on behalf of customers in cases where DMBs fall short of their CSR obligation. Nigerian DMBs engage in CSR, purporting to give back to society, and their view of CSR is that it is more like a charitable cause that is not legally binding. The current corporate governance framework does not support customers' enforceability of CSR initiatives. Customers are often subjected to DMBs' charitable gestures without adequate stakeholder involvement; this is a significant issue limiting stakeholder recognition and the protection of their interests, and as previously argued, enforcement should be a core component of banking regulation. Due to Nigeria's challenging institutional context, there are several issues with the current enforcement mechanism; therefore, an alternative enforcement framework is aimed at fostering effective corporate governance within the Nigerian banking sector. Further analysis of the suggested enforcement framework will be discussed in the following section.

8.7 Enforcement Mechanisms for the Functional Stakeholder Model

Developing a new corporate governance code tailored to the banking sector is necessary to address the absence of an enforcement framework, as this will provide a solid legal and regulatory foundation for implementing and enforcing the proposed FSM. The new code should clearly outline the responsibilities and duties of the board regarding its CSR obligations and substantiate them through legislation to ensure enhanced regulatory effectiveness. Moreover, the corporate governance code should encompass the standards that banks are anticipated to adhere to, along with delineating the available remedies and the procedures for enforcement in

50 *People v. Grasso* (2007) N.Y. Slip. Op. 3990
51 *People v. Grasso* (2007) N.Y. Slip. Op. 3990
52 *People v. Grasso* (2007) N.Y. Slip. Op. 3990

case of non-compliance. The FSM identifies several key stakeholders involved in enforcement, including the bankers' association, the Attorney-General, legal practitioners, courts, and customers in host communities. Their powers and responsibilities are discussed next.

To ensure effective compliance with corporate governance regulations in the banking sector, the CIBN will have additional enforcement powers to regulate banks. CIBN will maintain a dedicated whistleblowing telephone line that will enable stakeholders who may suspect any code breaches to register their complaints without fear of their identity being exposed. Stakeholders' reluctance to report breaches of the corporate governance code and other banking regulations is attributed to the absence of a legal framework safeguarding whistleblowers within the Nigerian banking sector. Therefore, if stakeholders complain to the CIBN directly, such complaints will be duly investigated by a dedicated committee of the CIBN. Suppose any directors or senior management staff fell short of the standard required of a competent banker given their qualifications and experience as stated in the banker's code of conduct; in that case, CIBN shall discipline those involved in line with its powers under its code of conduct.[53]

The Attorney-General under the Nigerian Constitution has unfettered powers. FSM advocates harnessing these powers in the public interest, particularly employees and customers who suffer the most when banks fail. The powers of the federal and state Attorney-Generals are provided for under s.174 and 211, respectively, of the Constitution of the Federal Republic of Nigeria (CFRN) 1999 as amended.[54] The Attorney-General is empowered to initiate and conduct criminal proceedings against any individual before any court in Nigeria.[55] Additionally, the Attorney-General can take over and continue criminal proceedings that a different authority or individual has initiated.[56] Furthermore, the Attorney-General holds the prerogative to terminate any proceeding before the court renders a judgment.[57] It is contended that despite the Attorney-General's unrestricted constitutional powers, there is an absence of documented instances wherein such authority has been utilised to address misconduct by directors and senior management personnel within the Nigerian banking sector.

Therefore, FSM supports the Attorney-General as the principal law officer[58] of the federation and the states, respectively, to take the lead in prosecuting banks' directors and senior management staff who are implicated in various corporate malfeasants resulting from the breach of the new code. Although the Attorney-General's powers to institute proceedings are expressly stated in s.174 and s.211 of the CFRN

53 Code of Conduct in the Nigerian Banking Industry: Professional Code of Ethics and Business Conduct, available at: <www.cibng.org/files/resourceDownloads/1559753366resourcehub-codes.pdf> accessed 25 July 2024
54 Sections 174 and 211 CFRN 1999 (as amended)
55 Sections 174 and 211 CFRN 1999 (as amended)
56 Sections 174 and 211 CFRN 1999 (as amended)
57 Sections 174 and 211 CFRN 1999 (as amended)
58 *State v. S.O. Ilori & Ors* (S.C. 42/1982) [1983] NGSC 37 (25 February 1983)

1999 as amended,[59] the FSM further reiterates that responsibility by mandating the Attorney-General to take action against banks' directors involved in corporate malfeasants. The prospect of prosecution by the Attorney-General is pivotal in ensuring a robust and secure banking system for the collective benefit of all stakeholders. When the Attorney-General cannot prosecute the matter due to not having time to prosecute it diligently, they can grant a fiat to any legal practitioner interested in initiating such prosecution.[60]

For the Attorney-General to deliver on it responsibility concerning the corporate governance of the Nigerian banking sector, the FSM recommends that banks be mandated to produce a detailed corporate governance report for the office of the Attorney-General every quarter. The Attorney-General shall study the report to ensure full compliance with the corporate governance framework for the banking sector. Where there is any breach, the Attorney-General shall institute proceedings against those directors and the senior management staff of the affected bank or permit any legal practitioner who has shown an interest in carrying out such prosecution to do so.[61]

A strong audit process is fundamental for effective corporate governance in the banking sector.[62] Therefore, to effectively strengthen the Nigerian banking sector's audit process, the FSM suggests that external auditors should be mandated to file annual audit reports with the Attorney-General's office. External auditors are expected to highlight irregularities and discuss such concerns with the Attorney-General. The new corporate governance framework under the FSM provides for external auditors' liability. They will be criminally liable if they cannot deliver their responsibilities with due diligence and a high professional standard. In those circumstances, the Attorney-General shall institute proceedings against them; if the Attorney-General cannot prosecute because of other commitments, they must grant a fiat to any legal practitioner interested in initiating such prosecution.[63]

Other contextual stakeholders that should be empowered to enforce the corporate governance code in the Nigerian banking sector are depositors who do not possess fixed deposit accounts. They are identified as relevant stakeholders in the Nigerian banking sector not because they only contribute to the banks' capital by maintaining savings and current accounts; however, if the banks fail, the government uses public funds to bail these banks out.[64] Given the importance of these

59 Sections 174 and 211 CFRN 1999 (as amended)

60 Section 56(1) Federal High Court Act Cap F12 2004

61 Section 56(1) Federal High Court Act Cap F12 2004

62 ICAEW, 'Audit of banks: Lessons from the crisis', 2010, available at: <www.icaew.com/-/media/corporate/archive/files/technical/financial-services/audit-of-banks-lessons-from-the-crisis.ashx?la=en> accessed 25 July 2024

63 Section 56(1) Federal High Court Act Cap F12, 2004

64 Deinibiteim Harry, Winston Madume, 'State intervention/bailout and economic stabilisation in Nigeria: Some lessons from the US', *Mediterranean Journal of Social Sciences*, 9(3), May 2018, pp. 71–78

stakeholders in the Nigerian banking sector, it is suggested that such banks' customers should be allowed to enforce corporate governance codes.

The rights accorded to these depositors under the FSM include the power to request detailed corporate governance reports from the DMBs, attend board meetings of DMBs, and the right to sue directors and senior management of Nigerian DMBs for breach of the code. DMBs will generally have 20 working days to respond to a request for the corporate governance report; for a request to be valid under the FSM, it must be in writing. If there are any concerns after receiving the report, the customer can request to attend the board meeting where their concerns will be discussed. However, their role at that meeting should be that of an observer, ensuring the complaint raised was given some consideration in the business of the day. Suppose they still have some concerns; in that case, a formal complaint should be made to the bank in writing, and the bank has eight weeks to deal with such a complaint. The customer must submit a complaint to CIBN and the Attorney-General within one month of receiving the bank's final response to their complaint or from the end of the eight weeks if they have not received any response from the bank. As prescribed by the FSM, the CIBN and the Attorney-General will have three months to resolve the issue from the date they received the complaint. The FSM has prescribed disciplinary actions and sanctions against the directors who are found culpable of the breach of the corporate governance code; such actions would deter others from engaging in illegal and unethical conduct. However, suppose the matter is not dealt with as stated earlier or within the timeframe stipulated. In that case, the customer is at liberty to approach the court for a writ of mandamus compelling the Attorney-General to commence proceedings against directors and senior management staff in breach of the corporate governance regulations.[65]

The courts also have a fundamental role in enforcing corporate governance in the Nigerian banking sector. Because of Nigeria's current legal and institutional framework, matters usually take several years to be heard. The reason for matters taking this long depends on several factors. For example, the courts are still writing in longhand, which has resulted in several backlogs of cases over the years; usually, cases take between 15 and 20 years to be decided. This is from the first trial at the High Court to the conclusion of the final appeal by the Supreme Court.[66] Another reason for the backlogs is that the courts entertain all disputes, including land, crime, civil, and family matters; as a result, they are overwhelmed with these different cases, making it difficult for the courts to deal with these matters efficiently due to lack of specialisation.[67] Consequently, the FSM proposes establish-

65 *Fawehinmi v. Akilu* (1987) 4 NWLR (Part 67) 797 SC, *A.G. Anambra State v. Nwobodo* (1992) 7NWLR (Pt 256) 711

66 Comfort Ani, 'Towards eradicating the problem of delay in criminal justice administration in Nigeria', *Legalpedia Online*, 29 May 2020, available at: <https://legalpediaonline.com/eradicating-the-problem-of-delay-in-criminal-justice-administration-in-nigeria/>

67 Enefiok Essien, 'The jurisdiction of state high courts in Nigeria', *Journal of African Law*, 44(2), 2000, pp. 264–271

ing a specialised court to deal specifically with banking law and ancillary matters. A similar system of having a specialised court was established in 1994, following a series of banking failures that undermined the soundness of the financial system as a whole.

In 1994, the Federal Military Government enacted the Failed Banks (Recovery of Debts) and Financial Malpractices in Banks Decree Number 18, which established the Failed Banks Tribunal to deal exclusively with banking law and related matters.[68] Eight directors were tried and convicted within two years after the Failed Banks Tribunal commencement.[69] Additionally, over 200 others, including directors, senior management staff, and their accomplices, were detained and prosecuted for offences relating to fraud, which caused the Nigerian banking crisis.[70] It is argued that the tribunal was effective due to its exclusive jurisdiction in dealing with banking fraud cases. Therefore, establishing a specialised court such as the Failed Bank Tribunal will help to protect all stakeholder interests. For instance, suppose a banking licence is revoked, like during the Nigerian banking crisis in 2009, when nine DMBs had their licences revoked. Even if shareholders challenge the revocation, having a specialised court in place is likely to speed up the process, and depositors would get their compensation under the deposit insurance scheme on time; unlike presently, cases take a long time to be resolved by the ordinary courts.

Following Nigeria's return to civil rule, the Failed Banks Tribunal mentioned earlier was dissolved in 1999.[71] Subsequently, all banking law and ancillary matters were transferred to the Federal High Court[72] and States High Court if those matters were related to customers' and bankers' relationships.[73] Some may argue that creating another separate court to handle banking regulation and related matters is unnecessary. This argument may seem reasonable; however, the High Courts are overwhelmed by the numerous cases before them and face several challenges, such as judges still writing using longhand, insufficient judges to handle the caseload, and most importantly, exploitation of legal loopholes by lawyers to prolong proceedings. For instance, lawyers to the litigants exploit the loopholes in the law to prolong the proceedings. For example, a prevalent tactic used by defence lawyers is to raise preliminary objections challenging the court's jurisdiction to entertain the matters.[74] The court would have to decide whether it has jurisdiction because

68 Failed Bank Decree No. 18, 1994

69 Chibuike Uche, 'The Nigerian failed banks decree: A critique', *Journal of International Banking Law*, 11(10), 1996, pp. 436–441

70 Chibuike Uche, 'The Nigerian failed banks decree: A critique', *Journal of International Banking Law*, 11(10), 1996, pp. 436–441

71 Tribunals (Certain Consequential Amendments, etc.) Decree No. 62, 1999 Laws of the Federation of Nigeria

72 Section 251(1) CFRN, 1999 (as amended)

73 Section 271(1) CFRN, 1999 (as amended)

74 Olayinka Aileru, 'Preventing delay tactics in criminal trials in Nigeria', *The Punch Newspaper*, 7 April 2016, available at: <https://punchng.com/preventing-delay-tactics-in-criminal-trials-in-nigeria/> accessed 25 July 2024

jurisdiction is fundamental to deciding cases. After all, jurisdiction is sacrosanct, no matter how sound the court's judgment is; if it has no jurisdiction, such judgment is invalid and of no effect.[75] If an act is void, then it is in law a nullity; it is not only bad but also incurably bad because you cannot put something on nothing and expect it to stay there. It will collapse.[76]

If the court dismissed the preliminary objections claiming to have jurisdiction, the lawyer for the defendants would then file an appeal to the Court of Appeal, praying the court *inter alia* for a stay of proceeding pending the determination of the appeal.[77] If the outcome of the appeal is not favourable to the appellant, they would further appeal to the Supreme Court, which in most cases dismisses the appeal. As these are interlocutory appeals, the cases are sent back to the original courts to continue the hearing of the substantive matters. The process usually takes several years from when the matters were first mentioned at the High Courts and when the Supreme Court dismissed the interlocutory appeals. An excellent example is Akingbola's case, which has dragged on for over ten years due to these trajectories.[78]

It is argued that establishing a specialised court to deal with banking law matters will eliminate the problem of determining which courts have jurisdiction. If one court is devoted to dealing with banking law matters in the Nigerian banking sector, it would eliminate the need to raise preliminary objections challenging the court's jurisdiction. Additionally, establishing a court to deal with just banking law and ancillary matters will help reduce the workloads of the High Courts. This will lead to the specialisation of judges who can efficiently handle cases in a timely manner due to their expertise in banking law.[79]

8.8 Conclusion

The chapter introduces ways to improve the recognition and protection of stakeholder interests in the Nigerian banking sector by proposing an alternative corporate governance framework, the 'functional stakeholder model.' Previous discussions have shown that Nigerian corporate governance is based on the shareholder primacy model inherited from the UK due to Nigeria's history as a former British colony. The shareholder primacy model in the Nigerian banking sector has revealed limited recognition and protection of stakeholder interests.

Based on stakeholder and institutional theories, the book suggested a different corporate governance model for the Nigerian banking sector. The aim was to

75 *Madukolu v. Nkemdilim* [1962] All NLR (Part 4)

76 As par Lord Denning in *Macfoy v. United African Company Ltd.* (1961) 3 W.L.R

77 *United Spinners (Nig) Ltd v. Chartered Bank* (2001) 14 NWLR (Pt. 732) 195 at 214

78 Felix Omohomhion, 'Supreme court dismisses Akingbola's appeal, orders case back to high court', *BusinessDay Newspaper*, 18 May 2018, available at: <https://businessday.ng/uncategorized/article/supreme-court-dismisses-akingbolas-appeal-orders-case-back-high-court/> accessed 25 July 2024

79 F. Adeyemo, 'Towards the creation of a specialist tribunal for banking law in Nigeria', *Financial Regulation International*, 20(7), 2017, pp. 18–20

improve stakeholder recognition and protection of their interests. FSM calls for the inclusion of non-shareholder stakeholders, such as employees and debtholders, in the board structure to foster effective corporate governance within the Nigerian banking sector. Furthermore, besides addressing board composition to balance stakeholder interests, FSM recommends an alternative enforcement regime, granting enforcement authority to other stakeholders such as the Attorney-General, CIBN, and customers in host communities.

FSM suggests integrating CSR into the corporate governance framework of banks in Nigeria. It is argued that a CSR mechanism incorporated into the banks' corporate governance framework will further align the interests of all stakeholders. Consequently, FSM recommends creating a board CSR committee to engage stakeholders, particularly host communities, through town hall meetings to select CSR projects for the benefit of all stakeholders. To ensure the effectiveness of CSR initiatives, FSM proposes allocating at least 2% of the bank's profit after tax for the past three years to the agreed CSR projects. Additionally, FSM suggests establishing a specialised court to handle banking law and ancillary matters, facilitating the specialisation of judges, and expediting the resolution of cases.

Reference List

Adeyemo, F., 'Towards the creation of a specialist tribunal for banking law in Nigeria', *Financial Regulation International*, 20(7), 2017, pp. 18–20

Aileru, Olayinka, 'Preventing delay tactics in criminal trials in Nigeria', *The Punch Newspaper*, 7 April 2016, available at: <https://punchng.com/preventing-delay-tactics-in-criminal-trials-in-nigeria/>

Amaeshi, Kenneth, Bongo Adi, Chris Ogbechie, Olufemi Amao, 'Corporate social responsibility in Nigeria: Western mimicry or indigenous influences?', *The Journal of Corporate Citizenship, Corporate Social Responsibility in Emerging Economies*, Winter 2006, pp. 83–99

Ani, Comfort, 'Towards eradicating the problem of delay in criminal justice administration in Nigeria', *Legalpedia Online*, 29 May 2020, available at: <https://legalpediaonline.com/eradicating-the-problem-of-delay-in-criminal-justice-administration-in-nigeria/>

Ayuso, Silvia, Antonio Argandoña, 'Responsible corporate governance: Towards a stakeholder board of directors?', IESE Business School Working Paper No. 701, July 2007, available at: <https://core.ac.uk/download/pdf/6536252.pdf>

Bernardi, Richard, Veronica Threadgill, 'Women directors and corporate social responsibility', *Electronic Journal of Business Ethics and Organization Studies*, 15(2), 2010, pp. 15–21

Carter, David, Frank D'Souza, Betty Simkins, Gary Simpson, 'The gender and ethnic diversity of US boards and board committees and firm financial performance', *Corporate Governance: An International Review*, 18(5), 2010, pp. 396–414

CBN, 'Nigerian sustainable banking principles', Central Bank of Nigeria, July 2012, p. 19, available at: <www.cbn.gov.ng/out/2012/ccd/circular-nsbp.pdf>

CIBN, 'Our principal responsibilities', available at: <www.cibng.org/institute-brief#corporate-info> accessed 25 July 2024

Code of Conduct in the Nigerian Banking Industry: Professional Code of Ethics and Business Conduct, available at: <www.cibng.org/files/resourceDownloads/1559753366resourcehub-codes.pdf>

Companies and Allied Matters Act, 2020

Constitution of the Federal Republic of Ningeria, 1999 (as amended)

Cook, Alison, Christy Glass, 'Women on corporate boards: Do they advance corporate social responsibility?', *Human Relations*, 71(7), 2018, pp. 897–924

Eisenbeis, Robert, George Kaufman, 'Deposit insurance issue in the post-2008 crisis world', in Allen Berger, Philip Molyneux, John Wilson (eds), *The Oxford Handbook of Banking* (2nd ed., Oxford University Press, Oxford, 2015)

Essien, Enefiok, 'The jurisdiction of state high courts in Nigeria', *Journal of African Law*, 44(2), 2000, pp. 264–271

Failed Bank Decree No. 18, 1994

Fawehinmi v. Akilu (1987) 4 NWLR (Part 67) 797 SC, *A.G. Anambra State v. Nwobodo* (1992) 7NWLR (Pt 256) 711

Federal High Court Act Cap F12, 2004

Financial Service Compensation Scheme, 'Compensation limit', available at: <www.fscs.org.uk/what-we-cover/banks-building-societies/>

Freeman, Edward, *Strategic Management: A Stakeholder Approach* (Pitman, Boston, 1984)

Gregory, Amanda, Jonathan Atkins, Gerald Midgley, Anthony Hodgson, 'Stakeholder identification and engagement in problem structuring interventions', *European Journal of Operational Research*, 283(1), 2019, pp. 321–340, available at: <https://doi.org/10.1016/j.ejor.2019.10.044>

Hagen, Inger, Morten Huse, 'Do employee representatives make a difference on corporate boards? Examples from Norway', in Gunnar Folke Schuappert (ed), *Perspective of Corporate Governance* (Nomos Verlagsgesellschaft, Baden-Baden, Germany, 2007)

Harry, Deinibiteim, Winston Madume, 'State intervention/bailout and economic stabilisation in Nigeria: Some Lessons from the US', *Mediterranean Journal of Social Sciences*, 9(3), May 2018

Hopt, Klaus, 'Corporate governance of banks and financial institutions: Economic theory, supervisory practice, evidence and policy', ECGI Working Paper Series in Law, Working Paper No. 507/2020, 2020, p. 10, available at: <http://ssrn.com/abstract_id=3553780>

Hyun, Eunjung, Daegyu Yang, Hojin Jung, Kihoon Hong, 'Women on boards and corporate social responsibility', *Sustainability Journal*, 8(4), 2016, pp. 1–26

Ibrahim, Nabil, John Angelidis, 'Effect of board members gender on corporate social responsiveness orientation', *Journal of Applied Business Research*, 10(1), 1 January 1994

ICAEW, 'Audit of banks: Lessons from the crisis', 2010, available at: <www.icaew.com/-/media/corporate/archive/files/technical/financial-services/audit-of-banks-lessons-from-the-crisis.ashx?la=en>

Indian Company Act, 2013

Iyerl, Rajkama, Manju Puri, 'Understanding bank runs: The importance of depositor-bank relationships and networks', *The American Economic Review*, 102(4), 2012, pp. 1414–1445

Keay, Andrew, 'Stakeholder theory in corporate law: Has it got what it takes?', *Richmond Journal of Global Law and Business*, 9, 2010, p. 249, available at: <http://scholarship.richmond.edu/global/vol.9/iss3/2>

Keay, Andrew, Joan Loughrey, 'The framework for board accountability in corporate governance', *Legal Studies*, 35(2), 2015, pp. 252–279, ISSN 0261-3875, available at: <https://doi.org/10.1111/lest.12058> accessed 25 July 2024

MacFoy v. United African Company Ltd. (1961) 3 W.L.R

Madukolu v. Nkemdilim [1962] All NLR (Part 4)

Nigerian Deposit Insurance Corporation Act, 2006

Omohomhion, Felix, 'Supreme court dismisses Akingbola's appeal, orders case back to high court', *BusinessDay Newspaper*, 18 May 2018, available at: <https://businessday.ng/uncategorized/article/supreme-court-dismisses-akingbolas-appeal-orders-case-back-high-court/>

People v. Grasso [2007] N.Y. Slip. Op. 3990

Rodriguez, Miguel, Joan Ricart, Pablo Sanchez, 'Sustainable development and the sustainability of competitive advantage: A dynamic and sustainable view of the firm', *Creativity and Innovation Management*, 11(3), 2002, pp. 135–146

Sharrock, Wes, John Hughes, Peter Martin, *Understanding Modern Sociology* (Sage Publications Ltd., London, 2003)

Srinidhi, Bin, Ye Sun, Hao Zhang, Shiqiang Chen, 'How do female directors improve board governance? A mechanism based on norm changes', *Journal of Contemporary Accounting and Economic*, 16(1), April 2020, available at: <https://doi.org/10.1016/j.jcae.2019.100181>

State v. S.O. Ilori & Ors (S.C. 42/1982) [1983] NGSC 37, 25 February 1983

Steger, Thomas, 'Context, enactment and contribution of employee voice in the boardroom: Evidence from large German companies', *International Journal of Business Governance and Ethics*, 6, 2011, pp. 111–134, available at: <https://doi.org/10.1504/IJBGE.2011.039965>

Tribunals (Certain Consequential Amendments, etc.) Decree No. 62, Laws of the Federation of Nigeria, 1999

Turner, Jonathan, 'Functionalism', in B.S. Turner (ed), *The Wiley-Blackwell Encyclopedia of Social Theory* (Wiley-Blackwell, 2017), available at: <https://doi.org/10.1002/9781118430873.est0135>

Turner, Jonathan, Alexandra Maryanski, *Functionalism* (The Benjamin, Cummings Publishing Company, Philippines, 1979)

Uche, Chibuike, 'The Nigerian failed banks decree: A critique', *Journal of International Banking Law*, 11(10), 1996, pp. 436–441

United Spinners (Nig) Ltd v. Chartered Bank (2001) 14 NWLR (Pt. 732) 195 at 214

Villiers, Charlotte, 'Corporate governance, employee voice and the interests of employees: The broken promise of a "world leading package of corporate reforms"', *Industrial Law Journal*, dwaa017, available at: <https://doi.org/10.1093/indlaw/dwaa017>

9 Conclusions, Recommendations, and Future Directions

9.1 Introduction

The main focus of this book has been to contribute to the debates on corporate governance regulation in Nigeria, particularly as it pertains to the Nigerian banking industry. The core discussion has been on how to improve the corporate governance framework in the Nigerian banking industry to allow for the recognition of stakeholders and protection of stakeholders' interests, given that Nigeria practices the Anglo-Saxon corporate governance model, which is always designed to enhance shareholder value. However, the relative success of the Anglo-Saxon model in the UK is premised on the presence of functioning institutions, and because of the challenging institutional environment in Nigeria, implementing the Anglo-Saxon model in the Nigerian banking industry has not yet prevented the series of banking failures effectively.

9.2. Summary

The general literature on corporate governance focuses on the different variations of corporate governance models: the Anglo-Saxon model, underpinned by the shareholder theory; the Continental European model and the Japanese *Keiretsu* system, both underpinned by the stakeholder theory. Nigeria inherited the Anglo-Saxon model because of its relationship with Britain as a formal colony.[1] However, a more practical issue of corporate governance in Nigeria is the failure and nonexistence of formal institutions like those in the Anglo-Saxon and Continental European countries. The institutional voids inherent in the country are connected with the poor corporate governance in the Nigerian banking industry despite the many banking reforms. One of the high points in contemporary corporate governance discourse has been whether directors should be accountable to all stakeholders, not just shareholders.

The shareholder primacy theory underpins the Anglo-Saxon corporate governance model. The shareholder theorists argued that directors should be accountable

1 Kami Rwegasira, 'Corporate governance in emerging capital markets: Whither Africa?', *Corporate Governance: An International Review*, 8(3), 2000, pp. 258–267

DOI: 10.4324/9781003474418-12

to only the shareholders because they bear the residual risk in the company. Directors are to promote the success of the company by maximising profit for the benefit of shareholders, and this has been the traditional view of the corporation.[2] According to Hansmann and Kraakman, it is not the position of corporate law to protect the interests of other stakeholders apart from shareholders; other stakeholders could seek to protect their interests through other spheres of law.[3] For example, they argued that directors should not be accountable to employees because employees could avail themselves of the protection offered by employment, contract, pension, and health and safety laws.

In contrast, stakeholder theorists contended that such a claim that corporate law should protect shareholders' interests alone is untenable in this era of globalisation[4] because employment, contract, pension, and health and safety laws are inadequate to regulate the corporation's relationship with non-shareholder stakeholders.[5] They argued that corporate law must protect the interests of all stakeholders.[6] There is also the problem of identifying the stakeholder group in the corporation. The shareholder theorists have argued that the stakeholder concept is more confusing because of the myriad definitions of stakeholders in management literature.[7] As a result, they argued that the stakeholder theory is unreliable and should be rejected.[8]

While there have been several studies on corporate governance in Nigeria, there are only a few studies in the Nigerian banking industry. Additionally, none of that research has focused on stakeholder recognition and protection of stakeholder interests, considering the challenging institutional environment in Nigeria, thereby evidencing the gap in the literature that this book has attempted to address. The main objective of this book was to explore the extent to which the Anglo-Saxon corporate governance model in the Nigerian banking industry allows for the recognition of stakeholders and the protection of stakeholders' interests. The book also intends to propose several ways of improving stakeholders' recognition and

2 Henry Hansmann, Reinier Kraakman, 'The end of history for corporate law', Yale Law School Working Paper No. 235; NYU Working Paper No. 013; Harvard Law School Discussion Paper No. 280; Yale SOM Working Paper No. ICF-00-09, January 2000

3 Henry Hansmann, Reinier Kraakman, 'The end of history for corporate law', Yale Law School Working Paper No. 235; NYU Working Paper No. 013; Harvard Law School Discussion Paper No. 280; Yale SOM Working Paper No. ICF-00-09, January 2000

4 Cynthia Williams, 'Corporate social responsibility in an era of globalisation', *University of California Davis Law Review*, 35, 2002, pp. 705–778

5 Cynthia Williams, 'Corporate social responsibility in an era of globalisation', *University of California Davis Law Review*, 35, 2002, pp. 705–778

6 Cynthia Williams, 'Corporate social responsibility in an era of globalisation', *University of California Davis Law Review*, 35, 2002, pp. 705–778

7 Samantha Miles, 'Stakeholder: Essentially contested or just confused?' *Journal of Business Ethics*, 108(3), July 2012, pp. 285–298; Roberts Phillips, Edward Freeman, Andrew Wicks, 'What Stakeholder Theory Is Not', *Business Ethics Quarterly*, 13(4), October 2003, pp. 479–502

8 Samantha Miles, 'Stakeholder: Essentially contested or just confused?' *Journal of Business Ethics*, 108(3), July 2012, pp. 285–298; Roberts Phillips, Edward Freeman, Andrew Wicks, 'What Stakeholder Theory Is Not', *Business Ethics Quarterly*, 13(4), October 2003, pp. 479–502

protecting stakeholders' interests in the corporate governance framework of the Nigerian banking industry.

The first chapter serves as an introduction to the book, establishing the necessary groundwork for understanding the background of the research problem. It delves into one of the fundamental causes of the problem: the legal transplantation of corporate governance regulations from developed economies such as the UK. The chapter argues that the relative success of the UK corporate governance framework is due to the presence of a functioning institution, which is lacking in developing and emerging economies such as Nigeria and South Africa. The chapter further outlines the nature and scope of the book, concluding with a brief overview of its structure.

The second chapter explored the conceptual and theoretical issues underpinning effective corporate governance. The chapter examined the dominant theories of corporate governance, the agency theory, stakeholder theory, enlightened shareholders value, stewardship theory, and institutional theory. The chapter explored the advantages and disadvantages of these different corporate governance theories and adopted the stakeholder and institutional theories to guide the discussions in this book.

The third chapter attempted to delineate banking regulation's conceptual and theoretical underpinning to justify the need for banking regulation. As a result, the public interest theory and the private interest theory of banking regulation were examined. The chapter argues that because of the unique nature of banks, there is a need for government intervention in the public's interests. Additionally, the approaches and strategies for banking regulation were examined, and as such, corporate governance was identified as a core component of prudential regulation; the chapter further argued that a hybrid regulatory approach is needed for banking regulation to be effective.

Chapter 4 addressed stakeholders in bank governance, corporate governance models in the banking industry, and the various mechanisms for promoting effective corporate governance in the banking industry. It argues that despite evidence suggesting the relative success of the Anglo-Saxon model in developed economies, it is not a case of one size fits all, as the application of corporate governance in any country is context-dependent. It argued that the Anglo-Saxon model is designed to promote shareholders' interest, and its success in the UK is premised on the existence of functional institutions. The chapter further argued that one way to ensure stakeholders' recognition and protection of stakeholders' interests is by embedding CSR in the corporate governance framework of banks.

In the fifth chapter, the book examines the corporate governance practice in the Nigerian banking industry to establish the extent to which it allows for the recognition of stakeholders and the protection of stakeholders' interests. It began by offering an overview of the corporate governance framework in Nigeria. It distinguished between the provisions of the CBN and SEC codes. It argued that both codes differ substantially, leaving DMBs with the problem of which code to adhere to. The chapter argued that the corporate governance model in the banking industry is designed to promote shareholders' interests. It explored the role of CSR in the corporate governance framework in the banking industry and whether the CSR initiatives are implemented to protect stakeholders' interests.

Chapter 6 delved into the examination of corporate governance in South Africa to delineate differences between the two jurisdictions and propose measures to enhance corporate governance in the Nigerian banking industry. The chapter posits that the corporate governance framework in South Africa is similar to that of Nigeria, as it is premised on the Anglo-Saxon corporate governance model practised in the UK. While acknowledging the context-specific nature of corporate governance, the chapter concludes that the South African corporate governance framework is akin to that of Nigeria, as evidenced by various banking failures despite implementing several banking and corporate governance regulatory reforms.

In the seventh chapter, the book presents a rationale for an alternative corporate governance framework, taking into account the conclusions drawn in the preceding two chapters. The prevailing corporate governance structure in both countries is built upon the Anglo-Saxon model as practised in the UK, which has achieved relative success owing to the functional institutional framework in that jurisdiction. Nonetheless, the chapter posits that the demanding institutional landscape in Nigeria and South Africa, characterised by the proliferation of corporate governance regulations, corruption, and deficient legal and regulatory systems, as evidenced by the numerous banking failures in spite of regulatory reforms, necessitates the development of an alternative corporate governance model tailored for the African context.

In the penultimate chapter, the book proposes an alternative corporate governance model to the Anglo-Saxon model, which considers Nigeria's institutional voids. The proposed FSM draws on institutional and stakeholder theories because the corporate governance framework should be context-dependent due to Nigeria's challenging institutional contexts. Additionally, contrary to the argument that the corporation must be managed for shareholders alone, the chapter argued that directors must be accountable to all stakeholders because of the interconnectedness of banks, as bank failures affect both shareholders and other stakeholders. It further argued for incorporating CSR in the corporate governance framework in the Nigerian banking industry, as such integration will help advance stakeholder recognition and protection of stakeholders' interests.

Chapter 9 summarises the main arguments from each chapter of the book. It also provides a summary of the key recommendations formulated by the FSM on how to improve stakeholder recognition and protect their interests within the banking industry, particularly those in challenging institutional contexts. Additionally, the chapter accentuates the book's contributions to the existing literature on comparative corporate governance, corporate social responsibility, and banking regulation. It discusses the practical and policy implications of the FSM for DMBs, legislators, auditors, governments, and academia, among others, and it concludes by suggesting potential areas for further research.

9.3 Recommendations

The corporate governance framework in the Nigerian banking industry currently has limited stakeholder recognition and protection of stakeholders' interests. This book provides recommendations for addressing these challenges and implementing effective corporate governance. In Chapter 8, the book proposes an alternative corporate governance framework called the functional stakeholder model for the Nigerian banking industry. It suggests involving key stakeholders, such as debtholders, employees, federal and state Attorney-Generals, professional bankers' associations, the CIBN, and other stakeholders, especially customers without a fixed deposit account, to promote effective corporate governance in the Nigerian banking industry.

The book suggests that having an efficient board is essential for effective corporate governance in the Nigerian banking industry. It argues that the board's composition is crucial for fulfilling its responsibilities. Thus, it proposes that by including debtholders on the board of directors would help mitigate the excessive risk-taking of executive directors and senior management staff. While the book emphasises maintaining a single board system, it recommends adding employees as stakeholders' directors to the board of DMBs. It suggests that having employee directors would represent the interests of all stakeholders and ensure that employees' voices are heard in boardroom decision-making. Additionally, the book argues that employee directors, being insiders, can provide valuable information to the board that may aid in decision-making, unlike outsiders, who may lack relevant information about the bank. Therefore, having employees on the board of DMBs could help address information asymmetry, which usually causes market failure.

One of the core recommendations of this book is that the federal and state Attorney-Generals be given enforcement powers due to the weak enforcement regime by banking regulators, particularly the CBN. This enforcement power will include the power to initiate legal proceedings against directors and remove directors who have been found guilty. It is argued that although Attorney-Generals have the power to prosecute criminal matters,[9] they are not proactive in prosecuting corporate law matters. If the Attorney-Generals cannot prosecute, the power can be given to any willing legal practitioner upon application to the Attorney-Generals. It is believed that if Attorney-Generals are specifically tasked with handling banks' fraud and board of directors' misconduct, bank directors will be more diligent, as they are unlikely to escape prosecution, as they will not be oblivious to the fact that if the Attorney-Generals cannot prosecute them for any reason, other legal practitioners can apply for permission to prosecute them.

It further recommended that other customers apart from debtholders should be given some rights, such as compliant rights/enforcement rights; such powers will enable them to sue directors that may breach the code. Additionally, it was suggested that contracting enforcement action be assigned to third-party organisations; for example, public agencies and members of the host community that are bank customers could be given the right to attend board meetings and be given the power to make public interest claims.

The book discusses the role of CSR in addressing socio-economic challenges in Africa by focusing on poverty alleviation, healthcare, infrastructure development,

9 Ss 174 (1)(a), 211 (1)(a) CFRN 1999 (an amended)

and education. It argues that CSR is essential for recognising and protecting stakeholders' interests. Consequently, it recommends integrating CSR into the corporate governance framework of the Nigerian banking industry to enhance information disclosure and maximise stakeholders' value, including shareholders. It also recommends establishing a mandatory CSR committee of the board to align key stakeholders' interests. As evident from the findings that banks are often hesitant to provide information on their CSR activities, it is recommended that corporate governance reports include detailed information on how banks engage with stakeholders for planning and executing CSR projects. It also recommends establishing a dedicated CSR committee of the board and including CSR in bankers' training programs to promote the importance of CSR. Additionally, it recommends that the CIBN provide regular CSR training as part of the banks' CPD requirements. Specifically, it suggests that all registered bankers undergo 12 hours of CSR training every fiscal year, ensuring a focus on CSR commitments and the board's role in setting the bank's CSR direction.

The book recommended that a board with more independent directors be established; it is important to mention that it recommends having gender equality on the board. It argues that board gender diversity is one way of ensuring the board's independence. There should be a fair percentage of women's representation on the board, as research shows that women are less likely to engage in excessive risk-taking.[10] Having a balanced board related to gender balance will improve the bank's performance and help mitigate excessive risk-taking, which is likely to occur if the board members are predominantly male.[11]

Another important recommendation is to review the current legal and regulatory corporate governance framework in the Nigerian banking industry. It argues that harmonising the codes will eradicate the discrepancies evident in the various codes applicable in the banking industry and will most likely ensure compliance with the code's requirements rather than shuttling between codes to see which code has the minimalist requirements.

Lastly, the book recommends that for proper enforcement of corporate governance in the Nigerian banking industry, a specialist banking law court should be established that deals with banking regulation and other related matters. It argues that the present framework with the High Courts dealing with banking regulation and other related matters is not fit for purpose. The courts are slow, expensive, and ineffective in resolving banking law cases. These matters often take a long time to reach trial because of the multitude of cases before them, which deal with various kinds of cases in different areas of law. The time it takes for cases to be heard in these courts delays the payment of compensation to depositors in the event of a

10 Bin Srinidhi, Ye Sun, Hao Zhang, Shiqiang Chen, 'How do female directors improve board governance? A mechanism based on norm changes', *Journal of Contemporary Accounting and Economic*, 16(1), April 2020, available at: <https://doi.org/10.1016/j.jcae.2019.100181>

11 Bin Srinidhi, Ye Sun, Hao Zhang, Shiqiang Chen, 'How do female directors improve board governance? A mechanism based on norm changes', *Journal of Contemporary Accounting and Economic*, 16(1), April 2020, available at: <https://doi.org/10.1016/j.jcae.2019.100181>

banking crisis.[12] However, establishing a specialised court to deal with banking law and ancillary matters will ensure that the cases are delivered in a timely manner by knowledgeable, independent, and impartial judges.

9.4 Contributions

This book has made significant and original contributions to the discourse on comparative corporate governance and regulations, especially in relation to DMBs and stakeholders. The key contributions of this book include the use of various theories of corporate governance to address poor corporate governance in the Nigerian banking industry, the use of different corporate governance mechanisms to analyse the corporate governance challenges in the Nigerian banking industry, and the development of an alternative framework by incorporating CSR into the corporate governance structure of the Nigerian DMBs. These original contributions to academic discourse require further discussion.

From a theoretical standpoint, this book has contributed to research in corporate governance using three different theories, namely, shareholder, institutional, and stakeholder theories, to explain corporate governance with deeper insight. Several pieces of research on corporate governance in Nigeria have focused their discussions on using the dominant shareholder theory; for example, most work by Chris Ogbechie has focused on the effectiveness of the shareholder theory in Nigerian companies.[13] In contrast, scholars like Adegbite have taken a different view from using the dominant shareholder theory to adopting the institutional theory in their analysis of Nigeria's corporate governance framework.[14] Nevertheless, what is common in existing scholarship on corporate governance in Nigeria is that most of the research only focused on the use of one corporate governance theory at any given time, as evident from the work of Ahunwan,[15] Okike,[16] Ogbechie,[17] and Ade-

12 Umaru Ibrahim, 'The challenges to deposit insurance law and practice', Keynote address delivered at The Sensitization Seminar for Court of Appeal Justices held at the Court of Appeal Complex, Abuja, 12 December 2018, available at: <https://ndic.gov.ng/keynote-address-delivered-by-alhaji-umaru-ibrahim-fcib-mni-md-ceo-of-nigeria-deposit-insurance-corporation-ndic-at-the-sensitization-seminar-for-court-of-appeal-justices-held-on-12th-december-20/> accessed 25 July 2024

13 Chris Ogbechie, 'Corporate governance practices and leadership in Nigeria', 7 June 2019, available at: <https://ssrn.com/abstract=3400913>; Chris Ogbechie, Dimitrios Koufopoulos, 'Corporate governance practices in publicly quoted companies in Nigeria', *International Journal of Business Governance and Ethics*, 3(4), 2007, pp. 350–381

14 Emmanuel Adegbite, 'Good corporate governance in Nigeria: Antecedents, propositions and peculiarities', *International Business Review*, 24(2), 2015, pp. 319–330; Emmanuel Adegbite, Chizu Nakajima, 'Corporate governance and responsibility in Nigeria', *International Journal of Disclosure and Governance*, 8(3), 2011, pp. 252–271

15 Boniface Ahunwan, 'Corporate governance in Nigeria', *Journal of Business Ethics*, 37(3), 2002, pp. 269–287

16 Elewechi Okike, 'Corporate governance in Nigeria: The status quo', *Corporate Governance: An International Review*, 15(2), 2007, pp. 173–193

17 Chris Ogbechie, 'Corporate governance practices and leadership in Nigeria', 7 June 2019', available at: <https://ssrn.com/abstract=3400913> accessed 25 July 2024

gbite.[18] This book contributes to the existing literature on corporate governance in the Nigerian banking industry, particularly since the 2007–2009 financial crisis. To the best of the author's knowledge, this is the only book to use the shareholder, stakeholder, and institutional theories as the theoretical framework underpinning the study of corporate governance in the Nigerian banking industry.

The use of three different corporate governance theories is significant because they help explain the limited recognition of stakeholders and the protection of their interests, as well as how to enhance stakeholders' interests in the Nigerian banking industry. The institutional theory allowed for exploring the institutional environment in Nigeria. The shareholder primacy theory forms the basis of the Anglo-Saxon corporate governance model, which was implemented in the Nigerian banking industry to maximise profits for the benefit of shareholders. However, this model failed to consider the challenging institutional environment in Nigeria. The book employed stakeholder theory to understand the different stakeholders in the banking industry and how to protect their interests, considering the unique nature of banks and the persistent failures in the Nigerian banking industry. It utilised institutional and stakeholder theories to identify and analyse the challenges of poor corporate governance in the Nigerian banking industry. It also applied stakeholder theory to address the limited recognition and protection of stakeholders' interests.

A significant contribution of this book to corporate governance discourse in the banking industry is establishing a nexus between corporate governance and banking regulation by identifying corporate governance as an essential aspect of prudential regulation in the banking industry. It highlights the risks involved in banking due to the collection of deposits and the subsequent lending and investing activities. The book discusses how corporate governance can be used to mitigate excessive risk-taking by the board of directors and senior management. It addresses corporate governance challenges in the Nigerian banking industry and provides insights into mechanisms that can enhance stakeholder recognition and protect their interests. The book employs various techniques to offer a comparative analysis of corporate governance across different jurisdictions, leading to a deeper understanding of mechanisms for improving stakeholder involvement and safeguarding their interests in the Nigerian banking industry.

In order to improve corporate governance practices in the Nigerian banking industry, this book proposes the FSM. In contrast to the Anglo-Saxon corporate governance model transplanted from the UK, the FSM takes into account the specific peculiarity of the Nigerian institutional environment. It suggests the inclusion of non-shareholder stakeholders, such as debtholders and employees, in the boards of DMBs as drivers of effective corporate governance; their inclusion will ensure that key stakeholders are recognised, and their interests are equally protected.

The book made an original contribution by incorporating CSR into the corporate governance framework of Nigerian DMBs. It suggested several ways in

18 Emmanuel Adegbite, 'Good corporate governance in Nigeria: Antecedents, propositions and peculiarities', *International Business Review*, 24(2), 2015, pp. 319–330

which CSR can be embedded into the corporate governance framework of banks to promote stakeholders' recognition and protection of stakeholders' interests. Additionally, FSM proposed alternative enforcement mechanisms for corporate governance, emphasising the assignment of enforcement powers to various stakeholders, including the Attorney-General of the Federation and the States, lawyers, CIBN, and customers. It is argued that despite various reforms, the CBN Nigeria's primary banking regulator has failed to meet its regulatory and supervisory responsibilities, as evidenced by the persistent banking failure in recent times. The CBN is more reactive than proactive, as evidenced by the series of bailouts in the banking industry. The FSM proposal of giving enforcement powers to other stakeholders means that CBN can focus on its other core functions.

9.5 Practical and Policy Implications

Given the similarities in the institutional environments, the findings and recommendations in this book will be highly beneficial to DMBs in Nigeria and other African countries. They will help DMBs understand the challenges that hinder the effective implementation of corporate governance in the banking industry and their responsibility to protect stakeholders' interests, especially through CSR. Moreover, these insights and recommendations will hold relevance for policymakers and government bodies, fostering an understanding of existing compliance gaps vis-à-vis codes and regulations and propelling them to fortify pertinent laws to ensure robust compliance. Equally pertinent is the value these findings and recommendations bring to legislators, poised to inform the development of legislation that upholds the welfare of all stakeholders, particularly in the context of CSR. Furthermore, the implications of this book are poised to offer substantial benefits to external auditors, enabling a deeper understanding of their role within the corporate governance framework of banks in ensuring an accurate portrayal of financial positions in audited financial statements. Finally, this book is relevant to academia, particularly for scholars engaged in research on comparative corporate governance, corporate social responsibility, and banking regulation.

9.6 Final Remarks

The research presented in this book delves into the assessment of the corporate governance framework within the Nigerian banking industry, focusing on the recognition and protection of stakeholder interests. It is important to note that the book does not aim to resolve all issues within the Nigerian banking industry; rather, its focus lies in addressing the restricted recognition of stakeholders and safeguarding their interests. Despite employing DMBs in Nigeria and South Africa as a case study, the applicability of the findings extends to banks in challenging institutional contexts, given the comparable challenges faced by customers and employees in the event of banking failures. Further investigation is imperative to ascertain the potential implementation of this framework within the broader spectrum of the Nigerian financial sector and in countries with similar challenging institutional contexts. Additionally, further research exploring the feasibility of implementing the framework in insurance, pension, and mortgage institutions would enrich the current findings. Moreover, further research is needed to expand the scope of stakeholders' recognition and the protection of their interests, especially in countries in the Global South with similar challenging institutional environments.

Reference List

Adegbite, Emmanuel, 'Good corporate governance in Nigeria: Antecedents, propositions and peculiarities', *International Business Review*, 24(2), 2015, pp. 319–330

Adegbite, Emmanuel, Chizu Nakajima, 'Corporate governance and responsibility in Nigeria', *International Journal of Disclosure and Governance*, 8(3), 2011, pp. 252–271

Ahunwan, Boniface, 'Corporate governance in Nigeria', *Journal of Business Ethics*, 37(3), 2002, pp. 269–287

Constitution of the Federal Republic of Nigeria, 1999 (an amended)

Hansmann, Henry, Reinier Kraakman, 'The end of history for corporate law', Yale Law School Working Paper No. 235; NYU Working Paper No. 013; Harvard Law School Discussion Paper No. 280; Yale SOM Working Paper No. ICF-00-09, January 2000

Ibrahim, Umaru, 'The challenges to deposit insurance law and practice', Keynote address delivered at The Sensitization Seminar for Court of Appeal Justices held at the Court of Appeal Complex, Abuja, 12 December 2018, available at: <https://ndic.gov.ng/keynote-address-delivered-by-alhaji-umaru-ibrahim-fcib-mni-md-ceo-of-nigeria-deposit-insurance-corporation-ndic-at-the-sensitization-seminar-for-court-of-appeal-justices-held-on-12th-december-20/>

Miles, Samantha, 'Stakeholder: Essentially contested or just confused?', *Journal of Business Ethics*, 108(3), July 2012, pp. 285–298

Ogbechie, Chris, 'Corporate governance practices and leadership in Nigeria', 7 June 2019, available at: <https://ssrn.com/abstract=3400913>

Ogbechie, Chris, Dimitrios Koufopoulos, 'Corporate governance practices in publicly quoted companies in Nigeria', *International Journal of Business Governance and Ethics*, 3(4), 2007, pp. 350–381

Okike, Elewechi, 'Corporate governance in Nigeria: The status quo', *Corporate Governance: An International Review*, 15(2), 2007, pp. 173–193

Phillips, Roberts, Edward Freeman, Andrew Wicks, 'What stakeholder theory is not', *Business Ethics Quarterly*, 13(4), October 2003, pp. 479–502

Rwegasira, Kami, 'Corporate governance in emerging capital markets: Whither Africa?', *Corporate Governance: An International Review*, 8(3), 2000, pp. 258–267

Srinidhi, Bin, Ye Sun, Hao Zhang, Shiqiang Chen, 'How do female directors improve board governance? A mechanism based on norm changes', *Journal of Contemporary Accounting and Economic*, 16(1), April 2020, available at: <https://doi.org/10.1016/j.jcae.2019.100181>

Williams, Cynthia, 'Corporate social responsibility in an era of globalisation', *University of California Davis Law Review*, 35, 2002, pp. 705–778

Index

FSC
www.fsc.org
MIX
Papier | Fördert gute Waldnutzung
FSC® C083411

Kolibri 360 GmbH
Ferdinand-Jühlke-Straße 7
99095 Erfurt, Deutschland
produktsicherheit@kolibri360.de